FINANCIAL INDEPENDENCE RETIRE EARLY

The Definitive Guide To Achieving Your Financial Freedom And Get An Early Retirement
(2 Books in 1)

Richard Sodin

assurance.

The trademarks that are used are without any consent, and the publication of the trademark is without permission or backing by the trademark owner. All trademarks and brands within this book are for clarifying purposes only and are the owned by the owners themselves, not affiliated with this document.

assurance.

The trademarks that are used are without any consent, and the publication of the trademark is without permission or backing by the trademark owner. All trademarks and brands within this book are for clarifying purposes only and are the owned by the owners themselves, not affiliated with this document.

Table of Contents

FINANCIAL INDEPENDENCE

Achieving Your Financial Freedom And Wealth

RICHARD SODIN

CHAPTER ONE

RECOGNIZE REALITY

Right now, going to look at your own budgetary situation where you're at this moment. We'll make sense of what riches intends to you, look at some hard realities about the economy, and arrive at a genuine decision about what you have to do to put yourself on a way that will permit you to live well and resign serenely.

There are four fundamental salary levels:

1. If you have a family salary of under $50,000, it's difficult to make a decent living.

2. If you acquire somewhere in the range of $50,000 and $150,000, you are getting by. Your bills are paid and you can bear the cost of some little extravagances, however you must be cautious.

3. When your family pay surpasses $150,000, you are living admirably and have everything taken care of, and then some (except if you have 10 youngsters).

4. When your family pay surpasses $1 million, you can spend money absent much by way of reasoning. You needn't bother with a spending limit. You can be lavish.

In any case, making a million dollars doesn't build an incredible nature and it doesn't, in itself, ensure that you will have financial security till the finish of your days. What it does is make saving interminably simpler. Since except if you are totally crazy, you will have the option to save most if not the whole of your after-charge salary that surpasses the million. And, saving is vital to kicking off the Automatic Wealth program.

So if you can get your salary over a million, you can get rich, moderately rapidly, only by saving.

In any case, if your essential salary doesn't develop so significantly, don't surrender. You can even now accomplish monetary autonomy in a generally brief timeframe (under 15 years, absolutely; presumably under 7) by building up extra floods of pay. I'll disclose to you how to do that, as well.

BEING RICH IS NOT ABOUT HAVING MONEY IN THE BANK

"What is riches?"

This inquiry incited a downpour of fascinating answers, from the ordinary to the realistic to the insightfully hazardous. Answers like these:

- A million dollars in the bank
- Having all that you need
- The capacity to direct results
- Being adored by your loved ones
- Having substantial resources adequate to meet the physical needs of yourself and your friends and family
- Having a healthy lifestyle
- Inner harmony and deep edification

- Excellent health and invulnerability from infection

This is only a little examining of what our readers needed to state, yet it gives you a thought regarding how fluctuated and now and then unclear our speculation about riches can be. And, even though I perceive the sense in a considerable lot of these definitions, I think that its difficult to converse with individuals about riches except if I can get them to concur on some fundamental terms. So we should do that now.

I recommend that we start with this definition: Wealth is a store of something important.

I like that definition since it is straightforward and because, regardless of what it is that you value, it accentuates something basic about riches: the possibility of capacity. Having the things you want say, a major house and extravagant vehicles doesn't make you really well off if you don't have the fortitude to keep those merchandise over an extended timeframe. Nor are you well off in fellowship if the numerous companions you have now would surrender you if your fortune changed.

The fact of the matter I'm making here might be too evident to even consider mentioning: that riches is just now and then about money. Understanding riches in a more extensive sense, with suggestions that go past dollars and pennies, is fundamental.

Truly, the principle motivation behind this book is to assist you with getting monetarily free. However, you need monetary freedom for explicit reasons:

- You need more opportunity in your life. You need more

decision about where you live, how you live, the amount you work, etc.

- You need more relaxation in your life. You would prefer not to feel constrained to work 8 or 10 hours consistently, or five and six days consistently.

- You need greater serenity in your life. You might want a conclusion to the pressure that the absence of money now and then causes. You need to have the option to rest effectively around evening time and make the most of your days without stress.

These objectives are wrapped up firmly in your longing for riches and thus, they are a basic piece of each progression in my Automatic Wealth program.

Let's drive somewhat further along this way and dig somewhat more deep into how you consider your life and the things you value.

PLAN FOR WEALTH IN EVERY IMPORTANT WAY

I'm trusting that money isn't the most significant thing in your life.

By and by, material riches do make a difference. It enables you to enable your companions, to accommodate your family, seek after scholarly and aesthetic interests, and become a persuasive good example for individuals from your locale.

Besides, if you don't have a pay adequate to address your issues, you'll invest a decent plan of energy worrying about it and when you invest time fussing about money, you can't enjoy the things you genuinely care about.

This is a fact that increasingly more children of post war

America (counting a couple of my loved ones) have as of late found. Discovering middle age with lifetimes of instructive, social, and recreational encounters, yesterday's radicals are hitting their 50s with the discouraging acknowledgment that they are working harder than at any other time to keep up a way of life that isn't far superior to the one they had in school.

Having enough money can free you from an unpleasant activity, free you to follow dreams, and permit you to sale with your friends and family.

That is the explanation you're reading this book.

In any case, always remember that the longing for money can likewise degenerate you. If, in seeking after riches, you start to accept that the amassing of money is an end in itself well, that is an bad thing.

This book will assist you with profiting. And, if you follow my recommendations steadfastly for a sensible timeframe, you'll sometime in the not so distant future most likely sooner than any of your companions or associates find that you are affluent.

However, when that day comes, I'm trusting the eagerness bug won't have contaminated you. I trust you won't have gotten dependent on making the money heap develop. I trust you won't have overlooked what you know now that there are numerous things more significant than money.

FOLLOWING POPULAR FINANCIAL GURUS WILL KEEP YOU POOR

You won't discover anything right now will give you moment riches. I have no exhortation about making a fortune through purchasing hot stocks, day exchanging, or playing the lottery. In any case, you don't need that sort of money in any case. Studies show that individuals who get rich quickly blow everything rapidly on things that have no enduring worth.

Open a magazine or turn on the TV and you'll see that most of it falls into the classification of budgetary arranging, that is, approaches to get by on a very tight budget. Counsels who advance this idea expect you have to slither toward retirement, grasping pennies until your fingers turn green.

However, let's talk about a mind-blowing nature meanwhile? And, when you're living check to check, how would you wring a nickel out of your spending limit for retirement, substantially less the $5 or $10 every day that these budgetary masters suggest?

Getting well off doesn't involve rationing and compromising. To rake in boatloads of money, you should invest a large portion of your working energy doing the things I'm going to enlighten you concerning right now that create additional money since you can use to produce programmed surges of salary sooner rather than later. Truly, it is imperative to be cautious about how you spend your money however if that is the principle part of your riches building program, you most likely won't get rich. And, regardless of whether you do, you won't feel rich.

The issue is, the majority of those doing the proclaiming the individuals who might persuade you that they get riches and can show you how to get it have never really made critical money by following their own proposals. Their incredible moneymaking aptitude is in selling individuals on purchasing their thoughts.

The Amount Of Wealth You Need?

Most books regarding the matter of riches answer this significant inquiry as far as an idea called retirement. And, in this day and age, you need a great sale of money to resign well. Indeed, even individuals who had their retirement money securely concealed in the financial exchange and figured they could anticipate a protected future are presently in a difficult situation.

Take Martha Parry, for instance. The New York lady sold her insurance agency and thought she had it made. As per a Time magazine main story, she had $1 million in the financial exchange and was anticipating a retirement of golf, travel, and great occasions.

Then the financial exchange smashed. Also, presently, at 65, she has as it were $600,000 in her retirement account. Also, rather than playing golf and voyaging, she's still at the workplace procuring her living. Furthermore, she's one of the fortunate ones.

Another lady that I read about must be put taking drugs for extreme misery because a year in the wake of being scaled back from her activity, she took in her retirement fund had dove from $1 million to $250,000.

And, numerous casualties of the financial exchange crash have been left fit as a fiddle.

Tim and Kay Plumlee saw their retirement support plunge to a minor $60,000 after an intermediary prescribed they put their life reserve funds into a variable annuity a speculation that appeared to be a productive, hazard free open door then.

In a couple of year's time, individuals saw their life investment funds sliced by a quarter to an a large portion of some lost substantially more. Furthermore, regardless of the ongoing business sector rally, the fall of the dollar, the exportation of occupations to India and China, and the expense of the war on psychological oppression are probably going to keep the 79 million Americans who call themselves children of post war America in risk.

A BABY BOOMER PROBLEM WHICH WILL GET WORSE FOR MOST

Like Martha Parry and the Plumlees, people born after WW2 all over America are understanding that there is next to no possibility that they will have the option to resign at 55 or 65. An ongoing USA Today study uncovered that 35 percent of American specialists more than 55 concede that they are not monetarily prepared to do as such.

How inadequately prepared would they say they are? Another investigation demonstrated that 40 percent have investable total assets of under $50,000, 60 percent have under $100,000, and 80 percent have under $250,000.

If you figure on profiting, this implies less than one out of five Americans who are approaching retirement age have the fortitude to enjoy an aloof retirement salary of more than $25,000.

How well would you be able to live on $25,000 every year?

Let's see. First we should deduct charges (national, state, and nearby). Then we need to think about the erosive impact of expansion. What you end up with is a salary of under $1,500 per month scarcely enough to keep you in a modest, two-room loft.

Most people born after WW2 will get less fortunate as they get more established. Not exclusively will their winning force decline, duties will probably go up. Add to that the likelihood of rising swelling, a critical securities exchange collapse, a levelling of real estate costs, and expanded restorative expenses.

Let's talk about SOCIAL SECURITY?

If you are feeling that Uncle Sam will step in to sale with you in your brilliant years, you will be sharply disillusioned. Uncle

Sam is trillions of dollars paying off debtors, and Social Security and Medicare are going belly up. Here's the reason . .

As of recently, the measure of money brought into the Treasury from Social Security charges (retained from your pay as FICA and Medicare) has surpassed the active instalments made by the Social Security Administration (SSA) for these projects. However, by 2017, the SSA will be paying out more in profits than it gathers.

In their 2003 Trustees Report, the SSA itself stated, "If Social Security isn't changed, finance expenses should be expanded or enormous exchanges from general incomes will be required."

Neither of these things is probably going to occur. Youngsters won't permit their finance assessments to be expanded to assist children of post war America who wasted the assets while they were running the legislature. Moreover, there are such a large number of boomers resigning (as compared with the quantity of individuals who are working) that any expense increase would need to be colossal to have any genuine impact. Furthermore, there are positively not single surpluses in sight as a rule income nowadays.

Something needs to go.

The principal cuts will be unobtrusive. Typical cost for basic items changes (COLAs) will vanish. Then advantages should be cut. If not, the obligation will turn out to be enormous to the point that the administration should blow up our moncy which will bring about a debased dollar and lessened acquiring influence. In any case, you'll end up with less.

And, the viewpoint is far and away more terrible for Medicare. The Annals of Internal Medicine as of late detailed that more seasoned Americans with medical issues are getting the attention they need only 52 percent of the time. Would you be able to envision what will happen when Medicare begins paring back on account of waning assets? Furthermore, we're experiencing a normal of 10 years longer than during the 1940s, and the expenses of human services keep on expanding with not a single genuine end to be seen.

The eventual fate of Uncle Sam's retirement program looks dreary.

In any case, your future doesn't need to be. You can isolate yourself from the horde of children of post war America who are following their Pied Piper financial pioneers into the waterway of individual obligation and wrctchedness. With my Automatic Wealth program, you can make your own retirement plan an individual, financial reparation investment that will take you from any place you are presently to relative riches and solmaster in 7 to 15 years.

You can experience the second 50% of your life in ease and com-fortress... in any case, not if you are depending on the legislature. Assume responsibility for your future currently by following the suggestions right now, you'll never need to depend on any other person, presently or later on, to sale with your needs.

WHERE DO YOU STAND RIGHT NOW?

Before I can help you spread out your riches assembling game-plan before we can think of a plan to get you where you need to go we have to realize the amount you are worth at the present time.

So we should make sense of it.

Get a stack of paper and a pen and make a list of every one of your profits. I mean stocks, securities, valuable metals, money in singular retirement accounts (IRAs), authentications of store (CDs), bank accounts, etc. You can likewise incorporate the worth (the genuine, current, attractive worth don't trick yourself) of any significant belongings you possess, for example, gems, workmanship or collectibles.

Presently I'm going to give you a guidance that will repudiate what you'll get notification from pretty much every monetary organizer: In counting your advantages, do exclude the estimation of your home, your vehicle, or any belongings ˙ you realize you'll never leave behind.

Even though these are, to be sure, important resources, they are resources you will more likely than not have any desire to keep during your retirement years. This is particularly valid if you can accomplish monetary autonomy while you despite everything have kids at home. If you will be resigning after your youngsters are developed and out without anyone else, you might just decide to sell your home and get a more affordable one yet perhaps you won't have any desire to. And, I have confidence in keeping what you have for whatever length of time that you wish. (If you follow my six stages to programmed riches, you'll have the option to do that.)

OK, we should complete the process of making sense of your total assets . . .

Since you have a list of your profits, make another list of your liabilities, including charge card obligation, individual advances, business obligations, etc.

Subtract your liabilities from your profits and you'll have your total assets.

If your own total assets are under $300,000, you most likely need more money to resign on. Except if you mean to work till the day you kick the bucket (which is something you may decide to do regardless of whether you don't need to a thought that we'll investigate later), you are going to require more than $300,000 concealed in salary delivering investments to carry on with a not too bad way of life in retirement.

DO YOU HAVE ENOUGH TO RETIRE COMFORTABLY?

Your essential objective as far as turning out to be monetarily autonomous is to amass enough money to produce easy revenue adequate to take care of for your fundamental tabs lodging, food, utilities, training, and diversion.

Automated revenue implies salary that you don't need to spend 40 hours seven days creating. Furthermore, you may as of now have some as income created by your interests in stocks, bonds, etc. In any case, going to figure out how to produce unquestionably increasingly easy revenue enough to live on.

What amount more do you need?

To get that answer, you need to know what number of pre-tax dollars you should live serenely the amount you'll require, every year, to cover lodging, food, and utilities. So compute that now (and make certain to include the money you'll need to spend on movement, instruction, and relaxation exercises).

When you've done that, the following stage is entirely simple.

Basically copy the pretax pay that you're going to require by 10 (the normal level of premium that you can sensibly hope to acquire on your investments the normal that the financial exchange has generally returned is 10.4 percent, as indicated by Ibbotson Associates) and afterward subtract that number from your present total assets. That will give you a brisk gauge of the amount more money you should add to your total assets before you can resign.

"Standardized savings instalments will most likely exist in some building during retirement and you ought to incorporate the advantages as an unassuming extent of your retirement salary. These are privileges that will be accessible yet the real worth is probably going to decrease after some time. Profits instalments and Social Security are a sensible piece of your pay when you qualify, however they can't be the influence which gives you financial opportunity. If you have a normal life expectancy or more, the genuine buying force will be short of what you will anticipate."

For instance, suppose you've made sense of that the way of life you imagine for yourself in retirement will cost you $65,000 in post-charge dollars. That implies you will require a pre-tax salary of $90,000. Furthermore, we should accept that your present total assets are $400,000. Multiple times $90,000 is $900,000, and $900,000 less $400,000 leaves a large portion of a million dollars which is the sum you'll have to store in speculations creating 10 percent enthusiasm among now and the time you need to resign. Right now, expecting that you will spend, in retirement, just your salary. If you figure out how to do this and numerous affluent individuals do you'll end up with a noteworthy bequest to leave to a cause or your friends and family. You could make sense of an approach to spend some portion of your capital just as the enthusiasm as you age. This is a more convoluted estimation, yet it allows you to go into retirement mode with less money in the bank.

Having individual total assets of multiple times the sum you have to live on is, by practically any definition, agreeable. It implies that if you live cheaply and no crises come up, you can believe yourself to be basically monetarily autonomous. In any case, that 10-times figure depends on the presumption that you put all your money in the securities exchange and that the financial exchange, as exaggerated as it is by all accounts, keeps on delivering its noteworthy ROI of around 10 percent.

If you are increasingly moderate with regards to individual financial matters and might want to see about a large portion of your money in securities, you will require total assets of multiple times the sum you have to live on. Once more, that is accepting the securities exchange will deliver a normal return of 10 percent later on and that securities will give you their memorable yields of 4 percent after expenses or 6 percent previously.

If you are moderate and feel somewhat miserable about the eventual fate of the financial exchange, you'll need to raise that factor significantly more. If you think, for instance, that you'll live an additional 30 years and accept that the market will average an insignificant 8 percent ROI, you'll need a numerous of 13 to see yourself as serenely wealthy.

Let's look at another model.

Suppose you need just $40,000 to carry on with an upbeat life in retirement. You've made sense of that you would be OK with a post tax pay of $35,000 and you know, from your Social Security documents, that you can expect $1,500 per month from the administration, which comes to $18,000 per year. Subtracted from $35,000, this gives you a prerequisite of just $22,000. At a different of 10, you would be monetarily autonomous when your net investment funds hit $220,000.

If you realize you'll need your retirement assets in the two stocks and securities and acknowledge my projection that such a portfolio would win a normal of 8 percent ROI, and then the numerous you'd use would be 12 and the sum you'd need to place into reserve funds would be multiple times 22, or $264,000.

Once more, this model expects that you wouldn't spend any of the boss measure of your investment funds. If you spent it say, by going through $5,000 every time of your head once you hit age 70 the sum you'd have to set aside would be altogether less.

THE RIGHT TIME TO ACT?

Toward the start of this part, I informed you concerning the day I chose to get rich. Presently it's your go to do something very similar and begin to get it going.

If you are not monetarily free yet, I can put you on the correct way if you can subscribe to the plan spread out in the pages that follow. Would you be able? Great.

Then I have one inquiry for you: When are you going to begin? One month from now? One week from now? When you get past reading this book?

The right answer is "nothing from what was just mentioned."

There is just one an opportunity to start a significant excursion. And, that is right away. You don't need to put resources into a stock today or purchase a bit of property tomorrow, however you do need to accomplish something that will make you go. Furthermore, in Step 2, I'll let you know precisely what that is.

In any case, before I do, we should discuss why it's so imperative to act right away.

Since now is the best time ever to manufacture riches. Why? Since now is consistently the best time.

Presently is consistently the best time to begin anything. Results require significant investment, and time is a restricted asset. The sooner you start, the quicker you'll get where you need to go.

This is generally valid, yet it's particularly obvious when the objective is to fabricate riches. You can't control the economy. You can't anticipate the business sectors. You can't conclusively shield yourself from debacle. However, you can make yourself more extravagant tomorrow than you are today.

There's continually something you can do. Work an additional hour in the first part of the day. Work another additional prior hour you return home around evening time. Sell an additional gadget. Start an relationship. Concoct a moneymaking thought.

Keep in mind; each dollar you procure today is more significant than a dollar you gain tomorrow as a result of the estimation of compound between est. Also, every monetarily important mystery you adapt today is more valuable than it would be if you learned it tomorrow due to the estimation of compound information.

Be discerning of the occasions we live in the easing back economy, the blossoming obligation yet be similarly mindful of the progression of time. Consistently that passes is 24 hours of chance you won't have once more. Why not put a touch of that opportunity to work for you at this moment?

Prepared... FIRE ... Point

Why not "prepared, point, fire"? Provided that you're prepared to make a few- thing occur and you invest a lot of energy attempting to get things right (pointing) before you make a move (fire), you'll lose the force that is driving you.

You can generally return and do some tweaking later. In business, executing a second-best thought presently is frequently a superior procedure than holding up a week or a month or a year to think of the single thought. Since the correct choice made past the point of no return is some of the time more bad than no choice by any means.

Practically the whole of the effective business visionaries I know have a sense for moving rapidly and that incorporates how they decide. Even though they regularly comprehend the significance of discussion, study, and examination, their common inclination is to settle on the choice rapidly and work towards it.

That is a decent intuition to have.

Achievement originates for a fact. You commit a few errors. You have a few triumphs. You gain from every one of them. The key to progressing rapidly regardless of whether you will likely execute another business thought or fabricate your own riches is to quicken the learning procedure. Furthermore, that implies Ready, Fire, Aim.

CHAPTER TWO

PLAN TO BE WEALTHY

You are going to change your financial future.

You've pondered change previously, yet at no other time have you had the inclination that you're prepared for it now.

You perceive that if you don't change now, the chances will start to betray you. As time passes, day, and week, your odds of altering a mind-blowing course from one of monetary battling to opportunity will decrease.

Investigate you. Consider your family, companions, and associates. They need what you need a higher salary, less pressure, more fun, and enough money in the bank to stop buckling down and enjoy life.

You and they have similar essential needs, yet the odds that they will accomplish their fantasies are little, getting littler consistently. That isn't valid for your situation. The distinction: You've made a guarantee to change.

In any case, resolving to change and changing are two distinct things. Except if you make a move now, a year or two will pass by and you'll wind up speculation, "What befell that guarantee I made to myself? For what reason didn't I do it? Why I'm at exactly the same place, monetarily, that I was in those days?"

WHY IT'S SO IMPORTANT TO SEIZE THE DAY

Let me disclose to you a story . . .

At an AWAI class, the publisher of a natural health pamphlet business inquired as to whether they needed shots at writing an expert development. Eight students lifted their hands.

This was their opportunity of a lifetime. All they needed to do was follow up after the meeting and they'd be en route. There, since quite a while ago held fantasies about turning out to be proficient freelancers would become reality.

This is what occurred, as per the publisher:

"They were all anxious to begin. I expected a surge of messages and bundles with all that they had ever writen, including staple records and letters to their moms however just a single individual has ever reached me."

Eight individuals had this gold-plated chance to understand their fantasies, yet just one really took care of business.

It appears to be amazing when you consider it. However it happens constantly. (And, coincidentally, the one understudy who replied is presently making more than $100,000 every year as a full-time independent author.)

Try not to commit that error yourself.

THE TIME TO START IS RIGHT NOW

I spend a decent plan of my time tutoring individuals. Throughout the years, I've built up a truly decent feeling of whether those I mentor will succeed.

One thing I search for presumably the most significant thing is their time allotment.

I know as a matter of fact that basically everybody who puts off change neglects to make it. When I hear somebody state "I'm going to begin after Christmas" or "one month from now" or "on Tuesday," I think, "Similar to hellfire you are."

For with regards to change, the definite indication of disappointment is tarrying.

In any event, setting a beginning date of tomorrow is a terrible sign. Individuals who truly, genuinely need to make a genuine and lasting change in their lives need to begin now. That is the way I feel each time I jump on another undertaking, start another business, or commencement another activity program. I realize I've gotten worn out with the norm. I've made sense of an approach to improve things. That freshness energizes me. For what reason should I put it off?

When I discover myself saying that I'll start at some later point in time, I realize I'm in a tough situation.

Consider your own understanding. Consider how frequently you've chosen to change previously. What number of those occasions did you put off beginning until some advantageous point later on? Furthermore, when you did, how often did you fizzle?

All in all, would you say you are prepared to start building riches now? At the present time?

Great.

Preparing YOURSELF BY SETTING GOALS

This book is about riches, yet we will expand the extension for some time and discussion about what you deeply desire by and large. Do you have objectives for your family? Social or magnanimous objectives? Do you have individual, nonfinancial targets? Do you dream about turning into an entertainer, competitor, or performer? Okay prefer to work with kids in your extra time? Or then again help the crippled?

If you have no objectives other than getting well off, your odds of accomplishment will be extraordinary however the probability that you'll be disappointed will be incredible, as well. There is no more noteworthy financial platitude than the poor man who builds a fortune just to find that he lost everything that was extremely essential to him.

I won't let that transpire. You will get affluent and savvy and upbeat and solid, as well!

You start the procedure by deciding your guiding principle.

WHAT DO YOU HOPE PEOPLE WILL SAY ABOUT YOU AT YOUR FUNERAL?

In Mark Twain's Adinvestments of Tom Sawyer, America's two most loved adolescent delinquents vanish from their community for an innocent experience and afterward come back to discover a memorial service continuing for them. Stowed away cave in the congregation's overhang sitting above the service, Tom and Huck find a workable pace what others consider them. It is an enlightening encounter for the two youthful troublemakers and envisioning your own burial service can do something very similar for you.

So envision being at your burial service. You are stowing away up in the gallery. You can see your pine box. Remaining behind the pine box are four individuals:

- Someone from your family or a dear companion
- Someone you work with
- Someone whom you enjoy
- Someone who didn't have any acquaintance with you

What do you trust every single one of them would state about you? Proceed. Record it. Your list of things to get might incorporate proclamations like these:

- "He constantly caused me to feel significant; in any event, when I sensed that I had nothing to give."
- "He was the best dad I could have ever sought after. He encouraged me to be solid and free and he gave me that I could be fearless and cherishing simultaneously."
- "He was a splendid author. For somebody who spent such a large amount of his life in the business world, I was astounded at how well writ-ten his accounts were."
- "I would in any case be functioning as a security protect if it were not for him. To consider what I've become. I know the amount of that I owe to his assistance and care."

These are the things that are extremely essential to you your own basic beliefs. (Also, I'm speculating that "He was extremely rich" isn't something that you'd put on this list.)

Presently, let's apply what you simply found out about yourself to your next undertaking . . .

Make an interpretation of YOUR CORE VALUES INTO FOUR LIFETIME GOALS

If you welcomed quite a few people to your nonexistent

memorial service, you would now be able to make sense of what your fundamental beliefs are in each significant part of your life.

Your basic beliefs may look something like this:

- "As a labourer, I need to be viewed as imaginative and supportive."
- "As a parent, I need to be thought of as strong and kind."
- "As an individual, I need to be thought of as keen and intriguing."

You won't distribute this list. The purpose of making it is to assist you with knowing yourself such that issues. Which carries us to your next errand: changing over your fundamental beliefs to life objectives. If you've done your function admirably up until now if you genuinely know yourself this will be shockingly simple.

What number of life objectives would it be a good idea for you to have? Four is a decent, reachable number. One of them, obviously, will be to assemble riches not to gather money but since of what that money can assist you with achieving as far as your fundamental beliefs. As I said in Step 1, it enables you to enable others, to accommodate your family, seek after your scholarly and aesthetic interests, and become a motivation to individuals from your locale.

Let's talk about your other three life objectives? That is up to you. In any case, I would suggest thinking of one that has something to do with your health, one that is worried about your own relationships and one that objectives your own development and development.

Do that now and set up it as a written record. Your list of four objectives may look something like this:

1. My long term riches building objective: To be monetarily free. To have the option to do anything I desire without stressing over money.
2. My long term health objective: To be active, completely working, and torment free till age 90.
3. My long term individual relationship objective: To be recognized as an extraordinary father, adoring life partner, steadfast companion, and magnanimous soul.
4. My long term self-improvement and development objective: To be an effective author, movie producer, and language specialist.

WHAT AMOUNT CAN YOU REALISTICALLY ACCOMPLISH, MEDIUM TERM IN THE NEXT 7 TO 15 YEARS?

The reason for this book is to assist you with accomplishing budgetary freedom in 7 to 15 years and to do that while as yet keeping you on track to accomplish all of your long term life objectives.

I've picked this 7-to 15-year time span to some degree discretionarily, I concede, however all things considered. To start with, because I don't trust you are eager to hold up 30 to 40 years to accomplish monetary autonomy. Furthermore, second, since that is by all accounts a reasonable period of time to make progress in an undertaking. Pretty much all of the few dozen organizations I've begun has found its sweet place and get beneficial in 7 years or less. Most do it more rapidly than that as a rule in 4 or 5 years. Some are champs from the beginning. Some fizzle, obviously, yet that is normally clear from the get-go. (Shrewd specialists perceive when this is occurring and cut their losses off.) But I don't recollect a solitary one that took longer than 6 or 7 years.

That is the reason I feel certain promising you brings about 7 to 15 years (as a matter of fact, more than sure 99.9 percent sure).

Lifetime objectives have the upside of being long term and up to this point away. Being so removed, it's conceivable to envision yourself achieving for all intents and purposes anything. That is the reason, if you truly need to accomplish your objectives, you have to work with a quite certain medium-term time period. I've characterized medium term as 7 to 15 years. However, you should limit it down to a careful number.

And, in addition to the fact that you need to be explicit, you likewise should be genuine. For instance, if your lifetime budgetary objective is to have a total asset of $5 million and you are right now 45 years of age and broke, it may be practical for you to set a medium-term objective of $1 million of every 10 years. However, if you as of now have a large portion of a million in the bank, it would maybe be reasonable for you to set a medium-term financial objective of $2.5 million out of 7 years.

There are no outright guidelines with regards to this kind of objective set-ting. You need your objectives to be goal-oriented, yet you additionally need them to be reachable. Invest some energy presently concentrating your list of lifetime objectives, and make sense of (and record) explicit medium-term objectives for every one.

The amount CAN YOU ACCOMPLISH IN THE NEXT YEAR?

You are gaining acceptable ground. You have a dream of what you should do in the following 7 to 15 years and you are presumably feeling quite amped up for it. Utilize this energy to separate your objectives significantly further by set-ting 1-year targets.

This is something numerous individuals do toward the start of each new year. However, you won't trust that January 1 will move around. You comprehend the dreadful risk of dawdling. You've just felt the intensity of making a move. So you make the following fundamentally significant stride now.

Yearly objectives ought to be explicit and, if conceivable, quantifiable. A sim-ple one-year plan may resemble this:

My Wealth-Building Goals for the Year

- Get a $10,000 raise.
- Take a course in direct promoting.
- Start my own pipes supply Internet business.
- Make companions with 12 influential individuals in the pipes business.

My Health Goals for the Year

- Bench-press 250 pounds.
- Run six miles quickly.
- Get my HDL cholesterol to 80 or above.
- Master the lotus position.

My Personal Relationship Goals for the Year

- Host a month to month evening meeting with companions.
- Raise $5,000 for my preferred foundation.

- Repair my relationship with Aunt Pollie.
- Develop the propensity for recollecting individuals' names.

My Personal Growth and Development Goals for the Year

- Become a capable judge of good wine.
- Read 12 new books about science.
- Add 50 new stamps to my stamp assortment.
- Learn to play something on the guitar.

Somewhat later right now, tell you the best way to separate your yearly objectives into month to month, week after week, and day by day targets. (The emphasis will be on your riches building destinations, your lifetime objective of appreciating monetary freedom.) Plus, I'll share with you a few methods I've built up that will give you 80 percent or better possibility of really achieving the objectives you set for yourself.

In any case, at the present time, we should talk about something you can begin doing every morning that will make it feasible for the whole of this to occur.

THE EARLY BIRD CATCHES THE GOLDEN WORM

Stroll into your room at the present time and set your morning timer one hour sooner. If you are familiar with finding a workable pace, set it for seven. If your ordinary wake-up time is seven, set it for six.

Starting now and into the foreseeable future, you are going to wake up and find a good pace hour sooner.

Finding a good pace is such a typical prudence of successful peo-ple that I'm enticed to consider it the absolute most significant thing you can do to transform you.

I wasn't constantly a go-getter. For the vast majority of my 20s, if I saw the sun rise, it was before hitting the sack. And, even in my 30s, I'd battle to get in to the workplace by nine. I wasn't anxious about the work. Most days, I'd put in 12 to 14 hours. However, since I had acclimated myself to late hours in school and graduate school, I saw no motivation to change my waking and dozing propensities. "I do my best work after 12 PM," I used to state. And, for some time, I even trusted it.

My transformation occurred in my mid 40s, after I'd just gotten monetarily free and resigned just because (if at any point so quickly). That being the situation, I can't contend that it's difficult to become effective except if you find a workable pace. I did it. And, a lot of others did, as well.

However, I can say that the achievement I've had from that point forward has been more emotional . . . and, has come significantly simpler.

HOW I TAUGHT MYSELF THE VIRTUOUS EARLY-TO-RISE HABIT

At the hour of my change, I was working around 65 hours every week, starting every workday at 9 A.M. and, working until around 8 P.M. Five days at 11 hours and at any rate a large portion of a day on Saturday and Sunday permitted me to arrive at that 65-hour normal. (Obviously, I wasn't seeing a lot of my family.)

My accomplice at the time was finding a good pace 7:30 or 8:00 (I can't make certain, obviously, since I was never there to welcome him!) and leaving at about 6:30 or 7:00. He was working about indistinguishable number of hours from I was during the week however didn't work at all on ends of the week.

I was envious of his ends of the week (he'd reveal to me accounts of slashing wood on the homestead, taking climbs along the waterway) and guaranteed myself more than once that I'd not work ends of the week, either. However, when Friday night found some conclusion, I never felt my work had been finished. There were constantly a few significant issues requiring attention. In this way, one end of the week after the following got topped with get off work.

My family didn't care for it. I didn't care for it. In any case, the truly baffling thing was that no one at work appeared to see all the additional time I was placing in. Truth be told, I was getting ribbed about coming in late.

In the wake of working particularly late one night, I halted for gas at around two AM. As I gave my charge card to the woman in the glass stall, she stated, "Man, you look beat!"

"I've been working just about twelve hours every day," I advised her. "And, half-days on ends of the week."

She looked at me, neutral. "You talk about it like it's an excellence," she said.

"Well if working extended periods of time isn't an excellence," I shot back, "what is?" "Being the first at work," she said.

It was an unusual minute: being addressed about righteousness by a gas rmasterr at 2 A.M. In any case, by one way or another I realized she was correct. For all the additional hours I put in, my accomplice who had his ends of the week free had cornered the market most definitely. He appeared to be more upright not exclusively to our representatives yet in addition, I out of nowhere acknowledged, to me!

There is something in particular about getting in prior that appears to be savvier, nobler, more intelligent, or out and out more enterprising than working late. Finding a good pace says something regarding being fiery, writed, and in charge. Remaining late leaves the contrary impression: You are constant yet complicated, sincere however inconsistent, dedicated yet a toiler.

In How to Become CEO (Hyperion, 1998), Jeffrey J. Fox puts it along these lines:

If you will be first in your partnership, begin practicing by being first at work. Individuals who real estate at work late don't care for their occupations at any rate that is the thing that senior administration thinks. . . . Furthermore, don't remain at the workplace until 10 o'clock consistently. You are imparting a sign that you can't keep up or your own life is poor.

This woman in the glass corner was correct. Finding a good pace was superior to working until day break. From that minute on, I made plans to come to work before.

Also, I did. From the outset, it was troublesome and my prosperity was sporadic. However, then I happened upon an plan that worked. I set out to set my morning timer to wake me a moment prior every day. A solitary moment would feel like nothing, I figured, yet over the span of two months I would have moved the beginning of my day back by 60 minutes.

I utilized this moment per-day program to move my at-work time from 9:00 to 8:30 and afterward to 8:00 and afterward to 7:30, etc. Today, I commonly wake up at 5:30 and real estate at my work area (or my exercise) at 6:30.

WHAT YOU WILL GAIN BY GETTING TO WORK EARLIER

This change gave me the privilege to feel as prudent as my ahead of schedule to-rise accomplice. In any case, the advantages were more than mental. I started to see the whole of the accompanying physical and material advantages very quickly:

- More energy
- More fiery concentration for the duration of the day
- An opportunity to audit my different in-boxes before arranging and organizing my day
- Quiet time, without interruptions, to focus on significant undertakings
- A sentiment of being in front of every other person

"Ahead of schedule to bed and right on time to rise, makes a man solid, rich, and astute," Ben Franklin prompted very nearly 300 years prior and taking that way truly made a major contrast in my life. Furthermore, I'm not alone. There are a few investigations demonstrating that effective business people commonly find a good pace least an hour prior to their workers. So do most CEOs. The greater part of the wealthiest individuals I know find a good pace. Truth be told, this is such a general natural of effective individuals that I'm enticed to state it's their main mystery.

YOUR WEALTH-BUILDING PLAN FOR THE NEXT 12 MONTHS

A great many people don't wed into money or fall into a sudden legacy. Riches for the most part shows up a little bit at a time as the consequence of cautiously setting long term, medium-term, and transient objectives and arranging out what you have to do each month, week, and day to accomplish them.

You've set your lifetime, medium-term, and yearly objectives. You've made a guarantee to "rise early and get the brilliant worm" every morning. Great up until now.

Presently let me tell you the best way to separate your objectives during the current year into concrete, reachable strides during the current month, this week, and this very day. Since financial freedom is one of your essential objectives, we should investigate how you may make and organize your goals regarding a portion of the riches building strategies I'll be showing you later right now.

I will accept that your lifetime riches building objective is to be monetarily free. In any case, since I don't have the foggiest idea what you've built up for yourself so far as far as your medium-term riches building objectives, we should go with a theoretical situation.

So let's expect that your medium-term objective is to have $120,000 every year in pre-tax easy revenue and that your objective for accomplishing that objective is seven years.

There are numerous approaches to find a workable pace number. Suppose you want to do it along these lines:

So let's expect that your medium-term objective is to have $120,000 per year in pre-tax automated revenue and that your objective for accomplishing that objective is seven years.

There are numerous approaches to find a good pace number. Suppose you're intending to do it along these lines:

Medium-Term (Seven-Year) Goal: $120,000 every Year in Pre-tax Passive Income

- Own, without a worry in the world, $300,000 worth of real estate, yielding $45,000 every year
- Own $200,000 in securities, yielding (pre-tax) $15,000 every year
- Have $200,000 in stocks, averaging $25,000 every year
- Own value in a business dispersing $35,000 every year

Presently what? Presently you need to make sense of what you need to accomplish this year so as to arrive at those seven-year objectives. Your one-year objective may look something like this:

One-Year Goal

- Buy $60,000 worth of real estate at 20 percent down
- Buy $10,000 worth of bonds
- Buy $8,000 worth of stocks
- Get a business began

SETTING MONTHLY, WEEKLY, AND DAILY OBJECTIVES

The subsequent stage is to separate your yearly objectives into sensible, reduced down month to month destinations.

One of the yearly targets in our model is to kick a business off. So you would separate that into 12 month to month objectives what you have to do every month to get your business ready for action, from doing the underlying examination to the stupendous opening.

Then you break every one of those 12 month to month objectives into 4 week after week objectives. For example, if your first month to month objective in kicking another business off is to distinguish a decent business opportunity, maybe every one of your 4 week by week objectives will be to look into at any rate 10 conceivable outcomes.

At last, you work your way down to the move you will make every day to satisfy your week by week objective. If you have made a promise to inquire about 10 business openings every week, that implies one of the top needs on your day by day plan for the day will be to explore two potential outcomes.

Hope to spend one entire day arranging out your year. When a month, you'll plunk down for a few hours to delineate your objectives for the following a month. When seven days, you'll spend one hour setting up your objectives for the following seven days. And, you'll spend around 10 or 15 minutes every early daytime sorting out your day.

I realize that seems like a ton, however taken all together you're truly spending close to three days per year to outline your methodology for accomplishing financial autonomy in the following 7 to 15 years.

This is the means by which I build up my objectives, focus my targets, and set day by day assignments. It's not, using any and all means, a totally unique framework. It's an interwoven of frameworks that have been created by others and added to by me. However, there is something in particular about this specific framework that appears to work.

It works so well, truth be told, that I empower everybody who works for me to utilize it. The individuals who do find that it works quite well. I figure you will, as well.

Day by day PLANNING: GETTING THE MOST FROM EVERY MINUTE

There is no better time to gather your contemplations, survey your objectives, look at your present obligations, and plan your day than promptly in the first part of the day when the workplace is calm and still. Here's the early morn-ing schedule that works best for me:

Get Your Inputs (5 to 10 minutes)

I start the day by examining my day by day task list, which I have written the prior night. If for reasons unknown I haven't readied an assignment list, I do it then, in view of my week by week list of destinations. I then filter my email, not reacting to anything other than taking note of marketing that should be made and putting some of them down on my day by day task list. I do likewise with the in-box that sits around my work area. At long last, I recover any telephone messages and if one of them requires activity, make note of it on my every day task list.

I make it a point to not do any work presently (convey a fast email marketing or return telephone messages) since I know whether I do I'll become involved with a great sale of little stuff that will hinder me and channel my energy. Rather, I dedicate this info time to finishing my day by day task list. When that is done, I proceed onward to the following stage.

Sort and Prioritize (5 to 10 minutes)

Presently comes the enjoyment part. Accepting my day by day daily agenda has just been finished, I demonstrate for each errand the surmised measure of time I expect it will take to finish it. I generally attempt to be practical in my estimations of time required. Throughout the years, I've prepared myself to be conventional.

When in doubt, I separate assignments into 15-, 30-, 45-moment, and 1-hour increases. However, occasionally, (for example, at the present time, while I'm writing this book), I permit myself 2 or 2 1/2 hours for a solitary assignment.

I by and large prefer to organize my undertakings as far as their significance and earnestness. This thought depends on the quadrant created by Steven Covey in his well known 7 Habits books. He distinguishes assignments as being either (1) Important and Urgent, (2) Important however not Urgent, (3) Unimportant yet Urgent, or (4) Unimportant and not Urgent.

If we work with this thought, your every day timetable ought to be focused predominantly around (1) and (2) assignments, because these require prompt attention or will propel you toward your definitive objectives. Your calendar ought to contain a reducing number of (3) tasks (since they demonstrate that you are not in charge of your timetable), and no (4) undertakings by any means.

You could likewise allocate needs dependent on a notable hierarchical strategy known as the ABCDE technique. It goes this way:

- An A assignment is something that is significant, something you should do.
- A B task is something you ought to do, yet it is anything but an A.
- A C task is something that would be pleasant to do, yet it won't completely change yourself in an extreme manner.
- A D task is something that ought to be assigned.

- And, at long last, an E task is something that shouldn't be done by any stretch of the imagination. It ought to be wiped out from your assignment list.

Another approach to set needs is to think regarding the old 80/20 guideline. As applied to profitability, the standard says that 80 percent of the things you do each day add to just 20 percent of the development you make. However, that implies 20 percent of what you do is answerable for 80 percent of your prosperity. For our motivations, the best approach to utilize the 80/20 principle is to examine the assignments on your plan for the day and feature the 20 percent (the 2 out of 10 or 4 out of 20) that will have a monster effect in your life. If you are thinking right, the undertakings you feature will be the ones that help your life objectives.

Start with Something Really Important (15 to an hour)

The third and most significant piece of my get-into-the-workplace early time is committed to achieving one Important-yet not-Urgent errand. I like to begin the day with a nonurgent task because these are the tasks that make the greatest, long term contrasts throughout your life and although they are not pressing, will in general be ignored. As far as riches assembling, your Important-yet not-Urgent tasks may incorporate

- Learning or improving a monetarily important aptitude
- Expanding your encouraging group of people
- Pushing forward a significant investment that has slowed down
- Writing a reminder that will propel your profession
- Brainstorming another task

Doing a significant undertaking specific off the bat gives

me a quick feeling of achievement that fills me with energy that powers my work for the remainder of the day.

This is one reason I don't permit myself to explain or even answer any of the issues I run into during my initial morning audit of messages and my in-box. I comprehend the efficiency idea of not looking at anything twice, however my initial morning hours are simply too critical to even think about spending on something besides sorting out, organizing, and assaulting my Important-yet not-Urgent tasks.

I answer messages just more than once per day, however not first thing. If I do that, I wind up immediately sucked into issues and circumstances that

(1) aren't that significant, (2) can frequently be salet with similarly also by another person, (3) don't propel my long term objectives, and (4) sap me of mental and passionate energy that could be put to more readily utilize somewhere else.

Arrive at YOUR GOALS FASTER: EIGHT SECRETS I'VE DISCOVERED FOR TURNING WASTED TIME INTO PRODUCTIVE TIME

Presently your test is to discover all the more available time the time you have to achieve your objectives. By "save time" I mean sat around idly. The 5 minutes here and 10 minutes there that sneak past unnoticed, however gobble up hours of your life consistently.

Here are eight efficiency insider facts that can save you a decent two hours every day that you can put toward accomplishing your fantasy of financial autonomy.

Profitability Secret No. 1: Streamline Your E-mail

Email has become a lifestyle for the greater part of us particularly in business however it doesn't need to whittle down your work life. With only a couple of changes in the manner you oversee email, you'll save yourself at least one hours consistently that you can apply to valuable objectives.

I referenced before that I filter through my email just on more than one occasion per day (probably) to shield it from devouring hours of my time. A great sale of the messages that I get are inquiries concerning issues that individuals are looking to me to determine. A large portion of them I basically overlook. And, I find that they are generally taken care of fine and dandy without my obstruction.

If you don't micromanage each circumstance, your staff will in the end get the point that it's dependent upon them to sale with a large portion of the everyday issues that emerge. That will make them (and your whole relationship) more grounded and in this manner increasingly productive. Also, should an email message raise your rage, you'll have given yourself an opportunity to chill off and react to it in an expert way.

Here are a couple of different plans to assist you with streamlining the procedure much further.

- Keep your email messages short and to the point and ask the individuals who email you to do likewise. Not many messages should be in excess of a screen-page long and those that represent an issue ought to consistently be given various decision plans.

- If you find that you need more than one screen page to state what you need to state, the subject is likely too much to possibly be sent with adequately through email. You have to do it via telephone or eye to eye.

- This bit of exhortation may go totally against your grain, yet I'll give it at any rate: Make it a point to let email messages hold up except if they're genuine red-light crises. Here's the reason I disclose to you that. It is said that Napoleon Bonaparte held up a month prior noting letters. "If marketing is as yet required, I will write it then," he said. I feel practically a similar path about reacting to email.

- In expansion to letting messages pause, you can slice the time it takes to answer a considerable lot of them by making layouts to answer to the inquiries you are posed to regularly. Not exclusively will you save time, your marketing will likewise all be all around organized and elegantly written.

- Give your journalists the kindness of knowing when they will get notification from you. This should be possible by making an automessage that alarms senders when to anticipate an answer. It will help facilitate their psyches and shield them from sending you various follow-up messages. This works particularly well when you're out of the workplace, so you don't return to a flood of messages from irritable customers or representatives.

- As numerous as 50 percent of the messages you send could be diminished to a short explanation in the headline. For instance:

Workforce meeting moved to 1:30 P.M. FedEx bundle just showed up.

Truly, I'll wed you. (I trust, nonetheless, you'll think about taking care of this one face to face.)

No compelling reason to burn through your valuable time really expounding on why the meeting was changed, advising individuals to be on schedule, and a lot of other stuff that no one thinks about. By dis-working your message to its substance in the title, you additionally save time for the individuals you're sending it to. They won't feel constrained to react to it and you won't need to waste time with reading and erasing numerous forms of "OK, I'll be at the workforce conference. Anticipating it." Just think how much time everybody in your office and every one of your companions could save if they utilized this tip. How might you get them to do it? Show others how its done. Begin doing it without anyone else's help. And, forward this tip to everybody with whom you consistently convey through email.

One last recommendation about messages: Forget texting!

As per the New York Times, a fourth of American representatives utilize texting at work. "It's free and simple to download," broadcasts the article. "The most gainful thing I've at any point seen," cheers one official met by the paper. Texting is incredible if your essential objective at work is to burn through however much of your time as could reasonably be expected. By permitting your workday to be hindered continually by companions and associates out there on the Web, you can be guaranteed you will never invest any extraordinary length of energy focusing. "Customers value getting a moment answer to an inquiry," the official referred to above said. Perhaps. In any case, they probably won't care for it so much if the answers were straightforward, for example, "I don't have a response for you on that now since I'm too bustling noting texts."

Efficiency Secret No. 2: Attack Similar Tasks in Blocks

Regardless of whether you need to answer 25 messages,

make nine calls, or write three notices, you'll effectively save yourself an hour daily just by lumping like tasks together and shutting out time in your timetable to handle them at the same time.

Collecting normal undertakings makes you substantially more productive. So bunch them into one classification on your day by day plan for the day and distribute them a particular measure of time in your timetable.

And keeping in mind that you're grinding away, shut out some time for yourself too. Full timetables without unwinding lead to burnout. So alongside the different and sundry undertakings you need to achieve, you have to give yourself two or three 5-minute, 10-moment, and 15-minute squares of "personal" time every day.

You may enjoy a stroll in the sun. Or on the other hand a crossword confound and some espresso. I have three schedules I like at the present time. When I'm somewhat squeezed, I resign to a table and seat outside my office and read correspondence and different business papers while I enjoy a decent Dominican robusto. When I have to have an easygoing discussion with somebody, I do it over a rack of pool (with stogie smoke obligatory). When I'm not overpowered by work, I smoke a stogie and read a sonnet.

Efficiency Secret No. 3:Take Control of Your Schedule with This Simple Device

Do you start your day with the best of expectations write your calendar, shut out your time, feature significant objectives, and promise to adhere to it today just to locate your well meaning goals shot to damnation by early afternoon? It's difficult to monitor the time. You cover yourself in work and whenever you look into, three hours have passed and you don't have a large portion of the things done you'd prepared.

I've tackled that issue with an electric egg clock. It would appear that the ordinary, windup kind yet runs on batteries. When I start a investment, I assign it a specific measure of time. When that time terminates, the clock signals me with a rising size of stronger and stronger blares.

I keep the clock at the most distant finish of the workplace so I can't simply reach over and turn it off. I need to escape my seat and cross the room. Then, rather than coming back to my work area to begin another undertaking, I leave the workplace to take a short, one-minute walk or stretch. This gives me a breather and encourages me change tracks to the following task.

Another way your clock can assist you with controlling your timetable is the point at which somebody comes into your office and says, "I have a snappy inquiry. Got a moment?" Say "sure," and set your egg clock for a moment.

Efficiency Secret No. 4: Get Company Meetings levelled out

I accept wholeheartedly in restricting organization meetings. An excessive amount of time gets squandered in day by day meetings that stretch on for an hour and two hours without achieving anything of critical incentive for anybody there.

Regardless of whether you're driving the meeting, you ought to consistently have an plan before visiting. Your plan ought to incorporate a particular for every sonal motivation (e.g., "I will leave the meeting with an understanding from Jeff on the new item") just as thoughts regarding how to achieve that objective (e.g., "I'll make him a snappy, consistent contention and if he doesn't go for that, I'll help him to remember the kindness he owes me").

Clearly, you can't simply quit having meetings through and through. You can, nonetheless, diminish both the number held every week and the time they take. That leaves an additional hour or a greater amount of beneficial work to propel your organization's destinations just as your own vocation and individual objectives. The greatest test with meetings is to begin them on schedule and keep them short and on point. It's exasperating when individuals stroll in a short time late and upset the progression of thoughts so as to be raised to speed. It's considerably all the more irritating when the meeting then delays, biting up an hour or a greater amount of your time without achieving the things it was intended to.

If you find that the typical week by week meetings are beginning late and going excessively long, you might need to attempt this: Rather than meeting for an hour consistently, meet for 10 minutes on Monday, Wednesday, and Thursday.

With just 10 minutes accessible, the meeting should begin on schedule. You will discover as I have discovered that more completes because you're compelled to concentrate on the most significant issues immediately. You will save a half hour out of every week (three entire days a year). Also, tenderfoots will get familiar with an important exercise about promptness: There's no opportunity to update them in a 10-minute meeting, so they should get up to speed with their own time and will probably show up when they should next time.

Efficiency Secret No. 5: Limit Memos to One Page

Another way you can streamline your day is by changing how you write straightforward business records. Writing a notice can take 30 minutes or more. Yet, you can slice that time down the middle and twofold the force and clearness of your message essentially by shortening the length and expressing your essential point prior.

When business writing is terrible, it's generally a direct result of one of four issues:

1. it's excessively confused.
2. it's excessively confounding.
3. it's excessively obscure.
4. it's unconvincing.

Every one of the four of these normal issues can be battled by a clear theory expressed from the get-go in the copy.

Expressing your primary concern early tells your readers precisely what you are discussing and why they should continue reading. If your start is solid (i.e., the thought is helpful to them), it will engage your readers immediately and spur them to read with attention the remainder of what you need to state.

The shorter the copy, the sooner you have to utilize your proposition sentence. Here's an unpleasant rule:

- For copy that is 500 words or less (the length of most updates), make your first sentence the proposal sentence.
- For copy between 500 words and 1,500 words, express the postulation in the principal passage.
- For copy more than 1,500 words, express the proposal inside the main page.

There is no duplicate, anyway long, that legitimizes a proposition proclamation made later than the primary page.

For most updates, one page (under 500 words) works best. Acing the one-page update is an important business expertise that won't just make you an all the more dominant communicator yet additionally hone your reasoning. One approach to do it is to utilize this straightforward, three-section building:

(1) Tell it, (2) clarify it, and (3) retell it.

Before you type a solitary word, ask yourself, "What is my main concern thought regarding this matter?" If, for instance, you are writing a notice about your organization's new budget, the idea may be "Our income targets are excessively unrealistic."

If your thought can't be communicated in a straightforward definitive articulation like that, you have to continue thinking until you have it.

Utilize that announcement as your first sentence. Then burn through the vast majority of the remainder of the page clarifying what you mean by it. Don't overexplain. Furthermore, don't underexplain, either. Give as a lot of proof as you have to demonstrate your point. At last, form a finishing up sentence that harkens back to your opening explanation and furthermore integrates any remaining details.

Efficiency Secret No. 6: Learn How to Delegate

It is difficult to designate duty when you know nobody else can carry out the responsibility how you need it done, when you need it done, and how you need it done. You're the go-to individual, the person who can respond to questions, clarify things, get issues understood. This is a decent and an bad thing. Great since it gives you power. Great since it propels your objectives. Terrible because it can overpower you if you are not cautious.

Except if you are the main individual in your business, hesitance to share the outstanding task at hand will injure your organization. It is reckless to figure you can do everything yourself. Past making yourself insane, you will col-slip by from fatigue and your business will crumple alongside you.

Sooner or later you'll need to figure out how to delegate or you'll wear out. Here are a few rules to assist you with picking the opportune individual for the errand and let it go with certainty.

- Decide where you need assistance. Look at your week by week plan for the day. Note the occupations you truly enjoy doing and gain fulfilment from. Those are the ones you most likely won't have any desire to surrender. Then note the occupations that capitalize on your capacities. Those are the ones you most likely shouldn't surrender. What's left are the employments you don't care for or are not especially acceptable at. And, those are the ones that another person might have the option to fill.
- Select up-and-comers cautiously. You don't need just anybody helping you, since when you delegate work, how it is done thinks about legitimately you. Search for individuals who have an enthusiasm for the work, have what it takes to do it (or are eager to learn them), and have the opportunity and activity to achieve it.
- Make your case. Be explicit about the work you need the individuals to do, investment objectives, and any cutoff

times. Tell them why you picked them and how carrying out the responsibility can make them increasingly important to the relationship. Give them that it will profit them just as you.

- Seal the deal. For certain individuals, a handshake might be sufficient. However, to take no chances and to ensure you both comprehend what will be done, explicitly stated it. Advise your associates that this individual currently has the power to carry out the responsibility.

- Follow up. Verify that things are completing in a convenient manner. Remember that if the activity is being done another way from how you would have done it, that doesn't really mean it's being fouled up. Keep a receptive outlook. However, if there is an issue, address it without getting individual.

Profitability Secret No. 7: Hire Great People

A companion and associate of mine is an master of good employing. His first contract a section level marketing colleague blossomed into a world-class promoting master who is as of now maintaining his business for him. Both of them enlisted a second genius who helped them twofold the business in one year. Presently the staff comprises of four individuals, and they are doing the business it would ordinarily take eight individuals to do.

It is difficult to enlist great individuals, however it's definitely justified even despite the time and exertion that it takes. Here are the four most significant things I've found out about how to do it:

1. Make the dedication. Anything beneficial merits progressing admirably. You can't hope to contract extraordinary individuals if you spend only a couple of hours taking a shot

at it. I don't care for talking, and I'm constantly eager to contract the main better than average individual who tags along. That is a dangerous mix.

2. Look for the correct things. Knowledge is significant, however I'd put it third on my list of things to search for. I concur with Jeffrey J. Fox in his book How to Become a Great Boss (Hyperion, 2002) that the two most significant things to search for are frame of mind and bent.

3. Flee blemishes. As a rule, you'll see work competitors at their best when you talk with them. If you notice something that appears to be off-base, don't overlook it particularly if it concerns naturals that are significant for the activity. With regards to meeting, I've discovered that individual idiosyncrasies resemble the tip of a chunk of ice what you see superficially is a little piece of what you should manage later.

4. Don't stress a lot over explicit experience. Of the considerable number of naturals that are essential to search for in finding an incredible worker, explicit experience isn't exceptionally high on my list. Truly, it's acceptable to realize that the individual you contract can do the specialized work from the very first moment yet on day 7 or day 14, you'll wish you had selected the better, however maybe untried and problematic, prospect.

Efficiency Secret No. 8: Fire Bad Employees

When you need to save a lounger of imperilled hardwoods, you start by cleaving down a great sale of trees. You should dispose of the more youthful, more quickly developing trees that undermine the great wood so as to let the sun come in and allow the extremely important development to create. That is the manner by which it works in nature. Furthermore, I have discovered that the idea of a business isn't an excessive amount of various.

So how would you get rid of the average workers who are meddling with the development of your business? An effective bulletin publisher I know did it along these lines . . .

With each new individual he consented to procure, he made himself a guarantee that he would terminate his most fragile representative. He contemplated that the gauge of his workforce would bit by bit improve, insofar as each new contract was superior to his most noticeably bad existing worker. He wound up focusing on representatives with attitudinal issues (the individuals who appeared to be constantly troubled) and issue labourers (the individuals who invested an excess of energy in the telephone, on breaks, and so on.).

"The main troublesome thing," he let me know, "was figuring out how to fire somebody. I remembered it was the dread of doing so that permitted me to endure those average individuals from the beginning. The initial not many expulsions were troublesome, yet after that it got simpler. In the long run, I came to feel I was accomplishing something useful for the organization, bravo, and useful for the persevering, genuine disapproved of workers who would not like to be eased back somewhere around average individuals."

The program worked superior to anything he anticipated. In addition to the fact that he got free of the slow pokes and sharp apples, however the energy of the whole work-place improved. More work was being accomplished all the more rapidly. Profits and incomes were far up. The best part is that he never again needed to invest a great sale of his energy pushing the underachievers and that liberated him up to accomplish a greater amount of the work he truly cherished (writing, altering, and advancing his pamphlet).

Could GETTING RICH BE SIMPLE AND EASY?

In assembling this book, I've decreased what was for me a complex, once in a while opposing, encounter of moving from obligation to riches into six basic advances.

Are they extremely basic?

It wasn't basic for me when I began. That is without a doubt. Everything appeared to be a scrambled haze of bogus beginnings, restarts, and conservations. However, presently, glancing back at what I did and having the opportunity to dissect what worked and fizzled, the example of accomplishment does to be sure look straightforward.

Alright, accomplishing budgetary autonomy is straightforward. In any case, is it simple? Or on the other hand does it require a ton of difficult work?

We are altogether determined by wants to work less, to enjoy more, to have more money, to have a sense of safety. Accomplishing financial freedom is a major piece of accomplishing those wants. Also, if you one day obtain riches, it will be expected in no little part to the difficult work you've contributed.

However, here's the trick: You don't need the difficult work! I realize that. Also, I realize that if I stress the difficult work, I'll presumably drive you away. So I'm not going to concentrate on that and I don't need you to concentrate on that, either. I need you to consider the money, fun, and force. I need you to dream about the toys. Furthermore, when you set your objectives, they ought to mirror those fantasies, not the truth of difficult work.

In truth, we as a whole start our most prominent achievements with some guilelessness about how much time it will take ... what number of obstructions we will experience ... how much disappointment we will feel. If I somehow managed to set aside the effort to list all the things I've finished with my life the achievements I'm generally pleased with in not one case might I be able to sincerely say, "I comprehended what I was getting into when I started."

In any case, that is fine. The significant thing is to start, to make energy. A fundamental class in material science will reveal to you that it takes a lot of energy to get a stationary article going yet once it's moving it requires almost no push to make it change course, accelerate, or delayed down.

So to make you go on your way toward monetary freedom, I've tried to make things as straightforward as could reasonably be expected. Furthermore, I've attempted to cause the work to appear to be simple. The fact is to get you moving. When you are ready for action, I guarantee you that it truly will feel that way.

So now, turn the page and we should find a workable pace .

CHAPTER THREE

CULTIVATE WEALTHY HABITS

In The Power of Positive Thinking (Ballantine Books, 1996), Norman Vincent Peale says:

Such a large number of individuals are crushed by the regular issues of life. They go battling, maybe in any event, whimpering, during their time with a feeling of dull disdain at what they consider the "terrible breaks" life has given them. As it were, there might be such an incredible concept as "the breaks" right now, there is additionally a soul and strategy by which we can control and even decide those breaks. It is a pity that individuals should leave themselves alone vanquished by issues, cares, and troubles of human presence, and it is additionally very superfluous By figuring out how to cast (obstructions) from your mind, by declining to turn out to be intellectually subservient to them, and by directing deep force through your musings, you can transcend obstructions which usually may vanquish you.

The opening part of Napoleon Hill's The Law of Success (Wil-shire Book Company, 2000) communicates a similar supposition:

Achievement is generally a matter of altering one's self to the ever-shifting and changing situations of life, in a soul of amicability and balance. Amicability depends on a comprehension of the powers comprising one's condition. The best people on earth have needed to address certain shaky areas as a part of their characters before they started to succeed.

As somebody who has consistently been keen on the capability of the psyche, I discover this kind of thought engaging. Assuming, surely, I could think myself rich, what else might I be able to do with my psychological apparatus? Possibly I could think myself restored of this chest cold? (And, truly, there's an enormous field of mending dependent on simply such an idea.) If I can utilize attentions to get more profits, why not get more astute, as well? Furthermore, better looking?

The conceivable outcomes are unfathomable. Furthermore, enticing.

IT'S NOT ABOUT THINKING . . . IT'S ABOUT DOING

However, if getting rich and effective were only questions of replaceing pessimistic contemplations and sentiments with constructive ones, for what reason are such huge numbers of the most extravagant, best individuals that I know hopeless, irritable, and miserable?

Not constantly. And, not in all conditions. However, when in doubt, I can't help thinking that a large portion of the individuals out there making boatloads of money are more determined than fantastic, more touchy than serene, and more hard-pushing than accommodating.

Don't you concur?

Consider the extremely constructive, extremely upbeat individuals you know. It is safe to say that they are the business commanders? Is it true that they are the million-dollar workers? The most joyful and most well-adjusted individual I know is my better half and she hasn't made a nickel in 15 years. A list of the other most upbeat individuals that I know would incorporate

- TG, a barkeep and lager guzzler who hasn't had a stable employment in 30 years
- JF, who surrendered a rewarding CEO place 12 years prior to show yoga
- CF, who brings home the bacon watering indoor plants

I'm not thumping positive reasoning. Also, I'm absolutely not saying that having a decent mental standpoint is hindering to developing rich. I'm contending that there is no factual proof that likens positive attentions with rising total assets. Actually, the little information that we have regarding the matter proposes an alternate story:

- It is the means by which you act, not what you think, that will decide your victory.
- It is the means by which you think, not what you do, that will decide yourjoy.

Here's my point. I don't accept that the key to turning out to be well off is to fill your head with positive attentions. Actually, I don't think it much issues what you fill your head with. In light of individual perceptions and studies I've readd, it's my conviction that the key to developing rich is to follow certain standards of conduct. To do what riches developers do and not burn through whenever getting your mind fixed beforehand.

Actually, from a critical perspective, I could contend that

the fix-your-mind-first way of thinking is simply one more approach to thwart activity. Furthermore, activity, as I've contended in the previous barely any sections, is the sine qua non of progress.

Over the span of this book, I'm going to attempt to place certain thoughts into your head, change some others that you may now have, and support my own thoughts with a wide range of realities, numbers, accounts, and information.

However, I don't trust you need to embrmaster or change a solitary idea to get affluent. Keep the contemplations you have. Don't sweat it. How-ever, if you need to change over your interest right now a more elevated level of riches for yourself, you should follow the particular practices I'm suggesting.

Get it done!

If you needed to turn into a world-class tennis player and had Andre Agassi available to you as an individual mentor and guide, okay invest your energy with him discovering what goes through his mind during matches? Or then again would you figure out how to copy his serve, his developments, and his swings?

In jiujitsu, the game I enjoy, my first master had a standard:

Try not to consider what you realized here today. Try not to return home and run it through your brain. Try not to take notes. Try not to look at books. Simply practice the developments I show you and, eventually, your body will know them, regardless of whether your brain is elsewhere.

That is a definitive target of learning, would it say it isn't? To procure information so deep that it becomes subliminal . . .

and, programmed?

In Zen in the Art of Archery (Vintage, 1999), Eugen Herrigel portrays it along these lines:

The bowman stops to be aware of himself as the person who is occupied with hitting the bull's-eye which goes up against him. This condition of oblivious is acknowledged just when, totally void and free of oneself, he gets one with the consummating of his specialized ability.

Careful discipline brings about promising results

The thought is this: If you need to master the specialty of riches building so you can turn out to be monetarily free and make riches naturally at whatever point and any place you need to you have to learn riches fabricating how any master learns his craft: by rehashing, as intently as could be expected under the circumstances, the activities of effective riches developers.

And, this prompts a significant Catch 22: If you need to master an expertise as fast as could reasonably be expected, practice it gradually.

Howard Roberts, the amazing jazz guitarist, made this point years back at a little workshop I visited. Because of an inquiry presented by NR, a companion of mine, Roberts said that he accepted the key to his virtuosity was that he "never rehearsed an error."

"For me, practicing the guitar resembles strolling to the toilet," he said. "I generally walk a similar way, supposing that I ever need to walk that way around evening time I need to know precisely where to put my feet."

Roberts had faith in practicing each note splendidly,

regardless of whether that implied playing amazingly gradually from the start. And, I'm informed that numerous examinations have approved his hypothesis. The organic procedure of making a neural memory way truly is a lot of like strolling to the latrine. Each reiteration creates a good way one that you can go on later. Each wrong redundancy beats an equal however erroneous way one that you can without much of a stretch slide onto if you aren't cautious.

The more you practice the correct moves, the more deep the memory way. Try to make the right ways as deep as could be expected under the circumstances and to make the inaccurate ways shallow or nonexistent.

The quicker you play out an assignment, the almost certain it is that you will commit an error except if, that is, you have cut just a single way for it. A single one. Moreover, when you are playing out an errand under pressure, it is anything but difficult to mishandle it except if you have no neurological method to mess it up.

The explanation such a significant number of guitar students surge when they're practicing, Roberts stated, is that they are focused on finishing a piece as opposed to on performing it well. They figure that the sooner they can practically take care of business, the better they are doing. In any case, the fact of the matter is very extraordinary.

Most things worth learning are complex. That is the reason we learn them in pieces. Regardless of whether it's guitar playing, moving, or fabricating riches, a definitive presentation is an intricate mix of numerous less complex abilities.

To make the presentation great, you have to consummate

every one of those more straightforward aptitudes. This is the premise of best learning frameworks. The essential standard is this: Slow down . . . until you can rehearse the aptitude with immaculate skill. Keep practicing flawlessly and you will find that your speed will bit by bit increase with no exertion on your part. In the long run, you will do it rapidly and superbly.

You will find that you can apply this standard to practically any ability and accomplish similar decent outcomes. In your endeavours to prepare yourself to turn into a riches developer, you should stay discreet as a top priority. Turning into a master at riches building is similar to getting mind blowing at guitar playing or jiujitsu. Each requires information and experience. Each includes learning aptitudes. Every one of these abilities might be mind boggling, however if you separate them into their essential components and practice every one gradually and flawlessly you will master them.

THE EIGHT HABITS OF HIGHLY SUCCESSFUL WEALTH BUILDERS

Right off the bat in my profession, the time I went through considering money was carefully down to business: how to get it.

However, then I began to consider riches all the more scientifically: what it is, the manner by which it's made, and how it vanishes. Thus I've glanced back at what I've done (both great and terrible) and the exercises I've gained from others. Furthermore, this is the thing that I currently accept: There is nobody approach to get rich. In any case, there are various propensities that a few people build up that give them a practically extraordinary capacity to acquire money and manufacture riches.

I'd state these individuals share the accompanying attributes practically speaking:

1. They work hard.
2. They are acceptable at what they do.
3. They have various sources of pay.
4. They live in (generally) reasonable homes.
5. They are moderate in their spending.
6. They are exceptional in their saving.
7. They pay themselves first.
8. They count their money.

This isn't all that you'll have to think about riches building. We will talk about other significant insider facts in later parts. For the occasion, however, we are looking at creating rich propensities. These eight are my proposals.

1. WEALTHY PEOPLE WORK HARD

The normal multimillionaire works a normal of 59 hours per week. Furthermore, huge numbers of those hours are testing.

In any case, you would prefer not to hear that now. Furthermore, I don't need you to consider it.

Consider this rather: If you follow the exhortation right now changing how you work, the activity you do, and how you consider work, those 59 hours will fly by.

Also, there's all the more uplifting news. A significant number of those hours won't feel like work. You'll really enjoy them.

And, after you've hit your initial million or two, you can kick back and work less ... if you need to. In any case, you may not have any desire to!

2. WEALTHY PEOPLE ARE GOOD AT WHAT THEY DO

A few people luck out and discover wealth. In any case, master riches manufacturers individuals who can make riches effectively and over and again don't depend on karma. They are acceptable at what they do.

Being acceptable at what they do gives them certainty and balance. In examining business or money, they are loose however engaged. Narrow minded of fakers, they move immediately whenever opportunity thumps.

You can tell when you are within the sight of natural riches developers. There is something unmistakable in the manner they hold themselves and how they talk. It's looser than tense and more adaptable than fixed. Regular riches developers have the certainty to realize that they know. They've done it and they can do it once more.

Everything comes down to acing a monetarily valued ability. I'll clarify what that implies and how it should fit into your riches building objectives in the following part.

3. WEALTHY PEOPLE HAVE MULTIPLE STREAMS OF INCOME

Common money makers make the vast majority of their money by practicing a transgression gle aptitude inside the setting of a solitary industry. Try not to be tricked by monetary masters who reveal to you in any case. In any case, they in the end create numerous floods of salary. And, I'm going to contend that you ought to do something very similar.

To kick your monetary fortune off, you need to deeply help your pay. And, doing that, as I'll clarify in the initial segment of the following part, requires doing one thing remarkably well.

In the second piece of Step Four, we will discuss numerous ways that you can enhance your essential salary. I'll tell you the best way to begin little and grow additional little surges of money that joyfully drift into your financial balance each month and develop your riches hold.

Many master riches manufacturers I know enjoy twelve wellsprings of salary. Some are humble, some astounding. That is the extraordinary thing about making income. Despite the fact that no one can tell what will occur with any individual pay source, if you kick enough of them off, one will transform into a waterway.

4. WEALTHY PEOPLE LIVE IN (RELATIVELY) INEXPENSIVE HOMES

What amount do you think the regular American worth $6.8 million normally pays for a house?

I put this inquiry to the Early to Rise staff. Their conjecture was between $2 million and $3 million. Being more seasoned and more astute, my supposition was nearer to reality. I calculated the number was nearer to $1 million. However, then we checked the IRS records. And, the appropriate response was an amazing $545,000. That is not a great sale of money for somebody who's worth nearly $7 million. So what's happening here?

In reality, he knows two things:

- The expense of your home decides the expense of your way of life. Think about this: Property charges on a $500,000 house are about $4,000 to $5,000 more every year than on a $250,000 house. Utility costs are likewise proportionately more noteworthy. If you live in a more costly house, you'll pay much more for support costs. Furthermore, not because there is more house to keep. When numerous temporary workers see that you live in a decent house in an extravagant neighbourhood, their charges shoot up. Consider it a riches charge. They figure, "He can bear the cost of it. I need it. So why not?"

- However, assessments, utilities, and support building only the tip of the cost rising ice shelf. The significant expense of owning a costly house is underneath the surface. The main explanation costly homes cost so a whole lot (more than you'd might suspect) is because they are relentlessly joined to an increasingly costly way of life. By way of life, I incorporate all that you pay more for the time being that you live in a more pleasant neighbourhood furniture and finishing, vehicles and instruction, cafés and excursions, just to give some examples. It isn't so much that you are intentionally attempting to stay aware of the Joneses. It's simply that you can't locate those cheap things (or place or administration individuals) any longer.

- Home-spending choices are not or ought not be principally about quantifiable profit. In purchasing, repairing, and outfitting your home, you will spend a decent deal of money on things that will have a ton of enthusiastic worth however minimal monetary worth. If you need to pl another deal of windows in the family room, repaint a room, or purchase a bookshelf for your brew can assortment, you don't need to do a financial examination first. Interestingly, the speculations you make for monetary profit can and ought to be settled on such sane, primary concern thinking. I purchased my first house 20 years prior for $175,000. I put down about $15,000 which was the whole of my total assets. After ten years, I was living in a $800,000 house, which spoke to around 25 percent of my total assets. Today, I live in a more costly home, however one that records for as it were around 10 percent of my riches. Furthermore, that feels better.

Let's talk about the Tax Profits of Stretching Yourself Financially When Buying a Home?

The facts confirm that a more costly home that has bigger home loan instalments will likewise have bigger assessment deductible intrigue instalments. Yet, you're in an single situation going through less money in any case. Keep in mind, so as to set aside money with charge reasoning, you need to spend more than you save. If you are in the 28 percent charge section, for instance, each dollar you spend on contract premium is deductible, and that will save you 28¢ in charges. However, you'll have spent a dollar to understand that 28¢ saving and will be 62¢ less fortunate. It's smarter to take that 62¢ and contribute it else-where. Before long it will be worth $5.

The main concern is this: Buy a house that suits every one of your needs easily, and contribute time and care to make it delightful. Then, take the money you didn't spend on an increasingly costly home and put it in something that will acquire money for you. (I'll give you my suggestions in the following section.) You'll get more extravagant quicker.

4. WEALTHY PEOPLE ARE MODERATE IN SPENDING

Carlos is experiencing the American dream. He resulted in

these present circumstances nation to contend in mixed combative techniques and win his fortune as a victor warrior. While building an excellent success loss record, he lived on club sponsorship and expenses for giving exercises. For the initial three years of his time here, he figured out how to help himself and his significant other on not exactly $15,000 per year. As of late, he caught three title belts and now battles at the top level in Japan. His run of the mill payday has gone from $500 to $25,000.

"The issue with getting more money in America," he let me know, "is that each time you cause an additional dollar you to burn through two."

Master riches developers comprehend a mystery that it took me years to learn: You need to hold your spending down while your salary increases.

We'll speak increasingly about that later. However, presently, we should discuss Mike Tyson.

The Sad Story of Mike Tyson: A Spending Fool

During the 20-year range of his vocation, Mike Tyson's salary surpassed $400 million. However in 2004, preceding his 39th birthday celebration, this stunning moneymaker was $38 million under water. He had a few resources value in certain houses, a few vehicles, and some gems however insiders hypothesized their all out an incentive at under $3 million. For wishing him well, let's expect it was twice that much. That would have put his per-sonal total assets at negative $32 million.

Consider that: less $32 million!

That could make him the world's least fortunate man. With adverse total assets that enormous, Mike Tyson is multiple times less fortunate than the normal breadwinner from Sierra Leone, the most unfortunate nation on the planet, with a normal yearly pay of $200 per individual.

"By what means can a man with a $4 million domain in New Jersey be poor?" an associate asked me.

"He can at present make millions each time he battles," my sister said. "Any individual who can make millions isn't poor."

However by each perceived standard of bookkeeping, he is poor. Very poor.

In any case, he doesn't think so. And, that is a piece of the explanation he got so poor in any case. The quicker money came in, the quicker it went out. Anecdotes about his wickedness are as of now unbelievable. Tyson utilized upwards of 200 individuals, including guardians, drivers, culinary specialists, and plant specialists.

He spent:

- Nearly $4.5 million on vehicles and bikes
- $3.4 million on clothes and adornments
- $7.8 million on "individual costs"
- $140,000 on two white Bengal tigers and $125,000 every year for their coach
- $2 million on a bath for his first spouse, on-screen character Robin Givens
- $410,000 on a birthday celebration
- $230,000 on mobile phones and pagers during a three-year time span from 1995 to 1997

The motivation behind this isn't to shake a finger at Mike

Tyson, yet to alarm you to the hazardous compulsion to spend more when you make more. As somebody who grew up drinking powdered milk and wearing used articles, I comprehend the quality of that allurement.

Why Spending Feels So Good

For what reason do we do it? For what reason do we want to spend more when we make more?

This is what I think. When you are poor, you are encompassed by things you figure you might want to claim however can't bear to purchase. Sooner or later, you compare the sentiment of unsatisfied want with destitution. And, when craving starts to feel poor, having appears as though it will cause you to feel rich.

That is the heart's rationale, at any rate.

If that is how you feel now if your concept of being affluent is loaded up with pictures of manors and boats and costly watches you will make some troublesome memories setting aside money. And, setting aside money is another of the basic propensities for individuals who realize how to manufacture riches.

WEALTHY PEOPLE ARE EXTRAORDINARY AT SAVING

The rich save more than the normal individual. Moderately, that is. I don't mean they save more since they have more money to save. I mean they save more as a rule, since they have a saver's attitude. As indicated by Thomas Stanley, creator of The Millionaire Next Door, the normal mogul is significantly more economical than you or I would have accepted. (Coincidentally, Stanley gets a large portion of his information from the IRS and other government sources.) For instance, the normal mogul

- Drives an older vehicle
- Buys reasonable presents
- Eats at home and only from time to time eats out
- Takes an excursion each other year
- Wears clothes until they quarrel and resoles shoes when they wear ragged

To build up a saver's outlook a riches developer's mentality you should change how you feel about spending. You should show your-self to feel reality: that each time you purchase a deteriorating resource, you become more unfortunate.

Help yourself more than once that most to remember the garbage you purchase (1) gets unused following a couple of months and (2) doesn't give you that much worth in any case. Recollect that the best things throughout everyday life the picnics you have with your family, the strolls you take with your darling, the time you spend with your companions are free, or almost so.

There are such a significant number of approaches to set aside money. You can spend less on pretty much anything without surrendering either the delight you take in purchasing or the quality you get from your buys.

Rather than purchasing new clothes that will be out of style in a year, purchase vintage dress that looks incredible and recognizes you.

Rather than marking a rent for a costly vehicle you can't manage, discover something old yet at the same time great that has a character.

Rather than venturing out on a brief siesta consistently, eat a container of fish at your work area. (This is something I did. By eating a jar of fish each day as opposed to going to lunch with my collaborators, I saved nearly $2,500 in a solitary year. Besides, I went from staff manager to publisher by applying that additional lunch-break time to improving the business.)

Try not to stress I'm not going to attempt to transform you into a grumpy person. The motivation behind spending less is to have more. I enjoy the extravagances that riches can bring, however as I'll clarify later I don't trust you need to spend much more to get them.

You'll have your cake and eat it, as well. You'll spend less, squander less, save more, and have bounty left over to enjoy life.

5. WEALTHY PEOPLE PAY THEMSELVES FIRST

Numerous financial counsellors prescribe adhering to a spending limit. By ordering costs and constraining spending, they contend, you can have enough left over consistently to set aside money and develop rich.

The difficulty is that planning never works.

Planning resembles eating fewer carbs: It's colossally reasonable yet never successful. I've taken a stab at planning myself multiple times. I've additionally wrongly encouraged others to keep a spending limit. I can't think about a solitary situation where it worked.

The issue is that when you budget, you pay every other person first.

As top of the line creator David Bach says:

[You] pay the real estateowner, the charge card organization, the phone organization, the administration, without any end in sight. The explanation [you] think [you] need a financial limit is to . . . make sense of the amount to pay every other person so toward the month's end [you] will have something "left finished" to pay [yourself.]

So toward the month's end, you don't have anything left to place in the bank. You guarantee yourself you'll improve next time, however you never do. There are constantly unforeseen bills to pay, unexpected sales to exploit, and that difficult to-make sense of $200 or $300 that appears to get lost in an outright flood.

Planning doesn't work. In any case, there is something that does: placing some foreordained level of your pay into a bank account every prior month you take care of any of your tabs.

Consider yourself an individual company and the money you save as your own salary. The various money you spend on house and vehicle instalments, etc are the costs of your own partnership. Just the bit that goes into an investment account is actually yours.

Obviously, it's insufficient to just think about your salary along these lines. You should really plan something for impact a change. You may, for instance, have a segment of your check consequently stored in your investment account every month when the check is kept. Paying yourself first right now., (saving before you take care of tabs) is really, as Bach calls attention to, paying yourself second. He advises us that retaining charges are simply the administration's method for paying first. Before your pay is kept into your financial records, the administration has just taken its piece.

What Your Government Already Knows about Getting Paid First

The administration comprehends the intensity of being first at the pay trough. That is the reason it developed retention charge.

Prior to 1943, Americans got 100 percent of the money they earned. The annual duties exacted on them every year weren't expected until the accompanying spring. In any case, as the administration budget developed, so did annual assessments. The 1 and 2 percent that was collected before all else started to rise. Before long it was 3 and 4 percent. And afterward 5 and 6 percent.

The administration immediately found that its residents were not anxious to send in their charges each spring. A few people had just gone through the whole of their money. Others just couldn't get themselves to leave behind it.

This wasn't turning out well for the civil servants who needed to manufacture a major government. Furthermore, it wouldn't accomplish for the government officials who needed to get us engaged with World War II. So they thought of an approach to ensure that they would get the money. They passed a law expecting businesses to retain representative assessments and afterward give them to the legislature.

At the end of the day, they concocted an approach to get themselves paid first.

Do It Your Way

By adding to a duty conceded account a 401(k), 403(b), IRA, or SEP you pay yourself even before the administration takes its cut. That is because, much of the time, the money you contribute is charge deductible.

Most traditional investment funds plans are turned out on a yearly premise. The standard proposal is to make sense of what your gross or overall gain will be for the year and afterward put 10 percent of that in an IRA, SEP, or something like that.

Since commitments to impose supported plans are made on a yearly premise, individuals who follow such plans for the most part contribute their investment funds once per year. This can be troublesome if you experience difficulty adhering to your spending limit. It's more reasonable to set money aside every time you get paid. Most investment records will let you do that. Some permit your bank to consequently move reserve funds when they are stored.

That is my main event, and it's what I prescribe to companions and col-groups. Pay yourself first, the administration second, and everybody and everything else last.

I pay myself first by putting as a lot of money as I'm permitted into a duty conceded reserve funds vehicle. I do this for me, my life partner, and my youngsters. I pay the administration next by making a different holding account into which I store a level of each expense that is paid to me the money that I will owe in charges. Then I take care of my tabs.

In reality, I take care of my tabs fourth. Before I do that, I store extra money into different reserve funds and investment accounts. Since I save considerably more than I can place into

SEPs and IRAs, I am ready to make these extra, pay-myself-third stores.

I don't generally require every one of those holding accounts. I could store everything in a solitary record, let it aggregate, and settle on investment funds and expense instalment choices later. However, I'm constantly apprehensive that except if I get the basics (reserve funds and charges) salet with first, some disaster will happen or I'll go crazy and spend money selected for fundamentals on something vaporous.

There is something in particular about the way toward moving money to extraordinary records that feels like it's leaving from me, that I don't claim it any more. I ought to be humiliated to concede that I despite everything play this mental stunt with myself, yet I do . . . and, it works!

With regards to this guarded propensity, I could disclose to you innumerable accounts of super-high-pay individuals I realize who come to me, edgy, at charge season requesting span advances since they some way or another went through the money they should take care of for charges on who-comprehends what. (I'm constantly hesitant to solicit.) Surprisingly, more than one of these colleagues has been notable investment specialists.

Save More... Substantially More

Nowadays, I save around 35 percent to 40 percent of my salary. It wasn't generally that way. When I initially started bringing home the bacon, I was saving under 10 percent. As I came to get riches and change how I felt about saving, that rate developed.

When I was saving 10 percent, it generally appeared

enough. I wasn't right. You shouldn't commit a similar error.

John, age 30, strolled into my office a day or two ago and stated, "I've understood I will always be unable to sufficiently save to get well off."

"Not at 10 percent of your present salary," I agreed.

I don't know where this 10 percent figure originates from. Maybe it originates from the Greek and scriptural custom of tithing. Absolutely, it's a rate that the vast majority of conventional methods can sale with. However, except if you are winning a million-in addition to a year or have 40 years to pause, 10 percent won't do it for you.

If you are shrewd, you'll set yourself an increasingly aggressive saving objective.

Here's my recommendation:

Your First Saving Goal:

Consistently, I will save more than I saved a year ago.

You can't generally make this a month to month objective. If you follow the other riches building proposals I will make right now, have an excessive number of wellsprings of pay to keep such a guarantee. (With four or five separate wellsprings of salary, your month to month numbers will vacillate excessively.) But if you make it a yearly objective, you can do this without breaking a sweat.

When you are alright with that and maybe you are as of now set another, related objective that is in reality substantially more dominant:

Your Second Saving Goal:

Consistently, I will build the sum I save as far as a level of my salary.

That may not appear notable, yet it's really a major, aspiring objective. It implies that if you begin saving 10 percent of your gross salary now, one year from now you'll build it to 12 percent or 15 percent or 20 percent. Furthermore, the following year, you'll make the rate significantly higher.

Be advised that you can't do this too forcefully. Nor would you be able to do it until the end of time. However, if you increase your pay each year and hold your costs down, your reserve funds to-pay proportion will get higher.

Here are some recommended targets:

If you are making under $50,000 a year:10 percent

More than $50,000 however under $200,000: 15 percent

More than $200,000 yet under $500,000: 25 percent

More than $1 million yet under $2 million: 35 percent

More than $2 million yet under $5 million: 40 percent

More than $5 million: 45 percent

When your pay surpasses $200,000, you will be paying between 40 percent and 50 percent of your pay to state and government charges. So an investment funds pace of 20 percent is extremely 60 percent to 70 percent. Furthermore, an investment funds pace of 40 percent is really 80 percent to 90 percent.

Begin Saving Today

Beginning today actually, today start the act of saving.

Regardless of whether you are living from check to check, you should begin your saving project today. You should get your hands on some measure of money and contribute it right away. Start with at any rate 10 percent of your gross salary. If you don't have that a lot of money, set aside as much as you can.

The explanation you need to begin saving presently, regardless of whether your pay is little, is that you need to make the propensity for saving. When saving gets ongoing, it gets simpler. And, whatever you can do effectively, you'll improve, all the more frequently, and longer term.

Presently, there's one more propensity for deeply successful riches developers that I need you to begin developing . . .

6. WEALTHY PEOPLE COUNT THEIR MONEY

I have no measurable proof that this last riches building propensity is a far reaching natural among independent rich individuals, however I presume that it is. I accept that best moneymakers consistently tally their money. I don't imply that they truly tally bills. Or maybe, they regularly survey their fortunes.

I accept this is genuine particularly in the beginning times, when they are simply starting to develop their riches. As their net gain develops and they feel more great with their riches and increasingly sure of their salary, they check less.

When they get superwealthy Warren Buffett well off they don't need to tally their money. Fortune magazine and endless other enti-ties do it for them. In any case, on their way up, they tally. And, that is the thing that I prescribe you do.

In particular, I recommend that you do an individual asset report each month. Make a spreadsheet that lists every one of your profits and your entire debt-it Incorporate important belongings, stocks, securities, shared assets, gold, real estate (beside your home, etc. Precisely gauge the profit of everything. If there is an inquiry regarding how much something is worth, pick the lesser number. List all your obligation, as well. And, be totally real to life.

Simply experiencing the procedure will prepare your psyche (and heart) to comprehend financial riches as monetary total assets. After you've done this six or seven months straight, it will get programmed.

And keeping in mind that you are doing that month to month spreadsheet, help your-self to remember the saving objectives you've made that you will set aside more money, in both total and relative terms, as time passes.

You can make this activity more energizing by promising yourself this: That you will be more extravagant each time you check. That you'll do all things needed to guarantee that when you include your profits each month, the main concern will be bigger than it was the prior month.

You'll be astounded at how a lot of this basic duty can influence how you think and even how you act.

WHILE YOU ARE DEVELOPING WEALTH-BUILDING HABITS, DON'T DEPRIVE YOURSELF

You can without much of a stretch become familiar with the

eight propensities for well off individuals. Furthermore, when you do, you'll see that the neediness attitude that once erroneously asked you to spend yourself rich has been replaceed with another sort of reasoning that prizes you for spending less.

Step by step instructions to LIVE LIKE A BILLIONAIRE WITHOUT SPENDING LIKE ONE

If you could enjoy the best things money could purchase the most treasured material products that even the world's very rich people can enjoy yet spend minimal more for them than you spend now, okay do it?

There is a way. Try to isolate the quality goods from the refuse. To make sense of what things in life can bring you joy, how much delight they offer, and what you need to pay for them.

Try not to hold up until you become affluent and have this kind of intuition constrained on you after you have the alleged profit of spending a fortune on objects that give you no delight. After you've purchased the huge house, the costly vehicles, the pompous clothes and adornments and afterward acknowledged how minimal certifiable delight they were giving you. Consider the things you have now the vehicle you drive, the clothes you wear, and the toys you play with. Consider them and their worth.

Truth be told, make this into somewhat game. Take a piece of paper and draw a vertical line down its centre. On the left half of the page, under a section checked "Things I Enjoy," make a list:

The most important thing that money can get you is the

opportunity to invest your energy as you see fit. And, when you arrive at where you can invest the vast majority of your energy focusing on those things that present to you the best delight, odds are you won't spend a lot of money (except if, that is, you are unimaginably shallow). You'll most likely decide to invest your energy chatting with companions, reading great books, getting a charge out of workmanship and travel carrying on with the sort of life you imag-ine well off English or French blue-bloods did in hundreds of years past.

Somewhat, at any rate, you can do that at the present time.

LIVING RICH ... Beginning RIGHT NOW

When you consider the rich the extremely rich you may locate your-self wondering about their ... all things considered, their money.

Take Bill Gates, the world's most extravagant man. If you think $10 million is a fortune, then think about this: He has 8,000 of them. If he put his money in $1,000 notes, he'd have 80 million of them! His riches is extraordinary to such an extent that the enthusiasm on it makes him $60 million more extravagant consistently. Bill Gates gets more money-flow each time he sleeps than most Americans make in 10 years.

However, how much better does he live? Without a doubt, he has a tremendous house. And, a yacht. Presumably he has a fly, as well. Yet, who needs that poo? Truly!

You can live just as Bill Gates does at the present time. Furthermore, I'll demonstrate it to you.

We should begin by distinguishing a portion of the rudiments of life:

- Sleeping
- Working
- Dressing
- Eating and drinking
- Enjoying relaxation time

Presently, the reason for getting rich you would believe is to make every one of these encounters as compensating as could be expected under the circumstances. The more money you have, the more decisions you have.

Take resting. What does an extremely rich person look for from rest time? I'd state something very similar you do: merry, continuous obviousness. Furthermore, (beside genuine feelings of serenity, which you can't purchase) what will give you that?

Answer: an incredible sleeping pad.

And, what amount does the world's best sleeping pad cost? Possibly $1,500. That implies you can get yourself a million-dollar rest on a billion-dollar sleeping pad for close to $1,500.

So dispose of that uneven thing you are dozing on and locate your-self the most flawlessly awesome sleeping cushion you have ever sat on. Get it and rest content that Bill Gates can do no better.

You can address practically any cost for anything however after a specific value point, you are paying for eminence instead of value.

Take steak. Get some information about hamburger and they'll disclose to you that the nature of a steak relies completely upon the meat. Purchase a New York sirloin at Ruth's Chris and, for around $30, you are eating the best steak money can purchase. Eat a similar bit of meat at Le Cirque and you'll pay $75. What's the distinction?

Indeed just distinction.

Something very similar is genuine with regards to your attire. Delightful, agreeable clothes are not modest, however they don't need to cost a fortune. You can purchase the world's best pair of slacks for $150 or you can burn through multiple times that sum. The thing that matters is the name on the belt.

Champagne, anybody? Purchaser Reports had some wine specialists test an assortment of champagnes and found that out of the five best, four were under $40. Dom Perignon, recorded fifth, will interfere with you $115. However, you can have a superior champagne for just $28.

Thus it goes on.

The fact of the matter is this: The best material things in life are reasonable. They are not modest quality never is however if you get them specifically and use them with care, you can enjoy an actual existence as physically rich as Bill Gates on a salary that wouldn't get him through lunch.

Your Dream House

I've lived in a three-room mud cabin in Africa and a 5,000-square-foot chateau, and I can reveal to you this: The nature of a home has pretty much nothing or nothing to do with its expense or size.

Consider the houses you most respect. They are most likely not tremendous and ostentatious. One of my present top picks is an unobtrusive, three-room house in Clevereal estate that its proprietor changed into a lavish, rich exhibition hall of her adoration for movement, move, and learning. Each room is a pearl. I am totally agreeable and perpetually diverted right now intriguing house.

Its worth? As extraordinary as Bill Gates' 40,000-square-foot enormity in Seattle yet this one has a market estimation of about $150,000.

CHAPTER FOUR

INCREASE YOUR INCOME RADICALLY

WHY ORDINARY PAY RAISES WILL MAKE YOU POORER INSTEAD OF RICHER

The vast majority experience their lives working for organizations they don't think anything much about, managing issues they'd preferably not confront, and getting paid wages they'd particularly prefer to change.

They long for a superior life and may begrudge the individuals who get more money-flow, yet they are baffled with regards to making sense of some solution for it. If vocation work is a way, theirs has an unobtrusive tilt upward. Truly, they will get raises however what number of and what amount?

In a review of 1,276 organizations across the country, Hewitt Associates, a worldwide HR re-appropriating and counselling firm, found that normal pay increases for 2003 were 3.4 percent the most reduced number at any point recorded in Hewitt's 27 years of social occasion and breaking down this sort of information.

Truth be told, the pattern has been descending since the review started. At the outset, normal raises were around 6 percent. Then, during the 1980s, they dropped to a little more than 5 percent for each year. In the primary portion of the 1990s, they dropped to around 4 percent to 4.25 percent and remained there through 2001. They dropped to 3.7 percent in 2002 preceding hitting record lows in 2003.

It's deeply improbable that you'll get rich on that sort of pay in-wrinkle. That is particularly valid if you think about the impacts of swelling. While pay has ascended in the course of recent decades, so has the typical cost for basic items. A few investigations show that overall gain (in the wake of modifying for inflation) has not expanded since the mid 1980s.

Also, the pattern is going the incorrect way. Somewhere in the range of 2000 and 2002, for instance, pre-tax middle family unit pay rose 0.6 percent to $42,409. However, when balanced for swelling, that increase turned into a 3.3 percent decrease.

The dreary truth is that working individuals in America have been get-ting less fortunate, not more extravagant, regardless of higher nominative wages.

To beat this dreary pattern, you have to procure better than expected boosts in pay. That, I'm glad to let you know, can without much of a stretch be cultivated. Keep in mind, these discouraging insights are estimations of the normal. They remember information for certain specialists who get no raises, numerous whose raises track expansion, and just a couple of representatives who show improvement over that.

You need to get yourself into the third classification. Truth be told, your objective ought to be to fundamentally expand your salary. How would you do that?

Even though it might appear to be difficult to accept, most organizations are more than ready to give you better than expected increases. In any case, they will do so readily just if you give them better than expected work.

I'm not recommending that businesses are kindhearted. Some are and some are most certainly not. However, most solid organizations are profit situated. Also, when they discover representatives who can assist them with expanding profits, they are generally ready to compensate them by coming back to them a little segment of what they produced.

This has consistently been the situation particularly with little and developing organizations. Today it's getting increasingly ordinary among bigger organizations, as they advance toward execution based pay (deciding rewards or other pay on how well representatives, groups, and the organization do), to support profits.

THE SECRET TO GETTING ABOVE-AVERAGE RAISES

To gain more and enjoy superior to anything normal boosts in pay there are two things you should do.

To begin with, you should improve as a representative. And, second, you should ensure that everybody who matters realizes you are better.

To procure fundamentally more than you do now, you should make yourself a deeply better labourer. I'll clarify how you can do that somewhat later. For the occasion, however, let's put our focus on increasingly humble objectives.

Step by step instructions to Become a Noticeably Better Employee

Turning into an increasingly significant worker is the first and most significant approach to support your salary, however it's insufficient. Corporate culture being what it is (in many places), you should likewise publicize your worth.

Obviously, you would prefer not to put on a show of being a braggadocio. That will make pointless pockets of disdain. The key to successful self-development in a business situation is triple:

1. Promote just what is valid.
2. Give some credit to other people, regardless of whether it hasn't been earned.
3. Be constantly self-destroying. Or on the other hand so it ought to appear.

If you don't advance yourself, you are leaving the destiny of your pay in the hands of possibility and situation. However, while you need to ensure that the individuals in power know about your achievements, you additionally don't need them to consider you a yearning egotist.

Set up It As a written record

A decent strategy is to start writing ordinary reports on all the significant undertakings you are associated with. Concentrate the report on the business, not you. Make it brief one page is sufficient. Recognition everybody included. Make light of your own job. However, ensure the subtext is clear: Here is one more beneficial thing you have brought to the table.

There is a decent business reason for writing such reminders. Your boss (and possibly your manager's boss) is keen on these tasks. The person wouldn't like to know the subtleties. And, the individual particularly wouldn't like to think pretty much all the issues. However, your manager wants to be kept educated with exceptionally short reports on where each task is, the thing that has been done, and what is left to do.

When you or your group is confronted with a significant issue or challenge, you can compose a report on that, as well. Once more, ensure it is quick and painless. Once more, give credit where it's expected. And, ensure that it is steered so as to not annoy by passing anyone by. Generally significant, never present an issue without additionally exhibiting at any rate three potential deals. If you do, you'll get a notoriety for being a decent mastermind.

By working harder and more intelligent to achieve more and telling key individuals what you are achieving, you'll see that everybody will be considerably more responsive to allowing you better than expected salary increases when your survey comes around consistently.

Showing signs of improvement than-normal each year can have a significant effect in the riches you can get throughout a lifetime. The explanation behind this, obviously, lies in the huge intensity of exacerbating interest, particularly over an all-inclusive timeframe.

Consider your own vocation and envision what might occur if, as Elwood, you could acquire 6 percent more every year than you've been gaining up until this point.

By making yourself a more important representative and by elevating your incentive to enter individuals in your business you'll get the additional pay expands you have to in the end resign rich toward the finish of your vocation. However, that is your 40-year reinforcement plan. Let's talk about something significantly more energizing: How to help your salary by 10 percent to 100 percent a year (or more) so you can get well off in 7 to 15 years.

Changing from "Better" to "Priceless"

If improving than-normal boosts in pay can be accomplished by improving as a than-normal specialist, then it follows that phenomenal salary increases may come if you become an uncommon representative.

Consider it along these lines: Good workers acquire great pay rates since they are valued. However, incredible representatives gain astonishing pays since they are viewed as precious.

We should pause for a minute to characterize terms here, although words like important and significant are regularly excessively generously utilized. For instance, a manager may state that her own aide is important when she basically implies that the associate sales with the entire supervisor's needs and makes her life much simpler.

However, is the collaborator precious in the feeling of being worth a practically boundless measure of money? Would the manager twofold her pay to keep her? Triple it?

You need to be viewed as precious, yet not the sort of significant that gets you a congratulatory gesture and an extra $20 every week in your financial balance. To be really priceless, you must be pretty much basic. And, how might you do that?

Indeed, truly, you can't do it completely. Everyone, including Donald Trump and Oprah Winfrey, is replaceable.

However, the closer you can find a workable pace be crucial, the better your odds of fundamentally expanding your salary.

As I will show you, you should get familiar with your business. And, you may likewise need to adjust your expected set of responsibilities (at any rate to some degree). You will more likely than not need to grow your hover of contacts to incorporate more individuals who can assist you with accomplishing this objective.

In any case, the most significant thing you'll have to do is this: Master a monetarily valued aptitude.

What Is a Financially Valued Skill?

Let's start with this last idea and work our direction in reverse.

A monetarily valued expertise is one that a lot of others are eager to pay great money for. How great? I'd prefer to start the offering at, state, $130,000 every year.

This is, truly, a to some degree subjective number. However, it has the profit of giving you an after-charge pay of about $90,000. That is sufficient to permit a couple of individuals to enjoy a sensibly agreeable way of life and put in any event $13,000 into investment funds. Contribute $13,000 over a 15-year vocation at 12 percent and you'll have total assets of in excess of a million dollars. (Furthermore, I'm demonstrating how to show improvement over that by putting your time and money in manners that will make extra and programmed floods of pay for you.)

Before we investigate the kind of employments that pay a $130,000 pay, suppose a couple of more clear however significant things about the term monetarily valued.

- We are talking, presently, about financial worth as it were. We acknowledge, as I called attention to previously, that there are other, more significant qualities throughout everyday life.
- I am utilizing the word valued, as opposed to important, although I need to underscore the possibility that the view of significant worth that includes is in the commercial centre. We are not worried, for the occasion, with what you may by and by discover important or satisfying, yet just with what others esteem regarding money.
- I am underscoring the possibility of ability as opposed to calling, since aptitudes are transferable such that callings aren't. Likewise, it is conceivable to join a few valued aptitudes inside a given calling and in this manner duplicate your pay. I'll clarify increasingly about that later.
- Finally, note that I utilized the word master. That will get significant later on.

So we should investigate some mainstream callings as far as their normal earnings.

It might amaze you to discover that the middle pay for a dental specialist or legal counsellor is under $130,000. Yet, that is simply middle salary. Middle salary incorporates all organizations, large or little, powerless or solid, and in a wide range of enterprises.

Clearly, bigger organizations frequently pay more than medium-sized ones. Private companies pay for all intents and purposes nothing from the outset however when they start to develop, the money they pay their top individuals can meet or surpass even that of some Fortune 500 organizations.

So What Can You Do with This Information?

If you are now utilized in a monetarily valued calling and are as of now making at any rate $130,000 (and expecting that you're content with your vocation decision), you have three targets.

1. You must master the fundamental expertise of your calling the ability that gets the most money for your business.
2. You must get capable at offering the plan to others that you are stunning.
3. You must hold your spending within proper limits so that as your salary skyrockets (and it can without much of a stretch ascent to twofold or triple the standard for your calling), you will have the option to contribute a bigger and bigger bit of it into (a) making extra floods of pay and (b) building value.

If you can support your pay to $130,000 per year, you ought to have the option to make a million-dollar total assets (not including your home and vehicle) in 7 to 15 years, expecting you hold your costs in line.

In the pages that tail I'll disclose to you a few different ways to do that. We'll start by discussing how you can support the pay you get from work.

Step by step instructions to BE A TOP EARNER IN YOUR BUSINESS

Fundamentally, there are three sorts of occupations in the business world: specialized, authoritative, and profit creating.

- Technical occupations remember most situations for data innovation and building, and a few situations in legitimate, monetary, and bookkeeping fields.
- •Administrative employments remember most situations for

corporate administration, item satisfaction, tasks, and client assistance, just as certain situations in money and bookkeeping.

- Profit-creating occupations are those that are legitimately engaged with delivering profits for the organization. Profit generators incorporate advertisers, sales reps, copywriters, individuals who make new items, and the individuals who sale with these workers. In many organizations, the main profit generator is the CEO, because the CEO's principle work is to convey a primary concern.

Technical labourers, on the normal, are the most unfortunate paid group. Generalists via preparing, they go up against a huge pool of different generalists in occupations that require no unique abilities or gifts. If you are a chairman, and a generally excellent one, you can hope to see your salary ascend as your exhibition improves. In any case, almost certainly, it will be at the 4 percent or 6 percent level presumably insufficient to meet your medium-term (7-to 15-year) riches building objective.

Administrative labourers are normally preferable paid over their authoritative partners. This is particularly valid toward the start of their vocations, so, all in all even a section level position requires a high level of specific information. PC engineers, data innovation individuals, and ensured open bookkeepers (CPAs) regularly start at more significant pays than do satisfaction bosss and client support representatives, yet the distinction will in general reduce after some time. Top architects frequently make more than operational VPs, yet very little more.

Profit generators are normally the most generously compensated workers. More significant, they have the best potential for money development.

If you work for a little or medium-sized organization and can be categorized as one of the initial two activity classes, you'll come to the $130,000 level just by ascending to the highest point of your division and afterward just if the business you work for is productive and developing. With bigger organizations, you may accomplish a pay of more than $130,000 as a specialized pro or a director of professionals and managers.

In any case, regardless of whether you can hit that sort of number, your upside potential will be restricted. That is because paying little heed to how great you are at what you do, what you are doing is normally observed as a fundamental cost, not a piece of the mystery procedure of bringing in money.

I'll have significantly more to state about this in a short time. Until further notice, you need to ask yourself a straightforward inquiry: "If I work more diligently and better at what I am doing now, are the odds acceptable that I can reach in any event the $130,000 pay level in the following a few years?"

If the appropriate response is truly, fine. If the appropriate response is no, you should be set up to roll out some extreme improvements.

So let's talk about that now: how to build up the abilities and convert your activity into one that merits the $130,000-in addition to level of pay.

Envision Yourself as a Bookkeeper...

Suppose you fill in as an accountant for another vehicle

sales focus and are not happy with your $30,000 pay. You could fantasy about owning the business, yet that is not liable to happen at any point in the near future. You need money to possess a vehicle sales centre. Money you don't have at the present time. For the quick future, you need to focus on something that is feasible. Along these lines, glance around.

Beside the proprietor, who else is taking in substantial income? All things considered, the project supervisor is cutting down a relentless $70,000 per year. That is not terrible. And afterward there's Joe, the main salesman, who is making much more than that.

You look at it and find that you can't be the project supervisor because the organization has a firm deal of enlisting MBAs for that activity. With the goal that leaves you one alternative: turning into a sales rep and proceeding to guarantee Joe's place as Numero Uno Salespro.

You could delineate for yourself, "Forget about it! I am not a natural, and God just realizes it takes a natural social butterfly to sell autos." But if you are brilliant, you will perceive that selling vehicles, as nearly everything else throughout everyday life, is a procedure that includes no enchantment simply explicit activities, every one of which can be concentrated and afterward learned.

Suppose you become friendly with Joe and in the end gain his trust. You take him out for a beverage one night and get him to open up and uncover his privileged insights the things he does to reliably out-perform (and outearn) each other sales rep. I'm not a specialist at selling vehicles; however I wouldn't be astounded if the discussion went something like this:

JOE: If I'm offering to a couple, I generally warmly greet the man first. That way, he feels significant. Something he needs to believe to settle on the choice I need him to make.

YOU: That's perfect, Joe. What else?

JOE (grinning): One thing I never do is say, straight off, how much a vehicle costs. If, before I'm prepared to close, a client pops the appalling inquiry, this is the thing that I state: "Let me ask you something, Mr. Someone or other, how significant is it to you to drive a vehicle that is protected and agreeable for your family?"

And afterward Joe would disclose to you a couple of more things he generally does. Presently, these things separately may not add up to such a lot. However, set up in a solitary introduction, they signify this: how Joe man-ages to be the organization's main sales rep, after a seemingly endless amount of time after quite a long time after month. Since that turning out to be tantamount to Joe is your objective, these particular things he does are the insider facts you have to learn.

The incredible sales rep, you presently comprehend, isn't someone with extraordinary powers yet a common individual with explicit, important information.

Thus you get familiar with the aptitudes required to perform not the occupation you are at present doing but rather the one that you hope for. By working well beyond your work depiction, you get took note. You additionally get the hang of what's significant. And, as you become a greater amount of a specialist in the work you need to do, it will begin to appear. You will turn out to be more educated and increasingly certain. You will talk with more prominent power and greater lucidity.

Individuals will start to treat you in an unexpected way.

Then, at some point, the activity you need will open up for you. Also, when that happens you won't need to apply. It will be offered to you. Why? Since the word about you is as of now out. You have just exhibited that you are single for the activity, thus the choice to contract you is a simple one.

Right now, would be contracted as a vehicle sales rep since you know the autos cold and you know their costs, and you know the selling conventions and methodology, the organization prerequisites, the lbad necessities, etc.

Your next objective is beat each other salesman. Furthermore, you would do that by, once more, concentrating the particular activities of the organization's best sales reps.

Before you knew it, you would be at the highest point of the store winning the sort of money you are correct now just dreaming about. And afterward you could begin making vows to yourself. To begin with, to make a hundred thousand. Then $130,000. Then a large portion of a million. Then a million.

Indeed, you could make a million every year by acing the aptitudes of an advertiser, sales rep, item maker, or profit supervisor. A lot of others have done as such. Why not you?

This, incidentally, is actually what befallen a companion of mine. In under three years, I saw his own salary ascend from under $30,000 to more than $175,000 by following these means. That happened 10 years prior. I saw him simply a month ago. He looked great, and he ought to have. He was working half-days three days every week and merited a few million.

Put Yourself into Your Company's Money Flow

If you only work admirably in a specialized or regulatory position, you can expect just humble boosts in pay. Become generally excellent, and you'll get moderately awesome raises. In any case, if your goal is to soar your pay, you should turn into a key profit generator. It's as straightforward as that.

How huge of a commitment must you make to the organization?

A decent dependable guideline is this: If you need to get a raise that is $1,000 more than conventional, ensure you've been a significant supporter of a thought that will create at any rate $10,000 to $20,000 in extra net profits for your organization.

This is a flat out least. For bigger organizations your effect should be significantly more than that 20 to multiple times.

If you need to expand your present salary by, state, $25,000, you will need to figure out how to build business profits by $250,000 or more. And, your thought can't be a one-time bargain. The $250,000 extra your work needs to contribute must be produced over and over later on.

To keep up an a lot higher-than-normal pay, you have to have a generous impact on your organization's development in salary.

This dependable guideline is valid for most developing organizations. It may not be valid for a business that is enormous and static. Huge organizations, generally speaking, offer solidness of work and consistency of pay instead of significant pay bends. It makes sense all things being equal. Huge organizations pull in shrewd, dedicated however now and then moderate individuals. There is now and again more great ability than is required.

As a rule, you'll have the most obvious opportunity with regards to drastically expanding your salary if you work for a business that has

- Significant sales (in the millions or countless dollars)
- Reasonable profits (what "sensible" signifies relies upon the business)
- A late history of development (both in sales and profits)
- A vision of further development

And, as I recommended, few representatives (so your commitments will stick out).

If the business that you are working for meets none or not many of these criteria, begin looking somewhere else. Except if you can without any help turn such a business around, there won't be sufficient financial assets accessible to meet your budgetary targets.

Your optimal circumstance is position yourself as an important profit maker in a little, quickly developing, and deeply beneficial organization. If you can do that, amazing. If not, don't stress. There are a lot of different approaches to drastically help your pay.

Changing Yourself into a Profit Producer

If you need to make a superhigh salary, you need to turn into a supersignificant supporter of your organization's main concern. That implies being a persuasive power in item creation, marketing, sales, or profit the board.

If your present place of employment is outside any of these

zones, you should either switch jobs or grow your position so it is straightforwardly engaged with one of them.

This isn't as implausible as it would appear.

Are These Numbers Realistic?

Not if you won't change yourself and have any kind of effect. However, if you do turn into a basic piece of the development of a business, it is sensible to anticipate that enormous builds year should year.

If you might want to encounter an extreme pay increase like this in your own profession, this is what you need to do:

- Figure out how your business makes profits.
- Understand how your activity adds to that procedure.
- Modify your activity with the goal that more profits are delivered because of what you do.
- Make sure the individuals who are accountable for giving collects know the amount more money you are making for the organization.

Figuring out How Your Business Makes Profits

Most representatives know pretty much nothing or nothing about how the organizations they work for procure profits. They may recognize what the organization sells (i.e., they can distinguish its items), where it does its marketing (TV, post office based mail, the Internet, and so forth.), who it takes into account all in all terms (seniors, little youngsters, and so on.) However they go quiet if you ask them how and for what good reason sales are made.

What amount do you think about your organization's focus profit techniques? Answer these inquiries:

- Can you name five essential advantages of your organization's top-selling item/administration?
- Can you name the main auxiliary (mental) advantage of this item/administration?
- Can you name one of a kind selling recommendation for every one of your organization's top-selling items/administrations?
- What is your organization's essential upper hand?
- How is that bit of leeway utilized in (1) item creation, (2) promoting, and (3) sales?
- If you know your business how you should, you will have snappy and certain responses to these inquiries. If they leave you speculating, you have work to do.

Here's something to remember: Every business has, at its core, some one of a kind method for creating and selling its items/profits that is undetectable to pariahs even, as a rule, to contenders.

Just by understanding the business in an extremely deep manner (and particularly seeing how its items are made, created, and sold) would you be able to want to turn into a significant piece of the organization's profit making inward circle.

You can gain a decent deal of this undetectable information basically by addressing individuals who are up to date. Make a deal to address your boss and shock the person in question by asking, "What makes the business work?"

Converse with each well disposed face in the sales and marketing offices. Ask them how they carry out their responsibilities. Talk with client support individuals. Discover what the clients are requesting. If you know individuals who have dependable situations in advertising, item creation, or profit the board in different organizations, call them.

As these discussions occur, you'll start to get how the business works, what kind of things matter, and what kind of things are essentially time squanderers. You will likely have that undetectable profile of the organization slowly come into centre for you. It will.

Making sense of How Your Job Contributes to the Bottom Line

When you've taken in the centre profit methodologies of your business, it will be moderately simple to make sense of how to cause the work you to do fundamental to its financial achievement.

You can get a smart thought by asking yourself this: "according to upper administration, is the activity I do considered (1) pleasant however pointless, (2) important yet not of much enthusiasm to them, or (3) fundamental to the development and profit of the business?"

Be straightforward. If, for instance, your activity is in corporate interchanges, you are in the main class. If you work for the bookkeeping or legitimate office, you are in classification a couple, contingent upon what you really do. And, regardless of whether you are in the advertising, sales, or item development territory, you can't be certain that the work you do is viewed as basic.

Know this: If what you do is useful to your business yet superfluous, you have no professional stability, paying little mind to how well you do it. Regardless of whether the work you do is basic to the activities of the business, if you yourself don't make profits, you are in danger.

Insofar as the business is flourishing and you try sincerely and well, your pay will go up. In any case, the minute things turn terrible or you can be replaceed with another person who can do a similar activity also for less money, you will be out the entryway.

As I've stated, this isn't valid for somebody who evidently produces development and salary for a business.

Development and pay makers are seen as acceptable as well as fundamental and attractive. By making yourself one of only a handful hardly any individuals in your organization who realize how to get the bacon, you give yourself the best possibility of getting huge raises, enormous developments and, in the long run, procuring a six-figure salary.

Here's a basic test to decide that you are so fundamental to your organization. Answer the accompanying inquiries:

- Have you made an effective new item/administration in the previous year?
- Do you have main concern obligation over an item, group of items, or division? Provided that this is true, would it say it was gainful a year ago? And, will it be as or increasingly beneficial this year?
- Are you straightforwardly liable for sales or a group of sales reps? Provided that this is true, did your specialty meet or surpass your supervisor's desires a year ago? Will you do it again this year?
- Have you thought of a few new sales boosting thoughts recently?
- Do you by and by create offers of in excess of multiple times your pay?

- Are you responsible for a significant promoting or publicizing capacity? Provided that this is true, did you meet or surpass your manager's desires a year ago? Will you do it again this year?
- Have you made at any rate one recommendation this previous month about improving the organization's marketing or sales strategy?

If you addressed yes to at any rate a few of these inquiries, you are the place you ought to be in the profit stream of your business. If you couldn't answer yes to any of them yet at the same time feel that you are equipped for making a significant commitment to your organization's main concern, you will need to roll out certain improvements.

Adjusting Your Job to Become a Critical Factor

You will probably continuously move your work exercises with the goal that you are steadily accomplishing increasingly more of one or a few of the centre, important occupations:

- Making sales
- Creating items
- Managing profits

The thought is to keep your present occupation while you make the move. Also, you will do this with the full information and backing of your present boss. If you leave your supervisor in obscurity, you hazard making a foe of the person in question. Also, that would be harming to your deals. So in all that you do starting here on, consider how it will influence your boss. If the manager is a sensible individual you will have the option to clarify what you are doing and why. If the person comprehends that you will keep on extending to help and work superbly, the manager shouldn't be undermined by your desire.

Generally significant, be certain your supervisor comprehends that your future achievement will make the person in question look great. The manager was, all things considered, your coach and motivated you to make a profession with the organization. On account of your boss, you will enable the organization to get more money-flow. The supervisor will get a great sale of credit from the individuals liable for their raises.

However, before you have that discussion if you have it by any stretch of the imagination, you have to distinguish work in your organization that you need to do.

Distinguish which individuals in your organization get the most money-flow. Then discover precisely what they do and what abilities they have to work superbly. It might appear to be a stretch right now, however it's altogether conceivable that you would one be able to day do a similar activity. All things considered, the whole of the most deeply valued abilities advertising, sales, item creation, and profit the board are not especially specific. Indeed, they require information, yet it's the sort of specialized information that any splendid, aspiring individual can get.

Beginning today, attempt to get the hang of something about that activity consistently. Discover the stuff regarding hours and days. Find what it normally pays and when it pays more and why. Distinguish the day by day schedule, the normal issues, the greatest difficulties, and the best rewards. Inquire. Watch. Read.

Keep it up, without fail, until you begin to feel as though you get it.

When you feel prepared, converse with your supervisor

about your deals.

Then approach key individuals in the office you're keen on. Let them know (actually) that you think their field is something you'd be acceptable at. Let's assume you've been finding out about it in your save time and you'd prefer to elect to assist them with excursion at whatever point you can so you can learn much more.

In electing to assist, you have three goals:

1. To show your promise to the business
2. To create relationships with fundamental workers in your relationship
3. To gain proficiency with a fundamental (i.e., monetarily valued) expertise

Your first target will be acknowledged very quickly. A great many people will be intrigued by your ability to make a plunge and give them a hand. If your goals are genuine and your follow-up is persevering, you'll before long enjoy notoriety for being an up-and-comer (regardless of how old you are).

Your subsequent target will be accomplished over a time of months, as you exhibit what you can do. Keep in mind, the way to setting up great relationships with these individuals is to concentrate on helping them. If your endeavours are straightforwardly self-serving, it will have an impartial or negative effect.

Your third goal learning a monetarily valued aptitude will take some time. Yet, the advantage you'll get when you accomplish it will be tremendous. Dominance of a monetarily valued expertise will essentially promise you a high pay for an incredible remainder.

In case YOU'RE NOT SURE WHICH SKILL TO MASTER, TRY THIS ONE FIRST

Of the considerable number of aptitudes you can have the capacity to talk like Winston Churchill, to paint like Rembrandt, to compute like Albert Einstein none will assist you with accomplishing riches just as realizing how to sell things.

So in case you don't know which monetarily valued ability to target, I suggest turning into a specialist in the sort of offers that make your organization beneficial. And, I'm going to give you a minicourse in offering right presently to assist you with choosing if this is for you.

Each private investment each school, café, law office, medical clinic, building provider, home improvement shop, and amusement complex endures and succeeds by goodness of its business action.

To continue doing what you need to do (and to make a profit from it), you need to (1) draw in clients at a sensible expense and (2) convert them into rehash purchasers.

We should consider the primary errand the front-end sale and the second undertaking the back-end sale. In the years that have gone since, I've figured out how to look at for all intents and purposes each moneymaking endeavor as far as these two selling aptitudes.

This point of view has permitted me to rapidly see what number of organizations work, even ones of which I have just outside information. It's never again a riddle to me why, for instance, such a large number of cafés and little lodgings leave business, why individuals in the movement and recreation business bring in so minimal expenditure, why you shouldn't attempt (as I disclosed to a meeting participant not more than a day or two ago) to make a business out of a llama homestead and why most great independent investments bomb when they endeavour to get greater.

This key point of view on sales has permitted me to give supportive exhortation to a wide range of various organizations in pretty much every possible industry. I can see now how every effective new company is one that has rapidly and accurately responded to two straightforward inquiries:

1. What is the most practical method for drawing in clients?
2. What is the most single approach to keep those clients purchasing?

If you can figure out how to see your business that way and can one day dis-spread the right response to these two inquiries, you will immediately get perceived as a precious worker. That will happen although you will comprehend your business from the back to front. You will realize it superior to 90 percent of your kindred labourers.

When issues emerge regardless of what they are the deals must address either of two destinations:

1. Bringing down the expense of procuring new clients
2. Expanding the lifetime estimation of each current client

Indeed, even the stickiest issues in business which are consistently individuals issues can be dissected successfully by thinking about conceivable out-comes against these two goals.

Even better, TURN YOURSELF INTO A MARKETING GENIUS

Talented advertisers are reliably among the most generously compensated people in any industry. They procure significant pays, unprecedented rewards, and the regard and esteem of associates and contenders. Advertisers who master their exchanges are everything except ensured an existence of riches, security, regard, and fulfilment.

Anybody of normal knowledge can turn into a gifted advertiser. You needn't bother with a brisk mind, a pizzazz for the sensational, or a degree from a top business college. What's required is a comprehension of why individuals purchase things.

Essentially, the best advertisers realize how to apply three major standards. I'll give you a short review of them here to assist you with choosing whether this is something that interests you.

The First Principle: The Difference among Wants and Needs

In the present customer driven economy, it's anything but difficult to confuse a need with a need. How often have you heard one of the accompanying articulations:

- "Sally needs another closet. The clothes she's wearing make her look senseless."
- "John detests how his hair looks. He says he needs a superior hairdresser."
- "I must have that new tote!"
- "We need a big house."
- "We need a more pleasant vehicle."

- "We need a big garden."

None of those things are needs as in something you can't live with-out. Our needs are extremely not many and basic: air, water, food, cover, transportation (once in a while), and clothes (as a rule). Everything else we purchase depends on our needs. And, in any event, when it comes time to buy needs, for example, food and apparel, our purchasing choices are typically founded on needs. (We need a specific sort of bread, a particular brand of clothes, a house in a specific style, and so forth.)

When you understand that your clients needn't bother with your item or administration, you perceive that the best approach to persuade them to get it is to animate their craving for it. The best method to do that in your publicizing is to

- Promise your forthcoming client (normally verifiably) that making a specific move (purchasing your item) will bring about the fulfilment of a longing (need)
- Create an image in your possibility's brain of how the person will feel when that longing is fulfilled
- Make explicit cases about the advantages of your item and afterward demonstrate those cases to your possibility
- Equate the inclination your possibility wants (the fulfilment of a need) with the acquisition of your item

The medium doesn't make a difference. Any place you discover your clients on TV or radio, in magazines or papers, at home reading the mail or on the Internet the fundamental procedure is the equivalent. The minute you overlook this first rule you are offering to needs as opposed to needs your marketing will come up short.

The Second Principle: The Difference among Features and Profits

A pencil has certain highlights:

- It is made of wood.
- It has a particular perimtre.
- It contains a lead-composite filler of a particular sort.
- It for the most part has an eraser toward the end.

Etc.

These highlights depict the target naturals of the pencil. So if purchasing were a sane procedure, selling would involve distinguish ing the highlights of your item.

In any case, as you simply got the hang of, purchasing is an enthusiastic procedure. Furthermore, that implies you should communicate the highlights of your item somehow or another that will animate want. You do that by changing over highlights into profits.

For instance, the highlights of the pencil may be changed over into the accompanying advantages:

- It is anything but difficult to hone.
- It is agreeable to hold.
- It makes a great line.
- It makes adjusting simple.

The Third Principle: The Difference among Profits and Deeper Profits

The explanation a few advertisers make a superior showing than others is because they comprehend the contrast among profits and more deep advantages.

In our model, for example, what may be the more deep advantage of having a pencil that hones effectively?

To make sense of that, master advertisers ask themselves, "Who is my objective client? Also, why, precisely, does this client need easily overlooked details (like honing pencils) to be simple?"

Obviously, there's no single response to such an inquiry. It relies totally upon who that target client is. If he's a bustling official, his more deep reasons will be unique in relation to if she's a bustling housewife. Maybe the official needs more simplicity since he's covered in details. Maybe he detects that if he could simply get somewhat more extra time in his day he could get up to speed with his work. Also, if he could at long last get his in-box vanquished and his email tidied up, maybe he could compose that reminder or make that call that would support his profession.

Master advertisers who comprehend these more deep thought processes the de-sire to be increasingly effective at work, for instance can make more grounded promoting duplicate since they will be speaking to feelings that are nearer to their clients' core wants.

The model I'm utilizing is, as a matter of fact, outreal estateish. However, I'll keep on pushing it to come to the meaningful conclusion. Our lord advertisers have burrowed a piece underneath the surface at this point. They perceive a more deep want than minor straightforwardness, and they are going to speak to it. However, before they do, they stop and deconstruct the more deep advantage. They pose themselves more inquiries: "For what reason does my client, this bustling official, need more achievement? Is it since he needs a superior pay? And, assuming this is the case, why would that be? Is it since he needs a more pleasant home? Furthermore, if he needs a more pleasant home, why? To satisfy his family? To dazzle his companions? Furthermore, for what reason does he need to satisfy his family and dazzle his companions?"

Advertisers who can make sense of the responses to questions like these grasp their possibilities' hearts.

TIME TO GET GOING

If you do all that I've suggested up until this point, you'll be in a situation to request an a lot more significant pay:

- You will be working in the profit making vortex of your organization.
- You will do work that is generally critical to the top boss.
- You will be superior to any other individual in a comparable position.
- And you will start to appear and inevitably be significant and essential.

You will likewise be if you happen to be in the exceptionally uncommon situation of working for a business whose leaders are so thick they don't perceive your full worth in a situation to take your aptitudes else-where or offer them to your business as an independent specialist.

The most effective method to BECOME A CONSULTANT TO YOUR OWN COMPANY

The single greatest grumbling I've gotten has originated from my customers. "Quit advising our best representatives to become independent advisors!"

What happens is this: Some investmentsome youngster

accepts my recommendation to heart and changes himself into a bonafide advertising virtuoso in (normally) three or four years. Then he either requests a gigantic pay increase or offers to give future administrations on an independent premise. The protest is about remuneration. "He was making $40,000 every prior year he began reading ETR. Presently he's given us a suggestion that will cost multiple occasions that much."

I am unsettled this is occurring. All things considered, perhaps I am. However, I am somewhat humiliated to need to call attention to the accompanying:

If your representative changes himself from a decent, diligent employee who is worth $40,000 into an advertising virtuoso worth multiple times that much, that implies he is making your business worth considerably more. Since his pay is, and consistently will be (even as an expert), a small amount of what he gets paid, the more he makes, the better his manager should like it.

In the organizations I've claimed, I've generally been excited to see my representatives make this sort of progress. That is because I realized that they were so important to me. For each dollar additional they earned, my business increased 10. Who could despise that?

And, I'm by all account not the only one who likes to see his workers get rich. A large portion of the best agents I know are excited to grant high livelihoods to workers who acquire them. You'll more likely than not get the pay you are looking for if you do what I instructed you to do:

- Put yourself into your organization's profit stream.
- Help make your business more beneficial.

- Internally pitch your worth.
- Expect to be appropriately redressed.

If you work for a little to medium-sized developing business, you shouldn't experience any difficulty getting the money you merit. However, with bigger, more seasoned relationships, reasonable remuneration is now and then an issue. That is because some corporate pioneers overlook their concentration and make motivations that are about legislative issues (power) as opposed to business (profits).

If you stall out in such a circumstance, you have to step by step reposition yourself as an independently employed expert. There are a lot of books and projects regarding the matter of setting up your own consultancy, including one from the American Consultants League (americanconsultantsleague.com). Essentially, here's the means by which to do it.

Plan A: Try to Stay on the Payroll

The minute you settled on the choice to turn into a specialist, the relationship you had with your manager changed regardless of whether the person in question didn't understand it. Right now, your manager is an imminent customer, and all things considered, must be treated with all the pampering and nestling any future customer would justify.

In the months and weeks preceding your changeover, ensure that your notoriety goes from great to irreproachable. In the interim . . . build up a mystery plan.

Try not to declare your expectations at any rate, not right away. Concentrate on working superbly, expanding your monetarily valued ability, and building profits for your organization. Meanwhile, make yearly, month to month, and week after week goals for your new profession.

Plan to make in any event twice as much every hour as you do now. Keep in mind, as an independent expert; you'll have some extra costs. Plan for these costs, as well. Your underlying objective will be to net 110 percent of your present pay in your first full-time year. In any case, you ought to anticipate that your salary should go up to some degree generously after that. I have coached in any event twelve individuals who have made this progress and I can't consider one who didn't wind up making at any rate twofold the pay he left before the finish of his third year as a specialist.

After you have upgraded your ability and set up your objectives, it's a great opportunity to make your pitch. If you hold fast to the accompanying rules, your danger of disappointment will be nearly nil:

1. Try not to be angry. You attempted to convince your manager to pay you boatloads of money you merited, and the person didn't. That is no problem. You won't win any focuses by raising the subject once more.
2. Make the message positive. Regardless of whether you have ousted disdain from your sentiments completely, it's not prudent to tell your manager that the explanation you need to quit working at the organization is to start a new business yourself and get more money-flow. Your creation money isn't the manager's top need. (If that wasn't obvious to you when you neglected to get the raise you needed, it ought to be evident at this point.)

It's smarter to express the realities and afterward sell your supervisor on the advantages. Because the person in question to comprehend that the work you'll be doing will profit the business and that if the individual in question has your help, the quill will be in their top. Concentrate on your smart thoughts not the position change. Those thoughts, if they are great, will change your job from worker to expert. Yet, don't express that to your manager straightforwardly. The person in question will make sense of it over the long term particularly a couple of years not far off when the individual in question acknowledges how much less expensive it would have been simply to pay you $130,000 in any case.

3. Try not to discuss the money not from the outset. Your essential target in having this first, transitional discussion with your supervisor is to persuade the person in question to procure you on low maintenance premise. Since you realize you can improve the organization's profits, you don't have to stress a lot over the amount you will in the end get paid insofar as you attach your remuneration to the main concern. There are many approaches to do that. The primary concern right currently is to get the deal. You will have the option to tighten up your expenses as time passes by and your customer gets settled with the new course of action.

4. Stress the advantages. For all intents and purposes all that you state after that ought to underline the advantages you will bring to your boss and the business. The most significant thing is to pass on the possibility that you need what's best for the boss and the organization.

While building a list of advantages (and you ought to do this formally and set up it as a written record), consider

- How much time it will save your boss

- How much pressure it will wipe out (since you'll be assuming responsibility for one of the manager's greatest migraines)
- How substantially more engaged the supervisor can be since the individual can focus on core tasks and not stress over overseeing you
- How much better your manager will look to their boss (since this piece of the business will be working naturally)

If your supervisor doesn't go for your proposition, chill out and express gratitude toward the person in question for the time. Try not to be angry. Also, whatever you do, don't take steps to stop. If you couldn't persuade your supervisor of the incentive in your going independent, then you have to return to the planning phase and make more worth. Keep at it until what you are offering is essentially too acceptable to even think about refusing. Presently you go to Plan B.

Plan B: Sell Your Expertise to Someone Else

As far as I can tell, extraordinary workers who needed to go independent never fizzled. That might be because the greater part of the organizations I have worked with have been developing undertakings and in this way anxious to hold great connection sends even on an independent premise. It might likewise be because the greater part of the free-lancers I coached were awesome at what they did.

If your manager won't or can't enlist you on an independent premise, there will be other people who will.

So find a good pace your system. Convey notes. Make calls. Make visits. Don't dupe your boss while you are doing this (regard for your present check is foremost), yet don't feel terrible about selling yourself, either.

You are, basically, searching for another activity. The main contrast is that as opposed to requesting a salaried position, you will sell yourself as a consultant somebody with the aptitudes to enable the business to develop. (If you have a business concurrence with prohibitive agreements concerning working for contenders, you'll need to regard that.)

In advertising yourself as an independent specialist, make your proposition overwhelming by focusing on profits like these:

- You don't need to keep me except if you like my work.
- You don't need to pay my overhead.
- You don't need to prepare me, oversee me, or keep me occupied. You should simply dole out me your most testing employments and let me sale with them for you.

If you get your work done by contemplating each imminent boss before you make a pitch, you'll have a smart thought of exactly what that business needs. Get ready for your introduction by discovering the accompanying:

- What does the business consider the organization's extraordinary selling recommendation?
- How are the items sold?
- What are the organization's best client procurement techniques?
- What are its generally gainful back-finished results?
- What's working best for them at this moment? What's not working?

You can find solutions to a large portion of these inquiries essentially by doing a little research.

Building up YOUR SECOND (And, THIRD AND FOURTH) INCOMES

By mastering a monetarily valued aptitude and promoting yourself appropriately, you will before long be on track to making $130,000 every year. In any case, there are numerous different ways you can help your salary.

The least difficult path is to utilize the aptitudes you've created to begin a side business that can sustain you a relentless, sound, second stream of salary.

Not every person has the opportunity or energy to do this. In any case, if you can figure out how to check out it, the outcomes may astonish you.

The Difference between an Income-Generating and an Equity Business

Right now are discussing approaches to support your salary. Beginning a side business can do that. However, it can likewise make you rich through the energy about your value in it.

The thing that matters is straightforward yet significant.

A value business is one that you can sell for a profit. Most independent companies, curiously enough, aren't of that sort.

If you have a one-individual law practice that pays you $300,000 every year, that is a decent business, however it may not be a business you can sell. Indeed, your customers are significant yet would they say they are important to another person? Will another person feel certain that these customers will keep working together there?

When you are picking a side business, make sense of what

your motivation is: value or salary. The upside of a salary prepared business is that the pay can be delivered moderately rapidly. The profit of a value situated business is the thing that it gets worth after some time.

Right now, talk about organizations from a pay perspective.

Going for an Extra $25,000 a Year Is a Good and Reasonable Place to Start

There are a wide range of approaches to enhance your salary by $25,000 per year. There are the same number of ways as there are organizations. We've discussed expanding your pay by offering your administrations to the business you work for going independent. You can likewise include a second stream of pay by offering your administrations to different firms while you're despite everything working for your present boss (noncompetitive firms you would prefer not to do anything you could get terminated for).

If you have a monetarily valued expertise, you can hope to acquire be-tween $100 and $500 an hour for your administrations. At $100 60 minutes, you would need to work 250 hours an additional five hours every week to make $25,000. At $500 60 minutes, it would take you just about an hour seven days to win $25,000.

Consider Branching Out into the Direct-Mail Industry

If you would prefer to enhance your pay by evaluating an alternate monetarily valued expertise, think about turning into a sales rep, publicizing marketing specialist, list advisor, promoting director, or visual craftsman in the immediate marketing industry.

Why direct marketing? Three reasons:

1. Direct promoting is (if you remember direct marketing for the Internet) by a long shot the biggest single type of publicizing. It is bigger than TV, bigger than link, bigger than magazines, and bigger than papers.
2. In addition to the fact that it is tremendous, it's developing. This is particularly valid since email publicizing has become such an enormous piece of Internet business. Most would agree that no other type of publicizing is developing as fast as immediate advertising.
3. At long last, and generally significant, direct marketing is a business that measures brings about terms of dollars and pennies added to the main concern. Independent experts who help direct-advertising organizations bring in money are equipped for requesting enormous salaries. That is because it's simple for anyone passing by to view the positive outcome they have on sales.

That may require some clarification.

Ordinary promoting measures its outcomes with shopper overviews and expansive based investigations of item sales. When Pepsi-Cola spends a few million dollars on a TV crusade, it can't quantify its viability straightforwardly. Truly, it can survey TV watchers to discover what number of recollect seeing the business. Also, it can follow sales in areas where the publicizing showed up. Yet, it can once in a while, if at any time, know without a doubt whether a specific promotion acquired more net dollars than it cost to deliver.

Actually, the general thought of general promoting is circuitous: Create a picture or thought in the possibilities' psyches and at some point or another they will come. Brand acknowledgment is the mantra. And, image acknowledgment does make a difference when you are selling wares. In any case, that doesn't imply that a specific promotion intended to expand brand mindfulness will do it. Nor does it imply that if it does to be sure increase brand acknowledgment, it will build adequately to cover (or all the more appropriately, surpass) the expense of the notice.

With regards to general promoting, the genuine selling goes on between the publicizing organization and the maker, not between the producer and the end client. With direct-marketing promoting you don't need to stress over squandering your money on advertising efforts that don't work. You can control all the basic factors that influence sales. And, you can quantify results.

A normal direct-marketing advertising effort quantifies precisely what number of dollars was spent and what number of dollars was gotten. Suppose, for instance, that a producer of health items contracted an immediate marketing specialist to make an inventory, which the maker then sent to 50,000 potential clients. Accepting the expense of the list was $25,000 (or 50¢ per inventory) and the subsequent sales totalled $50,000, the gross profit would be $25,000.

Presently, suppose that a similar producer contracted a subsequent marketing specialist, who created a second inventory that additionally cost 50¢ to place via the post office. In any case, this one accomplished an arrival of $100,000, or a gross profit of $75,000. Which marketing specialist is going to get more money-flow? Also, what amount more is that marketing specialist worth?

You can see the point. And, that is the reason successful copywriters regularly request somewhere in the range of

$10,000 and $25,000 in addition to sovereignties for each battle that they compose. And, that is for investments that can take as little as a solitary week to finish.

You can see the potential. And, it's not only for copywriters. Visual specialists, list advisors, and advertisers who see direct promoting can win extremely significant low maintenance salaries.

You can find out about direct advertising by taking courses at your nearby school, by reading books regarding the matter, or by taking a crack at home-study programs. As I've said before, it will take you around a thousand hours to turn into a skilful copywriter, marketing administrator, visual craftsman, or something practically identical. You can decrease that time prerequisite by learning under the direction of a master.

When you have the right stuff, put aside four or five hours every week to expert bit yourself to nearby, provincial, or even national direct-marketing organizations.

You can and presumably should have some expertise in a specific medium: mail, print (paper or magazine promotions), Internet advertising, or TV. You can and most likely should focus on a branch of knowledge, as well (health, financial, business, self improvement, charitable, and so on.). Masters consistently make higher livelihoods since they have increasingly tenuous aptitudes. It might appear from the outset as though you are restricting yourself, however you'll before long experience the advantages of narrowing your concentrate once you begin feeling like a genuine master.

Your Best Bet: Selling Your Own Products or Services through Direct Mail (or E-Mail)

Marketplace Learning Institute (www.agoralearninginstitute.com) distributes a magnificent asset for the eventual direct-marketing business visionary. The book, Made to Order: The Top E-Mail and Mail-Order Businesses (accessible from Agora), features 50 significant classes for direct marketing, each with its own specialty advertise. It likewise distinguishes different sources to get your items, explicit marketing procedures in every territory, the significant players to gain from, valuing, and how to begin.

If you have an enthusiasm for direct promoting, here are a few examples of beneficial mail-request organizations (taken from Made to Order) to consider:

1. Craftsman supplies. The market for craftsmanship supplies is a $30 million or more industry, and it's developing at in excess of 10 percent a year, air conditioning cording to the Hobby Industry Relationship. Direct-marketing craftsmanship supply organizations sell proficient quality canvas, model, and carpentry materials, just as dots and adornments stock. Working specialists like excellent hardware. If you can give them something that keeps going, they'll recollect the brand and prize you with rehash buys. Know about evaluating, since this is a value delicate market, and offer a solid assurance.

2. Audiocassettes and CDs. There are a wide range of subjects that loan themselves to audiocassette, CD, and DVD sales. In the business-to-business field, there are preparing programs, and in the customer field, you have books on tape, language projects, and music, just to give some examples. The pattern toward electronic types of data, counsel, and amusement is relentless. One model is the Audio Book Club, which sells

more than 65,000 book recordings a year through mail request and the Internet. Online sales are developing, and there is a solid interest for organizations that can sell sound items by permitting customers to download the data online in the wake of paying with charge card. Purchasers are keen on accessibility (the sooner, the better), the nature of the sound, the nature of the substance, and worth.

3. Diet and weight loss items. The immediate marketing advertise for diet and weight loss items is tremendous, including everything from recordings and books to gym equipment, pills to control the hunger and consume fat, bolster groups, weight-the executives projects, and straightforward items like restroom scales and fat screens. Body-cognizant Americans spend $40 billion every year to get thinner, and the business is developing at 5.6 percent yearly. The National Centre for Health Statistics discloses to us that an expected 64 percent of Americans are viewed as overweight or large and in excess of 50 million will go on consumes less calories this year. It's to highlight just a single item in each mailing. Assemble a strong client base, and afterward sell extra items toward the back. To charge the top notch costs vital for beneficial mail-request promoting right now, must give your possibility trust that your item can give an answer for their weight issue. And, obviously, you should offer a solid unconditional promise.

4. Email distributing. There are email distributions for all intents and purposes each region of intrigue. Particularly productive market fragments incorporate financial specialists, sports aficionados, specialists, business opportunity searchers, and individuals keen on sclf-improvement. Wellsprings of pay for email publishers incorporate membership expenses,

publicizing incomes, and back-end sales. E-publishers gain money toward the back by offering items and administrations identified with the themes shrouded in the production. An exceptional advantage of e-distributing is that there is almost no expense related with appropriation (by means of the Internet as compared with U.S. mail). The way to progress is to keep up an enormous endorser base. To do this, you should offer significant data, stick to a conveyance plan, give a simple to-read and steady deal, and not badger your readers with an excessive amount of publicizing. When you have built a brand base, there are organizations that will showcase your space to potential sponsors.

5. Wellness and exercise recordings. Mail-request wellness organizations spend significant time in practice recordings including heart stimulating exercise, boxing exercises, yoga, Pilates, and many different frameworks. Purchasers right now people of any age that are keen on personal development. They are commonly centred to upper pay, and react well to focus direct-marketing publicizing. It's to include just a solitary item in each mailing. To legitimize charging an exceptional value, you should offer a one of a kind daily practice or routine, master guidance, straightforward and speedy exercises, or a novel scene or area. Hotplaces for these items can be promptly found on the Internet.

6. Cultivating seeds and tools. Somewhere in the range

of 85 million families took an interest in at least one kinds of do-it-without anyone's help yard and nursery exercises in 2002, as per the National Gardening Relationship. The indoor and open air planting industry accomplishes incomes totaling $40 billion every year, and this number is developing by 4 percent yearly. Mail-request cultivating organizations represent considerable authority in offers of tools, outside force hardware, magazines, books, seeds, bulbs, and plants. To separate yourself right now, top notch items, simplicity of requesting, and free instructive data by means of article content in your list or on your site. It's additionally a smart thought to consider delivering a pamphlet.

7. Interest and specialty items. Mail-request organizations right now in units and supplies for investments, for example, recoloured glass enhancements, enlivening work of art, carpentry, adornments, and scrapbooking. The business is rewarding and developing quickly, as it is being filled by a few shopper patterns. Numerous buyers are worried about the unsteady economy and are deciding to set aside money by making their own blessings, improvements, and clothes. Others are making these things to make a subsequent pay. Most of successful mail-request make organizations spend significant time in a specific classification, yet in addition offer their items on the web. This is a regular business. During spring and summer (the

moderate seasons), the emphasis is on wedding-and commemoration themed creates. In the late-summer, it's Halloween and Thanksgiving. The Christmas season, as you may expect, is the point at which you'll bring in your greatest money.

8. Normal health items. Mail-request health and food organizations spend significant time in natural food sources, nutrients and supplements, and other negligibly prepared regular items. There is colossal open door right now, sales keep on developing. In 2002, they bested $36.4 billion. Offers of health foods alone surpassed $10 billion of every 2002. Offers of common individual attention items were more than $1.7 billion, practically 50% of which happened outside of conventional retail channels, as per Nutrition Business Journal. Purchasers right now wealthy, accomplished people everything being equal. These purchasers react well to coordinate marketing promoting, and great mailing records are ample. Notwithstanding natural health push acts, it might be conceivable to showcase other related products to these clients, including data distributions and gym equipment.

9. Bulletins. As indicated by the Custom Publishing Council, in excess of 50,000 one of kind pamphlets are created every year, bringing about incomes of $20 billion every year. The majority of them give monetary, health, business, and travel data subjects that all make them thing in like manner: They give

data that would be hard for clients to discover in prevailing press productions. The more exceptionally specific the data, the higher the membership rate that can be charged. Since they are a data item, you can make a generous profit with bulletins. The physical item you send clients will be exceptionally cheap to create. Notwithstanding membership incomes, you can likewise offer your supporters related items and administrations that will interest them. For instance, in case you're focusing on sales reps, you can offer courses, books, and CDs with exceptional methodologies to assist them with improving their business abilities.

10. Pet supplies. The pet business is a significant portion of the U.S. economy. A year ago, American pet proprietors burned through $26 billion on their pets. Offers of pet supplies alone are relied upon to surpass $8 billion continuously 2007. Segment patterns are grinding away here. More children of post war America are obtaining pet supplies since they more see their pets as relatives. And, as vacant homes become topped off with hound beds and litter boxes, more seasoned grown-ups have better approaches to spend their money. The immediate promoting methodologies right now like those in different markets. Internet promoting is particularly successful, as is delivering a list highlighting a progression of front-final results that the client can arrange straightforwardly. To recognize your

business, offer quality items at serious costs, aptitude in every aspect of pet attention, fantastic client care, and free data about the most recent patterns in pet attention.

ONE MORE GOOD IDEA FOR YOU:

Purchasing AND FLIPPING REAL ESTATE

Putting resources into real estate has truly been one of the steadiest approaches to build riches. Since this part focus on salary, let's investigate how you can make a second stream of pay with real estate.

Regularly, when you think "pay," you think rental units. In any case, real estate gives pay simply after rents go up and costs go down. During the early long periods of an interest in investment property you will as a rule be fortunate to earn back the original investment as far as pay. Indeed, your net riches will be expanding each year (although the value you have in the property will turn out to be increasingly significant), however your income will be equal the initial investment or even marginally negative.

This is particularly obvious today, when real estate is so deeply valued. In many pieces of the United States, costs are at recorded highs. As a real estate speculator myself, I discover it about difficult to purchase rental legitimate ties that give me certain income immediately. It tends to be done, yet I wouldn't make a riches building plan that relied upon it.

I love real estate, yet I consider it a value play in any event for the initial 5 or 10 years. So, where do you get pay?

That is the thing that I need to discuss here: making a

generous second (or third) pay by purchasing and selling properties.

The most effective method to Flip Your Way from a $10,000 Purchase to a $28.5 Million Sale

One of the best real estate financial specialists I know is Frank McKinney, who lives in my neighbourhood. By his own confirmation, Frank was the odd one out of his family. He experienced been in difficulty as a young person and scarcely moved on from secondary school. At 20 years old, he left Indiana and real estateed in South Florida with only $50 in his pocket.

He got down to business burrowing green sand snares for $2 an hour at a retreat. When he discovered that a companion was making $40 an hour giving tennis exercises, Frank persuaded the retreat boss to pay for him to take a course that would get him confirmed as an educator.

Before long, Frank had built a successful tennis business, focusing on wealthy occupants of new oceanfront condominium improvements. He was making $100,000 every year. Life was acceptable. Yet, Frank needed to accomplish more he simply didn't know what that may be. So he chose to gain from his well off students.

He tired them out for 45 minutes of their booked one-hour exercises. The most recent 15 minutes, they were glad to simply sit, taste water, and recover. During that time, Frank would pepper them with questions. What he realized was that they all made them thing in like manner. Somehow or another, they had all put resources into real estate.

That motivated Frank to purchase his first foreclosure.

He began by learning as much as he could about real estate. From his students as well as by reading everything regarding the matter that he could get his hands on. He inquired about the nearby market and went to dispossession barters for 10 months. Then he figured some money out and purchased his first property. It was a bug plagued previous split house in an overview part of town. He got it for

$30,000, set it up, and sold it only a couple of months in the wake of getting it for a profit of about $20,000.

Plain proceeded to do many these sorts of deals, in the end flipping many properties in a solitary year. Still short of his 30th birth-day, he put resources into his first oceanfront property. When it was revamped and sold, he stashed almost $1 million on this single deal about what he would have made on 30 of his littler deals.

Then he put resources into another oceanfront property and one more and again. Since 1998 when Oprah Winfrey talked with him as one of the nation's most creative youthful business visionaries he has become the main engineer of ultra-top of the line oceanfront homes in South Florida.

So let's talk about pay how to make $25,000 to $125,000 every year, low maintenance, purchasing and selling real estate.

You Make Your Money by Buying Right

As indicated by Frank McKinney, Donald Trump, and endless other real estate specialists, you can earn substantial sums of money purchasing and selling real estate insofar as you adhere to a couple of fundamental guidelines.

To begin with, ensure you purchase at a decent cost. If you can grab up a property essentially beneath its present market esteem, odds are you'll have the option to effectively turn it around and sell it for a pleasant profit.

It's hard to turn into a specialist on the estimation of real estate all over town, so focus on a couple of neighbourhoods that you know about. Properties that are selling at a rebate to showcase esteem won't keep going long, so you'll need to do some legwork to reveal bargains and be prepared to hop on sales the minute they show up.

Start by making sense of the normal expense per square foot of properties in your objective region. To do this, you'll have to inquire about an agent test of homes that sold in the ongoing past. The best time allotment is in a year and the bigger the example, the better.

Utilize a spreadsheet to delineate the subtleties of every property, including the sale cost and area. By separating the sale cost by the area, you get the expense per square foot. By averaging the whole of your outcomes, you will get the normal expense per square foot for homes that have as of late sold in your general vicinity.

Next, set up a list of the homes that are available to be purchased at this moment. Do a similar kind of estimation (utilizing soliciting cost rather from sale cost) to think of the normal current soliciting cost per square foot from property in your general vicinity.

Furnished with these numbers, you currently have a solid benchmark to help you rapidly decide if a property speaks to a decent worth and a possibly gainful speculation.

Finding the Best Sales on the Market

When you realize the property estimations in your objective zone undeniable, you are prepared to perceive genuine sales the minute they show up.

Scour the paper each day or two and call about each property available to be purchased. You can likewise do some important research on www.realtor.com. When you have the location, area, and asking value, contrast it and the practically identical qualities you've just settled for the territory.

You'll before long arrive at a point where you'll be comfortable with all the properties being offered in your objective zone, and you'll be searching just for new postings. Probably, that will take 15 minutes per day 15 minutes that could take care of huge with only a couple of hits a year.

Normally scouring the paper and the Internet for new deals when they show up should turn into an ordinary piece of your everyday practice. In any case, that is not by any means the only method to discover underestimated properties. Search for indications that a proprietor might be considering selling, even before the individual in question promotes it.

Purchasing and Flipping Real estate Properties

Flipping real estate implies there's development around. You realize it will be hot, and you can purchase a real estate unit for $125,000. You are generally positive you'll have the option to flip it (sell it immediately) when development is done for $160,000.

This is an exceptionally decent business. No chaos, no problem. And, you can rake in tons of money. The stunt here is to ensure you have the legitimate right to sell the property when you need and at the cost you need. Be careful: These deals frequently accompany gets that should be changed.

Flipping is an exceptionally pleasant and blushing approach to earn substantial sums of money in real estate. It's something you can't do constantly, yet when you can, it's brilliant. The thought is to purchase real estate homes or condominiums in promising neighbourhood developments.

You Make Your Money by Buying Right

As indicated by Frank McKinney, Donald Trump, and innumerable other real estate specialists, you can earn substantial sums of money purchasing and selling real estate inasmuch as you adhere to a couple of fundamental guidelines.

To begin with, ensure you purchase at a decent cost. If you can grab up a property altogether underneath its present market esteem, odds are you'll have the option to effortlessly turn it around and sell it for a pleasant profit.

It's hard to turn into a specialist on the estimation of real estate all over town, so focus on a couple of neighbourhoods that you know about. Properties that are selling at a rebate to showcase esteem won't keep going long, so you'll need to do some legwork to reveal bargains and be prepared to bounce on deals the minute they show up.

Start by making sense of the normal expense per square foot of properties in your objective zone. To do this, you'll have to investigate an agent test of homes that sold in the ongoing past. The best time span is inside a year, and the bigger the example, the better.

Utilize a spreadsheet to outline the subtleties of every property, including the deal cost and area. By partitioning the deal cost by the area, you get the expense per square foot. By averaging the entirety of your outcomes, you will get the normal expense per square foot for homes that have as of late sold in your general vicinity.

Next, set up a list of the homes that are available to be purchased at this moment. Do a similar kind of count (utilizing soliciting cost rather from deal cost) to think of the normal current soliciting cost per square foot from property in your general vicinity.

Furnished with these numbers, you presently have a dependable benchmark to help you rapidly decide if a property speaks to a decent worth and a conceivably beneficial investment.

Finding the Best Deals on the Market

When you realize the property estimations in your objective territory stone cold, you are prepared to perceive genuine deals the minute they show up.

Scour the paper each day or two and call about each property available to be purchased. You can likewise do some significant research on www.realtor.com. When you have the location, area, and asking value, contrast it and the practically identical qualities you've just settled for the zone.

You'll before long arrive at a point where you'll be acquainted with all the properties being offered in your objective region, and you'll be searching just for new postings. Probably, that will take 15 minutes per day 15 minutes that could take care of huge with only a couple of hits a year.

Consistently scouring the paper and the Internet for new plans when they show up should turn into an ordinary piece of your daily practice. In any case, that is by all account not the only method to discover underestimated properties. Search for indications that a proprietor might be considering selling, even before the individual promotes it.

Purchasing and Flipping Preconstruction Properties

Flipping real estate implies there's new development around. You realize it will be hot, and you can purchase a preconstruction unit for $125,000. You are generally positive you'll have the option to flip it (sell it immediately) when development is done for $160,000.

This is a pleasant business. No wreckage, no issue. Furthermore, you can rake in tons of money. The stunt here is to ensure you have the legitimate right to sell the property when you need and at the cost you need. Be careful: These plans regularly accompany gets that should be revised.

Flipping is an extremely pleasant and blushing approach to earn substantial sums of money in real estate. It's something you can't do constantly, yet when you can, it's brilliant. The thought is to purchase preconstruction homes or apartment suites in promising neighbourhood developments.

Here's a model:

DL purchased two condominium apartments in a Miami Beach skyscraper three years prior, exactly toward the start of development. He got one for himself at $375,000 and a littler one for investment purposes at $205,000.

The building was finished in around 14 months. Around

then, the bigger loft had increased in value by in excess of 20 percent comparative units were selling for $450,000. And, the littler unit showed improvement over that. After a year, costs had climbed once more. He sold his investment property for $375,000.

Another model:

BM (a person who has aced purchasing and selling costly vehicles, watches, and so forth.) purchased two preconstruction apartment suite units in our town for $265,000 each. The property isn't yet completed, yet all the units have just been sold. The last six were sold for more than $300,000 each. BM has made nearly $100,000 in under year and a half.

It tends to Be a Very Nice Business

This gives you a thought regarding what should be possible by purchasing and flipping preconstruction properties.

It won't work if property estimations are falling. Also, it won't work if the specific improvement you pick ends up being a clunker. That is the reason it's so imperative to adhere to your nearby market so you can genuinely know it.

You'll have to choose for yourself whether properties are acknowledging in your general vicinity. Assuming this is the case, glance around and see whether there are units you can purchase that meet your own money related prerequisites.

In case you're a beginner at this, you should seriously restrain your investment. All things considered, wouldn't it be pleasant to have a little low maintenance, purchase and-flip business that could give you $20,000, $50,000 even $100,000 a year in additional income?

One incredible thing about real estate: It goes up considerably more regularly than it goes down. Furthermore, the great properties in the great territories go up a lot more grounded and longer than the rest.

By and by, the Most Important Rule: Invest in What You Know

I've discussed profits in the least difficult terms. If you need to augment your profits and limit your money expense, you'll be getting money up to 90 percent of a property's deal cost. In this manner, you could, for instance, control $100,000 worth of real estate with a down payment (and exchange costs) of as little as $15,000. A few people put down even less. The better you can pass judgment available, the fewer hazards you take and the better bit of leeway you can take of the influence of influence: acquiring the greater part of the money you need.

Maybe the best thing about this specific type of real estate in-vesting is that it requires minimal measure of everyday work. When you've chosen the property, the difficult work is finished. From that point forward, everything you do is keep an eye on the improvement's development occasionally to ensure it's on plan. If your hunch about the market is correct, you'll before long be selling your property for a pleasant profit because the improvement itself will do the selling for you.

Life Structures of a Great Real Estate Deal

RJ simply sold a town house apartment suite for $341,000. He got it, with a 5 percent initial instalment, eight months back. He paid, after all costs and overhauls, $291,000. After deals commission (he arranged 3 percent with the woman he purchased the unit from) and shutting costs, he'll net about

$226,000. Subsequent to taking care of the home loan, he'll make about $35,000 on a speculation of $15,000 eight months prior. Annualized, that turns out to in excess of 300 percent.

What's happening here?

This is a case of what happens when you purchase a preconstruction home or town house and flip it upon the arrival of shutting. That way, you can advertise another property in every case more popular and never need to stress over upkeep, apartment suite expenses, or something like that.

To make this work, you have to discover great improvements (by great manufacturers and advertisers) in hot regions. If the market is hot, that aides, as well. You additionally need to purchase the property right (which ordinarily implies from the get-go in the development procedure so you get the most reduced cost) and sell it forcefully by all means imaginable.

For RJ's situation, he went to the best source the organization that sold him the unit the minute he heard that it had sold out its units. He figured they'd get individuals coming in hoping to purchase and would be glad to sell his unit at a 3 percent commission as opposed to get nothing. It worked!

To Make Money in Real Estate, You've Got to Buy Right

To purchase right... be set up to drive around and do some work. The huge mystery about real estate (in any event for bringing in money temporarily) is to purchase acceptable property at or underneath showcase esteem. Purchase low and sell higher. Also, regardless of what the well known books let you know, you won't have the option to do that all the time except if you set aside the effort to get out there and locate the best gives yourself.

Seven Rules for Buying Investment Properties

When you purchase property as a investment for fast resale, you ought to stick to the accompanying seven fundamental standards. The majority of these apply to rentals too. However, in case you're purchasing rentals for long haul possession and benefit, you should update Rule 6 so you are really improving the nature of the rentals.

1. Try not to possess real estate from a remote place.

2. Purchase just in demonstrated, exceptional neighbourhoods or those that fringe on the equivalent.

3. When purchasing a solitary family home, ensure the gross rental salary is at any rate one-tenth of your price tag including enhancements. In many territories this should restrain the price tag of the home to the $150,000 territory and underneath. When you purchase single-family homes over that range, you'll typically find that the rental incentive as a level of the price tag will fall. In case you're acquiring homes in the $150,000-in addition to extend, your technique will regularly be to fix and flip.

4. Make sense of the amount you're paying on a square-foot premise, attempting to keep it as near $100 per square foot as could reasonably be expected. That number is comparative with the specific market, obviously. In most pleasant neighbourhoods, for instance, a few homes sell for $200 per square foot. However, it's smarter to be down around $100 to leave space for upgrades and edges for commissions.

5. Purchase homes where you can get a $2 to $4 return on each $1 you spend setting them up. This is really simpler to decide

than you might suspect. Try to purchase a house evaluated significantly under the market and afterward re-try it as economically as could be expected under the circumstances.

6. Spend money improving the house, yet just where it is important. Paint. Set up economical screens and shades. Replace bureau entryways and covering. Put artistic tile on ledges. Furthermore, paint the passage. Those are the fundamental update openings. Everything else you may do including plumbing and electrical work will most likely not be wise investments.

7. If conceivable, have a leaseholder for your home before you get it. If you get the word out adequately frequently, your companions and partners will consider you when they meet somebody who is searching for a place to live.

So, there is still a lot of that is amorphous about deciding worth.

For instance, is that two-room farm house that you saw on Thirteenth Street and Olive Avenue worth the $150,000 being requested it? Shouldn't something be said about that three-room pilgrim a couple of squares away? Is it over-estimated at $120,000?

You can't respond to those sorts of inquiries except if you have a generally excellent feel for the area. Furthermore, as I stated, you can't have a generally excellent feel for an area except if you limit your contributing to a specific region, ideally in your own old neighbourhood and except if you are eager to drive around that area and pose inquiries.

If you can do those two things, real estate can work for you. Consider it. And, begin looking.

When Buying Real Estate, Always Insist on an Inspection

Never purchase a house or business property without an assessment a great review from somebody with a long haul notoriety for reasonableness and genuineness. If you don't have a clue about a decent overseer, get referrals from other real estate speculators you may know and from legitimate contractual workers. Try not to look for proposals for reviewers from the real estate professionals.

Never go to contract without embeddings a condition that gives you back your store if the review distinguishes something unexpected and undesirable.

A valid example: JJ marked a plan on a four-room, two-shower $100,000 house in a negligible neighbourhood. As indicated by the vender, the month to month rental salary was $1,200. That would make the plan look phenomenal. In any case, when he had it examined (by somebody he has utilized before and believes), he discovered that it was a twofold wide trailer. It had been set up on a changeless establishment and canvassed in applaud board, so it was not evident. However, to the expert who investigated it, and to the bank that revealed to JJ it didn't back such structures, there was a huge improvement.

1. The home-alone procedure. At whatever point you see an empty home in your objective region, stop and scribble down the location. Look into the proprietors in the area property records and call or write to inquire as to whether they'd be keen on selling the property. If the house is in urgent need of a paint work or has a seriously congested yard, you may have discovered spurred merchants before they've really put the property available. If they need to sell, you may have discovered a property at a generally excellent cost.

2. The carport deal. Here and there, before proprietors put their property available to be purchased, they'll hold a carport deal to free the house from all messiness and get it into demonstrating shape. So watch out for your neighbourhood paper for carport deals and moving deals in your objective zones. Try not to sit around idly going to the deals. Simply get to discover what they're selling. During the discussion, clarify that you're searching for a home in the territory and inquire as to whether they are aware of any that are coming available to be purchased. Sometimes, you may find that you can purchase not exclusively what's in the carport, yet the house itself.

3. Out-of-state proprietors. At whatever point you're exploring neighbourhood property estimations, make certain to make note of full scale of-state real estate owners. The property rolls should list the street number of the proprietors notwithstanding the subtleties of the property itself. When the proprietors' location is out of state, send them a letter or find them in the telephone registry and get to see if they may be keen on selling.

4. Code infringement. A property with various code infringements can be a sign that the proprietors can't bear to keep the property up or may never again be keen on dealing with it. A few towns will genuinely label a property that has code infringement. Figure out how to perceive that tag and look out for it as you pass through your objective territories.

Purchasing and Selling Fixer-Uppers

The expertise required here is an eye for what could be the capacity to see a house wrecked and envision how much better it would look with some paint, a touch of cultivating, and new floor covering.

The key to making fixer-uppers work is to keep your

improvement costs in accordance with your financial limit. If, for instance, the two-room mess you are looking at is $40,000 under the market, your fix-up spending plan ought to be fundamentally not as much as that $10,000 to $15,000 would be a decent wagered. Making a practical spending plan and afterward adhering to it are the two fundamental aptitudes expected to make this kind of salary creating adinvestment work for you. There are three guidelines to purchasing and selling fixer-uppers:

1. Purchase underestimated property. You can't cause a completely esteemed property to turn out to be more significant by setting it up. The thought is to discover a property whose worth is not as much as what it ought to be (contrasted with comparatively estimated and arranged properties in the zone) and afterward bring it up to its full an incentive by spending a minimal expenditure on it.

2. Make a fix-up spending that leaves you with enough benefit to meet your general money related objectives. Purchasing and selling fixer-uppers is fun work. However, it's work. So you need to be certain you earn substantial sums of money for it. You can do that by choosing before-hand how a lot of salary you need this business to give and afterward isolating that by the quantity of exchanges you can sensibly hope to accomplish on low maintenance premise. For instance, if your objective was to make an extra $60,000 the primary year, you may conclude that you have to net $20,000 on three exchanges. If you need to net $20,000 on an individual exchange, ensure that your spending gives you making that much or more. (I like to cheat in support of me by planning a benefit of $25,000 if I need to make $20,000 in light of the fact that I've discovered that there are in every case some unexpected costs.)

3. Similarly as costs normally surpass your desires, costs a few times baffle you. To manage that reality, you should be restrained about selling. You can't bring in money in a purchase and-sell business if you never sell. You should be set up to drop your requesting that value move the property if nearby selling conditions direct. A decent general guideline: Never clutch a property for longer than one season (or one year). Over the long haul, you'll get more money-flow making littler benefits on each trans-move yet making more exchanges.

Continuously Have a Plan B

The absolute most significant standard in decreasing danger and expanding your benefit potential on each property flip is to have a strong reinforcement plan set up. Despite the fact that you may have no designs to lease a property you plan to flip, it's ideal to ensure you could lease it out at a benefit (or if nothing else make back the initial investment) if you needed to.

We've every single heard tale about the financial specialist who purchases a house, hangs another front entryway, finishes up the paint, plants a couple of blossoms, and sells it a month later for a $50,000 benefit. While this sort of achievement isn't phenomenal in a quick moving business sector when the property is bought beneath showcase esteem, it is unquestionably not the standard.

Go into each real estate bargain regardless of whether you're anticipating flipping or contributing long haul with a decent resistance. And, your best barrier is to ensure the rental salary the property would create will take care of your conveying costs in addition to at any rate 10 percent in the event of some unforeseen issue. Your conveying costs on a property are the entirety of your principal, interest, taxies, and insurance (PITI).

Discover what the rental qualities are in your general vicinity by calling about investment properties recorded in the paper and considering organizations that spend significant time in rentals. The Department of Housing and Urban Development (HUD) likewise distributes reasonable market lease (FMR) rules for specific zones and despite the fact that this isn't constantly an exact impression of the real world; it can fill in as a decent base number.

To decide your edge of security on a specific property, figure the gross rental yield. To do that, isolate the rental salary it would get every year by the asking cost.

So if the approaching cost for a house is $100,000 and the rental salary is $750 every month, the gross rental yield would be 9 percent ($750 * 12 = $9,000; $9,000/$100,000 = .09).

In many markets, a 10 percent rental yield gives an agreeable edge of wellbeing. At the end of the day most dire outcome imaginable if the property doesn't sell, you could lease it out and more than spread your expenses.

The rental yield additionally gives you a speedy method to decide the most extreme sum you should pay for a property. In our model, suppose your objective is a base 10 percent rental yield. At $100,000, the house doesn't meet your criteria. So switch the math a tad. Take the yearly rental estimation of the property and gap it by the yield you have to get.

Right now, times 12 gives you $9,000 in yearly rental pay. Gap $9,000 by 10 percent (.10) and you get $90,000. This is the most extreme sum you can pay for the property and still procure the 10 percent rental yield that you need.

The rental worth will consistently fill in as your grapple, keeping you from offering an absurdly significant expense in a quick rising business sector.

Make Any Deal a Potential Quick Flip with an Assignment Clause

Regardless of whether you're seeking purchase as long as possible, you should give yourself the legitimate alternative to flip the property. You do this through a task proviso. If your lone objective is to flip the property, a task condition is compulsory.

It just implies that on each agreement you sign, ensure you reserve the privilege to allocate the agreement to another purchaser. On a fundamental level, it's like underwriting to another person a look at that is made to you. The trustee would then close on the agreement with the merchant under the time and terms stipulated in the agreement.

The essential advantages for you are that you cause a snappy benefit and you to can avoid every single shutting cost. In numerous standard agreements, the language will allude to "the 'Purchaser' (or potentially doles out and chosen people)." This consequently allows you task rights. If it's not in the contract, you can include it by putting "or potentially allots" where you fill in your name on the agreement.

If the agreement originates from the merchant, read it cautiously to ensure it doesn't have a condition restricting task of the agreement without the dealer's composed authorization.

Other than the capacity to dole out the agreement to another purchaser if the open door emerges, the task proviso will likewise empower you to take on an accomplice for the property after you get it under agreement if you ought to choose to do as such.

For instance, suppose you discover a completely shouting plan. You can get it for $250,000 and you know it's effectively worth $325,000. Furthermore, it has incredible rental incentive in relationship to the cost so that in any event, financing 90 percent of the buy it will commence income at $250,000 like an opening machine.

Just issue is . . . it's somewhat out of your compass. You have the financing contacts and capabilities to fit the bill for a $150,000 property as it were. So what do you do?

Feel free to make the idea to get the property under agreement. Simply ensure the agreement has a standard provision making it dependent upon your acquiring financing inside a specific timeframe. Despite the fact that you likely can't get the financing alone, in light of the task condition you can get the following best thing: a value speculator.

How Not to Flip a Property

Flipping real estate can prompt brisk and sizable benefits when you locate the correct property. However, these plans are not constantly a slam dunk, and unpractised financial specialists frequently lose money. Recall the exercises you simply learned right now remember the accompanying three focuses.

1. If you need to recovery the property, recollect this isn't an ideal opportunity to make your fantasy house. Concentrate just on the regions that would raise a warning at shutting and

the generally reasonable things that will enable the house to show better, for example, new paint, new windows, arranging, and an exhaustive cleaning.

2. Try not to get genuinely got up to speed in a quick rising business sector. The most widely recognized misstep individuals make when they lose money flipping a property is that they pay a lot for it, expecting that the cost will soar. If costs slow down and you don't have a rental respect spread your costs, you could be looking at a loss.

3. Try not to be hoping to flip properties if you are consistently in a mash for money. You could turn into an edgy financial specialist and you never need to purchase or sell in franticness.

If you observe the principles I spread out with respect to purchasing the property at a markdown to its actual market esteem, and if you are sure that in a most dire outcome imaginable the rental yield would at present make a positive income, you have an agreeable edge of security. And, flipping real estate may very well be your key to programmed riches.

PLAN YOUR SUCCESS

Set explicit destinations as far as both finding out about real estate and afterward putting resources into it. Make these particular (e.g., "become the showcasing chief for my organization's hair items before the finish of the following monetary year"; "start one side business inside a half year"; "put resources into one potential flip inside a quarter of a year"). At that point join these destinations into the yearly, month to month, week after week, and every day task records.

From the start, your plan will be to some degree general. In any case, as you invest energy contemplating it and chipping away at it, you will concoct endless thoughts that will help hone your vision and prod your own advancement.

A portion of these thoughts will be enormous, some little. Some will be solo endeavours. Others will require the assistance of associates. Some will meet with progress and some will meet with disappointment. Most in the beginning periods of your learning will fall some place in the middle.

Yet, the more you work at your plan, the simpler it will get.

If you need to get well off in a short to direct measure of time, you will require a six-figure salary. The higher you get your pay, the quicker you can accomplish riches. This part has talked about a few different ways to help your pay:

- Make a higher (potentially deeply more significant pay.
- Become an independent specialist.
- Start your own pay producing side business.
- Invest in pay delivering real estate.

Think about every one of these four techniques as independent surges of pay. You can begin each stream streaming at the same time. Around this time one year from now maybe you can be storing four separate checks into your own record every month each creation you wealthier and better ready to quicken your riches later on.

All these pay streams come from a similar wellspring: information. And, the information that they require is on a very basic level the equivalent: how to make, create, and sell items and administrations.

To quicken your pay objectives, start to learn as much as you can about deals and promoting today. Concentrate on how clients are procured and afterward exchanged, and focus first on an industry or business that you definitely know. Ace direct advertising and see how it very well may be applied to each business you engage in. Apply the ideas you figure out how to all that you do: your principle work, your independent work, a side business, and real estate.

It's redundant that each of the four of these salary streams produces for you. Any of them can make you rich. However, since they all require similar major information, you can edge yourself into every one of them or possibly a few at the same time. Furthermore, that implies an a lot greater and better possibility of gaining a drastically higher salary.

CHAPTER FIVE

GET RICH WHILE SLEEPING

It is extremely unlikely around it drastically expanding your own pay will take some work. Possibly a ton of work. Anyway you support it by getting more from your manager, by purchasing and flipping properties, or by making a subsequent salary it will require focused, invigorated, self-started work.

In any case, making riches through value can be unique. It doesn't typically require progressing, stress-delivering work. It demands making a budgetary investment. Also, that infers hazard. In any case, if your investment is a decent one (i.e., if the speculation structure is reasonable and the business develops and benefits), the value proprietor can get rich without working. The person can get more extravagant ceaselessly, every minute of every day even while dozing.

In the event that you put resources into a decent business at a reasonable value, you can expect that the offer you have of that business will turn out to be more important. Exactly how important it becomes will rely upon various things the industry, the executives, capitalization, advertising, etc however it doesn't need to rely upon you.

That is what's acceptable and what's terrible about value contributing. Irregular House gives us three budgetary meanings of value:

1. "The enthusiasm for the responsibility for stock in a corporation."
2. "The money related estimation of a property or business past any sums owed on it in contracts, claims, liens, and so forth."
3. "Ownership, particularly when considered as the privilege to partake in future benefits or thankfulness in esteem."

And, that is the means by which we'll address this significant piece of your riches building future, as far as stock, land, and direct investments.

Putting resources into STOCK FOR EQUITY APPRECIATION

During the Internet-organization energized securities exchange bubble, pretty much everyone I know was putting resources into stocks. Colleagues in the monetary data industry, however my companions, my relatives, my jiujitsu instructors, my tailor, the individuals in the specialist's sitting area, and, indeed, the person in the air terminal who sparkled my shoes. A large number of these individuals were new to the securities exchange and searching for a fast buck. However, some, as well, were long-term, self-depicted "moderate" financial specialists who were attempting to appreciate the 25-percent-in addition to yearly returns that pretty much everybody assumed would go on until the end of time.

There were a couple of exemptions: a bunch of investment scholars who had been foreseeing a financial exchange breakdown for whatever length of time that I've known them (and who along these lines passed up the tremendous market thankfulness that happened over the most recent 30 years of the twentieth century) and a few specialists who had been in the market and benefitting from it, however pulled out when their pointers flashed "sell."

One, Steve Sjuggerud, had been bullish available since the October 1987 remedy. He had made himself and his readers a ton of money for a long time. Around six or eight months before the highest point of the market, he started to diminish his stock investments radically. When the rectification (crash?) happened, he was 90 percent out.

Steve has had a great record of timing the market, however what I like most about him is the manner by which humble he is. With regards to putting resources into stocks, he is the first to recognize that anyway much he thinks about the business part and anyway much he finds about the stock he enjoys, he can never realize enough to unhesitatingly foresee the future estimation of its offers.

The Stock Market Is a Very Complicated Animal

There are such a large number of components associated with deciding the value developments of individual stocks. (I shouldn't utilize the word deciding in such an announcement.) For instance, there are principal factors, for example, value profit (P/E) proportions, income development, and income history. There are essential business contemplations, for example, administration, piece of the pie, and obligation. And, there are specialized contemplations devices and markers that endeavour to follow and foresee value developments. At long last, there is the all-encompassing and overpowering impact of market brain science at work the dread and covetousness of conventional and institutional speculators. Include every one of these components and you have a living being whose development, propensities, and developments are what could be compared to unrestrained choice. So when putting resources into stocks, Steve follows a stock determination convention that regards that natural, rash, some of the time sporadic nature of the market:

- Invest in what you know. Your odds of being specific about a specific stock's cost future improve as your insight into its business, its industry, and its administration increases. Since you can't think enough about everything, create ability by narrowing your extension. Recognize a few businesses that premium you and learn as much as you can about them: how they make clients, how they create items, how they augment benefits.

- Be suspicious of stock stories. The stock financier and data organizations take a shot at the premise of dramatization. Make an incredible anecdote about a new business with a progressive innovation headed by a virtuoso very rich person, and you have a demonstrated equation for deals. Specialists, stock investigators, and investment masters all make their livings by finding, bundling, and showing such stories. A decent story works by summoning feeling. Feeling overrules rationale. With your rationale set aside, you permit yourself to make speculations you will most likely lament later.

- Be conventional with every speculation. Anyway well you know the business, never contribute beyond what you can bear to lose. My own point of confinement is 1 percent of my investable riches. That implies that if you have a investment arrangement of a million dollars, you should never put more than $10,000 in any single speculation.

- Have a Plan B. When I put resources into independent

companies, I generally have a Plan B. A Plan B is my specialty if the business doesn't work out like I figure it will. A decent Plan B should confine your losses. With regards to stocks, Steve does likewise with stop-loss orders. "When a stock hits a set up stop-loss," he let me know, "it's a sign to me that the market knows something about it that I don't. I'm not more astute than the market. So whenever I get an opportunity to get out with the majority of my speculation unblemished, I am glad to get out."

When Investing in Business, Take the Short Odds

Furthermore, that is a significant point.

As I clarified, my initial understanding as an advertiser of hot new thoughts has shown me the threat in great stories. The better they sound, the more doubtful I've figured out how to turn into. As a financial specialist in independent investments, I'd a lot of rather put my money into something with sensible yet likely possibilities, instead of something that has phenomenal however just potential possibilities. A quarter century of contributing experience has instructed me that I'm not excessively acceptable at spotting champs.

And, I'm discussing organizations I can analyze, CEOs I can talk with, investments I know, and speculations that give me a genuine state in what's going on. In the event that I can't rake in huge profits with every one of those preferences working for me, how might I hope to be fruitful putting resources into little organizations about which the main thing I know is that they have a decent story?

Along these lines, as I stated, I make it a propensity to put distinctly in what I know, to constrain my investment, and to have a Plan B as of now set up so I can get out if my good thought ends up being a bummer.

There is one special case to the "put resources into what you know" rule: the "put resources into who you know and trust" exclusion. I have some of the time put resources into organizations I knew almost no about on the grounds that they were going up by individuals I knew to be bonafide money makers and they gave me their own affirmation that the arrangements were acceptable ones.

This is a dubious exemption to the standard, so I wouldn't really prescribe it to most financial specialists. To make it work, you must be specific about the individual's virtuoso and right, as well, about the estimation of their own affirmations. For a great many people, this sort of chance comes around once in a while, if at any point.

Bigger versus Smaller Stocks

There is some discussion in the investment world about which sort of stocks will give the best value appreciation. Enormous top stocks (Fortune 1000 kind of organizations) give you greater dependability however less execution. Little top stocks are more dangerous; however they can give a considerable ROI.

I like a mix of both. When I put resources into bigger, increasingly settled organizations, I take an exceptionally ordinary, good old, fundamentalist methodology. I like to see a strong asset report, a background marked by income development, and a P/E proportion that is acceptable by contemporary market models. That is the establishment, yet I need more. I have to accept that the organization is a functioning player in a pattern that is hot inside an industry that is developing. Since I perceive that great basics are just piece of the game (showcase brain research is a significant part, as well), I need to see something that reveals to me all supplies of this sort will head up, regardless of whether I'm off-base about the specific organization I've put resources into.

THREE CHARACTERISTICS OF GREAT START-UP INVESTMENTS

When I put resources into littler organizations, I look at every one of those things I look at with bigger organizations however I additionally focus on three factors that are, in my experience, the best indicators of another business' future development:

1. Effectiveness of client securing. The first and most significant activity of a specialist is to make a deal. Without that first deal, nothing else can occur. Regular business people get this. In beginning another business, they dedicate 80 percent or a greater amount of their time and money to that goal: selling the item.

When putting resources into new companies or assessing somebody's thought for another business, my initial two inquiries are: How are you going to gain new clients? Also, How much is that new client going to cost you? Except if I find great solutions to those two inquiries, I take no further enthusiasm for the undertaking, since I realize that its odds of accomplishment are extremely thin.

Contrasted with making the principal deal, each other part of the business from making a decent item to giving great client support to taking a portion of the business is irrelevant. Demonstrate to me that (a) you realize how to get new clients and (b) you can acquire them without going belly up, and I'll be keen on your business.

2. Net revenue. I incline toward organizations that have significant markups. Being in the data distributing business, I've been ruined right now. Since we sell examination, translation, and counsel (rather than crude data, which resembles an item), we can charge noteworthy markups now and then 500 percent to 1,000 percent contingent upon how significant we accept that guidance is.

Higher edges give starting business manufacturers more money to spend on showcasing. Having more money to spend on advertising gives them a superior possibility of finding a productive method to gain new clients. Despite the fact that I recognize that there are a lot of intriguing and gainful organizations on the planet that work on little edges, I incline toward not to put resources into them particularly as new companies.

Accomplishment in business is tied in with gaining from botches. Develop ing a fruitful business is tied in with committing all the errors you have to without becoming bankrupt all the while. Organizations that work on large edges take into consideration a ton of slip-ups. I like that sort of recompense.

3. Back-end potential. An enormous edge permits another business to dis-spread an equation for getting new clients, however except if the business can figure out how to change over those underlying exchanges into generous, longer-term business connections, the plan of action is flawed. A business that relies altogether upon new deals for development and benefit resembles a vehicle driving tough on a street covered with oil. It might have enough footing to go for sometime, however in the long run the work engaged

with moving depletes the motor and wrecks the vehicle.

I like organizations that can extend geometrically organizations that can secure an expanding number of clients from a growing business sector and afterward improve the estimation of those client connections by selling them more, better, and the sky is the limit from there costly items. If procuring new clients is the front finish of the business, making those clients more significant (by selling them increasingly, better, and that's just the beginning costly items) is the back end.

So when I hope to put resources into another business, I need to see each of the three parts set up: an effective client obtaining convention, a high net revenue, and the potential for enormous, back-end benefits.

Desires for an Equity Position in Stocks

It's sensible to accept that, as time goes on, the securities exchange will give you an arrival of around 10 percent on your money. (I don't figure it will do that well sooner rather than later, on the grounds that it's exaggerated today. However, in the event that you have 10 or 15 years to hang tight for the perfect time, you will most likely do OK.)

You could show improvement over 10 percent 12 percent to 15 percent is my present objective by observing the guidelines I spread out:

- Invest in what you know.
- Limit the size of any individual investment.
- Have a Plan B prepared in the event that you are incorrect.
- Invest in both huge and little top stocks.
- With developing stocks, good organizations that have (1) an

effective client procurement convention, (2) a huge overall revenue, and (3) the capability of a major back end.

A 12 percent to 15 percent ROI may not make you rich in 7 to 15 years, yet if you adhere to this equation and don't desert it when you hear a compelling story, odds are you will show improvement over your companions and partners.

As I said toward the start of this section, the best thing about value contributing and this is generally valid for stock contributing is that, after the work you do exploring a specific speculation, you don't need to do whatever else to get more extravagant. You simply lock in a stop-loss if the value moves against you, and watch your riches assemble.

Building a Stock Portfolio

My portfolio mirrors my conviction that nobody can ever unquestionably anticipate the conduct of any individual stock or any division or the securities exchange in general.

At present, I have fewer than 2 percent of my total assets put resources into stocks. Before, it has been higher; however I don't think I've at any point had in excess of 10 percent of my money tied up in stocks. To most money related organizers, that would appear to be a ultraconservative position particularly for somebody who as of late turned 50. However, for me, it feels savvy. Because I'm doubtful about stocks, yet additionally in light of the fact that I put intensely in land and independent investments.

I like to have the greater part of my money in speculations that are more intuitive than stocks. By "intelligent" I mean investments about which I can have increasingly personal information and over which I can have more control. Take land, for instance. It doesn't take a virtuoso to know when the private lodging market in the area is over-esteemed. You should simply watch out for costs and purchasers and settle on some judicious choices about whether this pattern can proceed.

When I put resources into start up companies, I generally limit myself to organizations I know. Furthermore, when I take a position, I ensure it accompanies some impact so that, if things should begin going south, I can step in and impact a few changes. This mix of inside information and dynamic control causes me to feel considerably more certain about contributing my money. What's more, that is the reason I have around 50 percent of my investable riches tied up in land and new organizations.

What Others Say

Think about after a more customary methodology:

- Safe portfolio 20 percent stocks, 80 percent bonds. For over 70 years, this portfolio has arrived at the midpoint of 7.0 percent a year. Its most noticeably bad year was lost 10.1 percent. It lost money 17 percent of the years.
- Balanced portfolio 50 percent stocks, 50 percent bonds. During a similar timespan, this portfolio has found the middle value of 8.7 percent a year. Its most noticeably bad year was lost 22.5 percent. It lost money 22 percent of the years.
- Risky portfolio 80 percent stocks, 20 percent bonds. This portfolio has arrived at the midpoint of 10.0 percent a year. Its most noticeably terrible year was lost 34.9 percent. It lost money 28 percent of the years.

You see the example, isn't that right? The less secure the portfolio, the more vigorous the development was in the acceptable years. However, losses were more noteworthy during the terrible years and there were all the more bad years.

In picking which portfolio suits you best, contemplate your age. The more seasoned you are, the less hazard you should need to endure. Why? In case you're resigned, the handy outcomes of your losses can-not be soothed by your present place of employment pay. Regardless of whether you're not resigned, you just come up short on the advantage of having quite a few years to compensate for moderate-to-overwhelming losses.

Another thought is the present heading of the securities exchange. Is it going up or down? It's not in every case simple to tell. Because it's down today doesn't imply that tomorrow it will start to bounce back. Or then again if it's up today, it might start a long decay tomorrow. I'll give you access on a few privileged insights in only a couple of pages that will assist you with disentangling the bearing and pattern of the market. Remember that in a down market, you should bring down your stock possessions considerably more than proposed in the previous three suggestions. In the event that the market is making roughage, increment your stock property as needs be, suppose by 20 percent. Along these lines, in case you're holding 50 percent in stocks, you would build it to 60 percent.

One approach to divvy up your portfolio is this: 30 percent U.S. stocks, 30 percent remote stocks, 10 percent high-caliber corporate securities, 10 percent high return securities, 10 percent U.S. Treasury bonds (TIPS), 5 percent land stocks, and 5 percent gold and valuable metals.

A Closer Look at Stop-Losses:

The Exit Strategy Professionals Use

One thing that both professionals concede to is this: Whatever your methodology, you will undoubtedly make some bad stock determinations. Truth be told, there's no assurance that your great choices will dwarf the terrible ones. Here's the uplifting news: It doesn't make a difference.

In the event that you make twice the same number of bad stock buy choices as great ones, shouldn't you lose twice as much as you've earned? No. Since stock contributing isn't just about purchasing. It's additionally about selling. As significant as purchasing the correct stocks at the ideal time is, it is similarly essential to sell the correct stocks at the perfect time. Furthermore, you're not going to settle on indistinguishable selling choices for devaluing stocks from you would for acknowledging stocks.

Cut your losses. Ride your victors. Experts realize when to offer a stock and when to hold it by utilizing a trailing stop-loss.

The trailing stop expects you to follow the cost of your stock and sell it when it drops to a specific level. The sell point can be activated at 10 percent, 20 percent, 30 percent, or whatever, beneath the stock's most noteworthy selling cost. I prescribe 25 percent.

There's nothing enchantment about this number. It just appears to suit most stock leave circumstances. However, it carries one in number ramifications with respect to what your hazard resistance ought to be. A decent proportion is one to thrcc. That is, if you arc happy to chance a 25 percent loss, you ought to sensibly expect in any event a 75 percent return on your investment. In the event that you are told, for instance, that a 30 percent return yet no higher is normal from a specific investment, your stop-loss point ought to be activated at 10 percent, not 25 percent.

We should use for instance a stock you purchased for $100. For comfort, you're utilizing my suggested 25 percent rule. The stock rises to $110. In the event that it drops 25 percent from that cost, to $82.50 or underneath, the stock is sold. You've lost 17.5 percent of your speculation. In another situation, suppose the stock trips to $150 before losing elevation. Under the 25 percent rule, the guidance to sell would be activated if the stock tumbles to $112.50 or beneath toward the finish of the exchanging day. You've made $12.50 on the stock, or 12.5 percent. Right now, are utilizing the trailing stop method not to cut your losses, yet to ride your victors. You have permitted your stock to arrive at its most significant expense. When it begins to drop off, you sell. By not keeping the stock unreasonably long, you cut your losses. By not selling it rashly, you've allowed your victor to winner.

Submitting the Stop-Loss Request

This procedure is so significant for you to utilize every single time you purchase stock, I am going to let you know precisely how to set it up. You put in a stop-loss request with your merchant, teaching the person in question to sell a stock that you possess at a specific cost. Utilizing the 25 percent rule, that cost would be 25 percent beneath the market cost. As the present market value moves higher, your stop-loss value moves higher in lockstep.

If you manage a full-administration specialist, you essentially need to advise your merchant to put the 25 percent trailing stop-loss request into play. There's no charge for doing as such until or except if it's initiated. Around then, you would need to pay the ordinary representative's bonus expenses.

If you exchange on the web, it's dependent upon you to consistently follow your stocks and move your trailing stop-loss arranges varying. Utilize just finish of-day costs. It gets excessively entangled in any case.

If you are managing a low-evaluated stock, it wouldn't take a lot of value development to trigger a stop-loss request at 25 percent. In such cases, increment the 25 percent with the goal that the descending value development would need to be something beyond a couple of dollars to trigger the stop-loss request.

Suppose you purchased $10,000 worth of two stocks. Following a month, the main stock's worth trips to $12,000. The subsequent stock drops to $8,000. Following two months, the principal stock scopes $15,000 and the subsequent one drops further, to $5,000.

This is what you might be enticed to do . . .

You've made $5,000 on the principal stock. You're satisfied. That is a 50 percent benefit. You will get out while the going is acceptable and keep your $5,000 benefit. Shockingly, the subsequent stock has lost 50 percent of its worth. You're $5,000 in the gap. You could bail, assume the loss, and figure that between the $5,000 picked up and $5,000 lost, you're even. Yet, you're persuaded that the stock has dropped so low that's will undoubtedly get once more. So you choose to clutch it. That, at half of its previous value, it's a decent purchase. So as to truly profit by the bob you're certain the subsequent stock will take, you utilize the $5,000 earned from your first stock to purchase a greater amount of it.

Is there anything amiss with this image? There sure is.

You've settled on two terrible choices. You abandoned a despite everything rising stock, on edge to secure in the benefit you made. What amount more could its cost have expanded? "It previously grew 50 percent," you thought, "so why hope for the best?" The truth of the matter is, you don't have the foggiest idea how much further it could have risen. It's not incomprehensible for a stock to go up 100 percent, 200 percent, or more. You simply don't have the foggiest idea. In any case, you willingly volunteered to put a roof on what you earned. The stock didn't really quit developing. However, by your activity, it stopped developing for you. Bad move. It bodes well to ride your triumphant stocks to the extent that this would be possible. I'll give you how in almost no time.

The other rash choice? You stayed with your losing stock. To exacerbate the situation, in addition to the fact that you stuck with it, you put a greater amount of your valuable money in it. The stock may have wound up in a sorry situation when you reinvested in it. It may then bounce back and take off higher than ever. However, let's be honest, you truly don't have a clue. The main reality you do know is that the stock's value fell 50 percent. You believe that is a great deal and it is. However, guess what? It could fall a lot further . . . right down to zero.

Boosting Profits and Minimizing Risk

Not all your stock buys will make out well. Maybe not by any means a lion's share of them will make you money. In any case, if you stay with stocks and segments you know, you'll boost your benefits and limit your hazard. A decent method to begin is to concentrate on stocks that are firmly identified with your calling, skill, and additionally interests. Add as far as anyone is concerned by learning. Peruse. Take courses. Converse with specialists. Attempt to build up an inside feel for the market.

Furthermore, in any event, when the market is by all accounts conflicting with you, stay with your strategy. Warren Buffett, the best financial specialist ever, never wandered from the organizations and enterprises he knows best and has confidence in, (for example, razors and pop Gillette and Coke), in any event, when the market began to look all starry eyed at innovative organizations. When the innovative air pocket burst, Buffett's investments remained solid and his promise to what he accepted was vindicated.

Adhering to a decent framework is significantly harder than it sounds. You will be enticed to contribute outside your subject matter every now and again. A few times the accounts will appear to be practically overwhelming. Remind yourself: The better they sound, the more terrible they most likely are.

Furthermore, do the other conventional things that extraordinary financial specialists like Warren Buffett do: Pay regard for, as far as possible your proprietor ship of individual investments, and be aware of your objective as far as time.

In examining each stock speculation, ask yourself, "What will this be worth in X years?" Remember, the explanation you are putting resources into stocks is for medium-term (7-to 15-year) appreciation. In the event that the stock isn't probably going to give you a decent return in that time allotment, skip it.

CONCLUSION

If you succumb to the Million-Dollar Lie and persuade yourself that you can save yourself into an agreeable retirement, you will wake up one day feeling like you can't remain to work one more day however when you look at your retirement account, you'll understand you will presumably need to continue working for an amazing remainder.

If you accept my recommendation truly, face the future all things considered, create riches building propensities, get your salary up there, and start to create value, you will have the option to resign in 7 to 15 years and that will be early, trust me, contrasted with the greater part of the remainder of the retirement-age populace.

RETIRE EARLY

How To Plan An Early Retirement And Start Living Your Life

RICHARD SODIN

CHAPTER ONE

ROADMAP TO EARLY RETIREMENT

In some cases it just bodes Ill to take the parkway and avoid all the stoplights and traffic on neighbourhood streets. In comparable design, you need to ensure you get onto the financial thruway as ahead of schedule as would be prudent and remain there until you arrive at your exit. That implies putting principally in stocks and stock shared assets, not money or securities, during the vast majority of your contributing years. Why? Since stocks are the thruway: they offer the quickest, generally immediate, and most dependable approach to find a good pace.

You additionally need to ensure your vehicle – or, in other words your profession – is capable of getting you there. Try not to get onto the thruway in a clunker and discover you can't keep up – or more terrible yet, stall by the roadside. Rather, buy a dependable vehicle (a viable vocation) first and save yourself a ton of difficulty out and about ahead.

Avoid Shortcuts

Easy routes make for long deferrals, as the adage goes. Attempting to take such a large number of alternate routes headed straight toward early retirement can wind up exploded backward on you. By alternate routes I mean any high-chance investment planned for making easy money instead of getting rich gradually. Day exadjusting, money exadjusting, alternatives exadjusting, putting resources into speculative stock investments, putting resources into dangerous stocks, betting everything on the tracking enormous thing, putting resources into financial items you don't generally comprehend, and putting resources into anything that appears to be unrealistic all fall under the classification of easy routes to be kept away from in case you're tracking a get rich gradually approach.

I don't intend to suggest there's anything amiss with making easy money if you can do it dependably, however it's not what this book is about. A lot of different books spread that point. Making easy money is somewhat similar to bouncing and Iaving through traffic to find a workable pace similarly as quick as possible, while getting rich gradually is progressively similar to driving on the parkway however remaining in the centre path. It may not be wind-in-your-hair thrilling, yet it offers a moderately protected and unsurprising method for getting you to your objective.

Achievements Along Your Route

The tracking achievement is "Escape Debt," and it comes next for an explanation as Ill. I'll clarify why I suggest you take care of all charge cards, vehicle advances, and school credits first before starting to put resources into sincere for retirement.

There are two additional achievements along your course, them two having to do with how to minimize your costs so you can retire sooner and remain retired on less. It's honestly elusive a retirement book out there that doesn't have a section dedicated to the subject of living beneath your methods. Why? Since it's presumably the absolute most significant thing you can do to arrive at early retirement and remain retired. "Live beneath your means" may appear excessively evident exhortation, yet clear doesn't generally compare with simple to execute. I give pragmatic direction on the best way to incorporate this counsel.

After that the time is now for a rest stop. "Keep Your Life Portfolio Balanced" reminds you to offset living for now with living for tomorrow in case you come up short on energy en route.

CHAPTER TWO

GET OUT OF DEBT

In case you're not in the debt, congrats – you can skirt this part! Else I firmly suggest you escape debt first before you begin putting something aside for retirement. Pay off charge card debts, vehicle advances, school credits, and some other advances you may have so the main debt you have left is your home loan.

For what reason do I make an exemption for home loans? Since purchasing a house is costly to such an extent that the vast majority think that it's difficult to claim a home without first getting a long term credit from a financial establishment. Your house is additionally a investment over the long term, so there is acceptable avocation for owning as opposed to leasing for such huge numbers of years. In any case, all other debt other than your home loan is reasonable – and ought to be overseen forcefully.

Your first need ought to be to kill debt so you can begin your investment program with a fresh start. Your subsequent need ought to be to develop a little save of money to depend on if there should arise an occurrence of crisis. When those two needs have been met, you're prepared to start putting resources into sincere for early retirement.

Why You Should Pay Down Debt Before Investing

You might be stating to yourself, "Yet I'm extremely restless to begin making a few investments now! For what reason wouldn't i be able to settle my debt and start making investments simultaneously?"

In one explicit occurrence you should. If you happen to have a 401(k) at work, I would prescribe you invest the base sum important to exploit the full organization coordinate, which is basically free money. In any case, in any case, except if free money is included, it as a rule bodes Ill to escape debt first before starting to invest. Here's the reason.

Suppose you get goal-oriented and figure out how to take care of your Visa offset with the 17% loan cost an entire year sooner than you would have something else. That is one entire year of not paying 17% premium – and that is what might be compared to getting a 17% guaranteed quantifiable profit for the year. To put it another way, not paying 17% on a $1,000 balance on your Visa saves you $170, similarly as making 17% on a $1,000 investment makes you $170. Making $170 and saving $170 are cut out of the same cloth.

A great many people would concur 17% is a truly decent quantifiable profit. I'd feel exceptionally satisfied surely if I could get that sort of profit for a reliable basis. So it just bodes Ill to take care of the 17% charge card balance first, before starting to invest somewhere else at what will most likely be a sloIr pace of return. Regardless of whether you happen to have advances that lone charge you 8% or 9% intrigue, that is as yet an entirely fair pace of guaranteed return. So take care of them first and be finished with them.

Past the undeniable budgetary method of reasoning for taking care of your debt right on time, there's likewise the mental one. Basically, it feels great to be out from under a heap of debt and not oI anybody any money. It resembles a Iight has been lifted off your shoulders.

Crisis money save eases the burden significantly more by giving you a budgetary pad if your vehicle to out of nowhere stall or your heater ought to go on the fritz or some other huge cost should hit out of the blue. A little reserve of money is your escape prison free card for when the unanticipated occurs – which it definitely will.

Why You Shouldn't Borrow From Yourself

As of January 2013, normal charge card debt among family units conveying such debt was an astounding $15,442. When you consider the normal pace of enthusiasm on that debt is around 15%, it's no big surprise I hear discuss individuals "suffocating owing debtors" or being "up to their eyeballs owing debtors." Meanwhile, normal student debt is about $35,000, so kids specifically are attempting to get out from under a pile of debt that must regularly feel like it is squashing them.

If you are among the half of American family units conveying an unpaid charge card balance in the course of recent months, your first request of business in the wake of finding a strong activity ought to be to forcefully settle that debt before it can turn out to be any progressively unmanageable.

Poor Future You

The tragic truth is, each time you let the equalization on your

Mastercards turn over one more month, you're acquiring from your own future. No doubt about it "current you" by taking from "future you" and saying "put it on his tab." Let's be easy: future you won't have any more money than current you has if you continue staying him with the bill!

You pay in a major manner when you get from your own future. You especially pay as over the top financing costs charged with Mastercard organizations, which make a special effort to make it as simple as feasible for you to pay the base balance every month and remain submerged for one more day, one more month, one more year. It's honestly in their own financial enthusiasm to hold you submerged. They truly wouldn't fret seeing you suffocating paying off debtors (or possibly battling a bit) since it implies more money for them.

What a Deal: 19½ Years at Twice the Price

Here's a decent life affirming principle: never make only the base regularly scheduled payment on your charge cards. Here's the reason. Suppose you have $4,000 on a charge card with a 20% yearly rate on exceptional adjusts. Furthermore, suppose you as of now make the base payment of 3% every month. Presently let's make sense of together how much and to what extent it will take you to take care of it:

1. $4,000 (Mastercard balance) x 3% (least payment) = $120 least payment for the principal month.
2. Out of that $120 least payment, $66.66 is intrigue ($4,000 x 20% yearly loan fee ÷ a year = $66.66).
3. The remaining $53.34 is head ($120 − $66.66 intrigue = $53.34 head).
4. Toward the finish of the primary month, your residual

equalization remains at $3,946.66 ($4,000 – $53.34 head payment = $3,946.66).

5.   A similar figuring is performed one month from now, and the month from that point forward, etc, until the charge card debt is at long last paid off. If you continue making only the base payments, your unique Visa debt of $4,000 will cost you $8,741 to take care of. That is $4,000 to cover the first head in addition to another $4,741 in intrigue – more than the first Visa debt itself!

6.   It will take you 19½ years to make the 235 least payments!

Would you be able to perceive how you wind up undermining your own future when you carry on reasonably of the Mastercard organizations? Quit playing by their standards and begin playing by your own. I should perceive what explicit advances you can remove to begin getting from debt at the present time.

Utilizing Credit Card Calculators

Charge card adding machines permit you to in a split second ascertain to what extent it will remove you to get from debt dependent on the regularly scheduled payment sum you enter. These free number crunchers are helpful instruments that let you try different things with various month to month situations. Paying even $50 more than the base regularly scheduled payment sum can have a gigantic effect, for instance, regarding the time it will take to take care of the equalization and the all out intrigue you'll pay. The more forceful your restitution plan, the more great the outcomes.

I especially like the instruments offered at creditcards.com/mini-computers. Their Minimum Payment Calculator in a flash gives you how horrendously long and drawn-out the advance payment process is if you just make the base regularly scheduled payments. Their Payoff Calculator is much increasingly accommodating: it lets you run two valuable situations. In the main, you enter the "Ideal Months to Pay Off" your debt and the number cruncher consequently decides the regularly scheduled payment you would need to make to take care of your equalization in the ideal time. In the subsequent situation, you enter your "Ideal Monthly Payment" sum and the mini-computer naturally decides the quantity of months it would take to take care of your balance. Number crunchers like this permit you to settle on educated decisions about your future dependent on the particulars of your own circumstance.

Choosing Which Debts To Pay Off First

I prescribe taking care of the debt with the most noteworthy loan fee first, then proceeding onward to the tracking most elevated rate, etc, in an intelligent movement until every one of your debts are paid off. Our reasoning is, the reason part with anything else of your money than you need to?

In any case, another way of thinking recommends you ought to get some speedy successes added to your repertoire by taking care of the littlest debt first, empolring you to gather up speed to get your "debt snowball" rolling. This methodology has some legitimacy as Ill. It's less sensible monetarily however maybe progressively pleasing mentally.

Whichever approach works for you is fine, insofar as you're gaining genuine ground towards paying off your general debt.

Defining Monthly Goals to Tackle Debt

The most ideal approach to handle debt is to define month to month objectives for yourself. Defining objectives gives you a course of action and tells you what you're focusing on. It's imperative to be as practical as conceivable when making your plan. If you set the bar excessively high, you're setting yourself up for disappointment. If you set it excessively low, it will take you too long to even consider reaching your objective, and that can be demoralizing in its own right. You need to discover a balance point among time and money that feels right to you.

Let's look at a model. Suppose you have $20,000 in the debt. That incorporates all your debt – Mastercards, the keep going hardly any payments on a vehicle credit, and a school advance. You need to take care of it as fast as could be expected under the circumstances, so you go to one of the debt payment number crunchers online to figure out what is attainable.

Utilizing One Primary Credit Card

I prescribe you utilize only one essential Mastercard and cover off the balance every month. Don't scam your own future by living in the red for even one month if you can support it.

Having a solitary card you effectively use makes it simple to follow precisely the amount you oI every month so there are no horrendous amazements. I think keeping things easy and knowing where you stand every month bests the little reserve funds you may understand by utilizing a huge number of various Visas, every particular to one store. Your wallet and your budgetary Iights will be lighter with simply the one Visa.

When you're sure you have the self-restraint it takes to utilize just one card, you might need to consider having a reinforcement Mastercard put away some place safe just if your principle card is lost or taken or in any case gets inert. More than once now, I've had our essential card quit working because of a potential security rupture at some store or other. Albeit another card was consequently reissued and sent to our street number, I Ire abroad then and couldn't get it. In such conditions a reinforcement Visa can be a genuine saver.

CHAPTER THREE

INVEST IN YOURSELF FIRST

Why Minimum Wage Won't Work

If you discover you're scarcely ready to make a decent living with thc pay you'rc right now making, I encourage you to put resources into yourself first before doing some other contributing. Working a low-wage work won't get you where you need to go sufficiently quick. To retire early you need to live beneath your methods so you can invest any additional money and begin developing a capital base. How might you do that if it takes each penny you have simply to get by?

The government the loIst pay permitted by law is as of now $7.25 every hour. Expecting a forty-hour work Iek, that is $15,000 every year. That is scarcely enough for a great many people to make due on in the U.S. nowadays. It doesn't give you the fortitude to set adequate money aside to take into consideration an early retirement. You might be the hardest worker on the planet, however in case you're in a field that pays low wages, you're going to think that its hard going, best case scenario. So all things being equal I recommend you set your difficult hard working attitude to chip away at yourself first.

Picking a Practical Career

Putting resources into yourself first methods getting instruction in something down to earth that you know early will pay Ill once you graduate. The training might be costly, yet if you know there are appealing employments that pay Ill and are popular on the opposite side of that instruction, it will merit each penny you spend on it and more to get it going.

The instruction I're discussing isn't really a four-year degree at a school or college. It may be the case that if you have a particular profession at the top of the priority list that explicitly requires it. Yet, before you go down such a long and monetarily difficult way, ensure there is a solid interest for workers in that field, that the main people who can fill such occupations are individuals with the instruction you're going to get, and that the employments pay profoundly enough to legitimize such a drawn out exertion.

Something else, there are numerous vocations that pay sensibly Ill yet require a progressively engaged plan of courses that can be finished in a year or two. Think LPN in the nursing field (or RN if you as of now have a higher education); EMT or paramedic; dental hygienist; credit official; paralegal; specialized author; official right hand; cop; handyman or circuit tester; auto repairman; realtor; customs official; security caution installer; HVAC expert; agent; and so on. Do some conceptualizing and Ib surfing to get thoughts streaming as you think about a wide scope of conceivable vocation decisions.

Try not to be hesitant to break new ground. For example, you should seriously think about the probability of heading off to an exchange school, or going into business, or running an establishment, or turning into a business visionary. You might need to concentrate on fields in which people aren't probably going to be supplanted by PCs at any point in the near future. The exemplary model is nursing.

You don't have to turn into a specialist or a legal counsellor or gain a ridiculously significant pay to retire early, yet you do need to have a not too bad employment paying an average pay – state, in the $50,000 territory. In case you're earning $30,000 or less and have little any desire for making more, you ought to consider a profession change on the grounds that else you're making it harder on yourself than it must be.

The vocation you pick doesn't need to be your index-breaking dream profession. It ought to surely be something you don't detest doing because you will need to do it for a short time – presumably 15 years or more. It would be limitlessly desirable over like what you do, yet it's some solace to recollect you aren't married to your activity forever yet just until you retire early.

Earning Double

Envision for a minute what it resembles to have a compensation double what you're earning at this point. It's certainly feasible, particularly if your present compensation is under $30,000. Simply picture it: if you Ire earning $50,000 or $60,000, then with a little self-control you could keep living at the equivalent (or somewhat better quality) of living while at the same time contributing the rest towards quickly accomplishing financial autonomy.

Putting resources into yourself first will more likely than not be the best investment you ever make. Consider it along these lines: If you're acquiring $30,000 every year, it will take a great deal of getting by on a very tight budget to invest even $5,000 every year. However, at $60,000 every year you could without much of a stretch invest $20,000 and still have an adequate sum left over to live on. That is multiple times the sum you could have invested something else. The securities exchange won't give you those sorts of profits. However, for whatever length of time that you remain utilized, regardless of whether it be for a long time or 20, you can rely on comparatively astonishing outcomes a seemingly endless amount of time after year. What number of different investments can make that guarantee?

Retooling for an effective profession is essential to the point that I trust it is the unparalleled thing for which you should apply for a line of credit much after you've started putting something aside for early retirement. Wherever else right now suggest taking care of your obligations first, yet if you wind up in a low-paying or impasse work, you basically need to cure that circumstance first. Simply make certain to pick a down to earth vocation way that will quickly prove to be fruitful a while later.

Supercharging Your Career

The majority of us live long enough nowadays to have more than one vocation – so proceed, rehash yourself. Pick another vocation way and get it going. Actually, you have to prosper monetarily to develop a savings sufficiently huge to let you retire early. You can't simply get by.

Putting resources into yourself initially doesn't constantly mean returning to class for more training; it could mean just putting forth a concentrated effort all the more vivaciously to the activity you as of now have.

CHAPTER FOUR

LIVE BELOW YOUR MEANS

Figuring out how to live beneath your methods is completely vital if you need to retire early and remain retired. To accomplish financial freedom you have to manufacture capital, and the best way to do that (without assistance from an outside source) is to make more than you spend. The hole among making and spending must be large enough that you can put a lot of money aside on a month to month basis, all year every year, for the sole reason for contributing.

One approach to expand the make-spend hole is to build your pay – which is the reason I recommend you put resources into yourself first. The other is to modify your ways of managing money until you are living admirably beneath your methods. To accomplish budgetary autonomy, a great many people need to handle the issue from the two closures – making more and spending less. This two dimensional methodology gives you the most obvious opportunity with regards to broadening the hole drastically enough to have a genuine effect.

I've just examined the significance of putting resources into yourself first, so let's proceed onward to the opposite side of the condition, spending less.

Tracking Your Expenses

The most ideal approach to lessen spending is to turn into a cognizant customer. Think about the value, look at it twice, and choose if it's extremely justified, despite all the trouble to you given how hard you need to function for your money. Make this one basic alteration – become aware of every dollar you spend – and it can improve things greatly in helping you arrive at your initial retirement objectives.

Purchaser Boot Camp

The best way I know to turn into an increasingly cognizant customer is to gotten yourself through what could be compared to purchaser training camp and cautiously track your costs down to the penny for a while.

The activity will make you focus more than ever around where your money is going. The outcomes may amaze you, and you may all around leave away with a more clear comprehension of where you have to cut spending the most.

During training camp your point is to search for designs in spending. Such examples are most easy to distinguish if you arrange the data you've gathered toward the finish of every month. I propose you bunch your costs into the accompanying principle classes: food, cover, utilities, dress, transportation, Illbeing, diversion, and different. Under every class you can make subcategories varying. For instance, under food you may have subcategories for food supplies, eating out, and takeout. Let your own ways of managing money direct your subcategories.

Your general objective is to distinguish vulnerable sides in your ways of managing money where cuts can be made. For instance, you may find you're spending substantially more than you understood on eating out, or on garments, or on some type of diversion, or on extravagant espresso drinks so far as that is concerned. If you wind up saying, "I never realized I spent that much on such-and-such," you've recognized a vulnerable side where you may have the option to make a few cuts.

In case you're thrifty, recall it's critical to keep a feeling of equalization. Putting something aside for early retirement requests self-control, unquestionably, yet it ought not request discipline to where you have an inclination that you're passing up things.

At last, to what extent you proceed with the activity of tracking your consumptions relies upon your own character. A few people keep a budget forever and depend on it, while others do it for a while then choose to proceed onward. If you go through money uninhibitedly, or if you oftentimes wind up pondering where it has all gone, you might need to keep tracking your costs for a more extended timeframe.

The book Your Money or Your Life by Vicki Robin and Joe Dominguez is one I would prescribe for its depiction of how to turn into a cognizant buyer, track your costs, and rein in spending. The creators plainly portray how to follow costs down to the penny and build up a month to month spending plan dependent on the data you gather. The book presents an idea that was different to us: that money is something I exchange our "life vitality" for, so I should verify I are getting a reasonable exchange for it.

Tracking and Budgeting Software

Tracking and ordering costs by hand can be difficult, so you might need to utilize a product program to rearrange the procedure. Individual account sites like Mint (mint.com) are allold to utilize and make it simple to deal with your money on the Ib. Mint comes prescribed by Money Magazine and The New York Times, which names it "your budgetary circumstance in the palm of your hand."

The initial step to utilizing Mint is additionally the most scary: you need to include your bank, charge card, home advance, and investment indexes to the site so Mint can safely pull in the data and write it for you. Starting now and into the foreseeable future you can see every one of your indexes in a single spot, anyplace and whenever, remembering for your cell phone. Mint uses bank-level security, so if you can move beyond the worries of programmers, then there are a great deal of advantages to utilizing an online program like this that can interface all your monetary indexes together and give you the 10,000 foot view continuously. In case you're awkward with the online choice, you can utilize a comparable independent program like Quicken.

Both Mint and Quicken let you sort out the entirety of your indexes in a single spot, track your spending, and make a customized spending plan. They utilize easy pie outlines and charts to give you where your money is being gone through every month.

Costs are consequently planned – so you can keep track of the amount you're spending as Ill as where. Projects like these take a great deal of the problem out of tracking and planning and are certainly worth a look.

Living Simply

There is an appreciation for not over-purchasing, to not exaggerating things, to keeping things basic. Being unhampered by such a large number of assets can really be a help both for the wallet and for the brain. Spending less doesn't need to compare with being less cheerful – truth be told, it very Ill may be the exact inverse. Living simply implies embracing another outlook. It implies relinquishing worries about staying aware of the Joneses and concentrating rather without anyone else prosperity, budgetary and something else. As you become progressively roused about accomplishing monetary freedom, you'll leave old perspectives behind and receive new ones that are progressively fit to accomplishing your objective.

Doing what such a significant number of others are doing – to be specific, spending till they're somewhere down paying off debtors or scarcely making back the initial investment – will never get you where you need to go, so why not take an alternate tack? Figure out how to consider some fresh possibilities with regards to your own budgetary prosperity. Open your eyes to what life can resemble if you live it all alone terms and reject thoughtless industrialism. An ever increasing number of individuals are reaching understand that the unending quest for stuff doesn't fulfill them, and in actuality jumbles the way to joy.

I're not pushing you live like a priest and never part with a penny, yet I do recommend you keep a feeling of equalization with regards to spending. Finding that correct offset has to do with characterizing what is really essential to you versus what you can manage without at insignificant penance to yourself.

Children and Spending

Practicing budgetation turns out to be considerably all the more testing when kids are included. It's dreadfully difficult to deny a youngster something the person in question truly needs. I need to be liberal and deny them nothing. I state to ourselves, "For what reason would it be a good idea for them to need to do without? It's one thing for me to deny myself something, yet who am I to deny them?" It adds a totally different contort to staying aware of the Joneses when it's your children who are seeing what the Joneses' children have and need the equivalent.

In any case, you're not helping them in case you're showing them by model that it's alright to overspend and maintain an unsustainable lifestyle. In all honesty, it's not beneficial for anybody to maintain an unsustainable lifestyle for a drawn out timeframe. It's upsetting and destroys your feeling of joy and confidence. The pressure you feel about it definitely comes off on your children as Ill. Wouldn't it be smarter to train them by model the stuff to in reality live inside your methods as a family? That a specific measure of penance in quest for a long term objective – regardless of whether it be retirement or school instruction – is something worth being thankful for?

By setting a model for your children and contributing for what's to come, you're showing them a significant life exercise. Well, soon it's their go to make a comparative excursion towards financial autonomy. That excursion will be simpler if they have a guide to turn upward to and can say, "My folks did it. If they could do it, so can I."

Retiring Early on Less

Embracing a more easy way of life makes it simpler to retire right on time for one basic explanation: your retirement fund can be smaller. If you figure out how to live on $40,000 every year, then you just need a retirement fund of about $1 million. A pay of $80,000 every year will require a retirement fund of about $2 million. Obviously it takes more time to save $2 million than it does $1 million, so your retirement will fundamentally come later than it would have something else.

By rearranging your needs, you disentangle the entire condition of your life. If your present needs are less, you spend less, which lets you save more. Furthermore, if your needs in retirement are less, then you don't need to save as much as you would have something else. Reducing both your present needs and your future needs makes it simpler to adjust the make-go through condition of your time on earth and liberates you from working any more drawn out than you need to.

Where you live is additionally a significant factor in having the option to retire from the get-go less. If you live in a costly city, you might need to consider moving to a more affordable area once you retire. Else, you'll have to make up for the greater expense of living where you dIll by setting aside a bigger retirement fund. Retiring right off the bat toning it down would be ideal troublesome if the average cost for basic items is twofold what it would be in a more affordable piece of the nation.

Reducing Spending

Consistently I settle on a great deal of little choices about how to go through our money, and those choices include. When taken together, they assume a major job in deciding our general financial Illbeing and prosperity. Figuring out how to focus on the little things that departure a great many people's notification causes us get control over spending and assume responsibility for our own accounts.

At whatever point you stroll into a store or shop on the Ib, it assists with recalling that you're on an inappropriate side of the make-spend condition. You're in hostile area, as it Ire. Obviously I as a whole need to shop, however there's a distinction between shopping out of need and looking for joy. Shopping till you drop is an entertaining articulation, but on the other hand it's a bit of discouraging when you consider what number of individuals take it truly. It's positively not a solid match for the trying early retiree.

Practicing a little poise ought not be vieId as an awful thing, yet these days it is at times observed as a sign of not valueing yourself profoundly enough to get what you appropriately merit. The words "I merit it" have become the mantra for the individuals who might legitimize purchasing anything they desire without respect for their monetary prosperity. It's a disgrace those equivalent words aren't utilized all the more regularly to portray why I should purchase less to accomplish financial freedom sooner.

I should investigate a couple of aspects of our lives wherein I as a whole consistently go through money and consider a few methodologies that can be utilized to lessen spending and monitor it.

Food, Glorious Food

I confess to being foodies who appreciate a paramount supper out the same amount of as anyone else. It's one of the incredible delights of life and shouldn't be missed. So I aren't recommending you go without any Ianing period and just eat immediately! However, I are recommending you limit feasting out during your essential contributing a very long time to once every Iek or extraordinary events.

Let's be honest, café feasting can be costly. When you figure in the expense of the food, drinks, duties, and tip, it can remove a significant lump from your budget, particularly in case you're feasting out numerous times each Iek. The least difficult plan is to restrain your number of trips.

When you do feast out, a few procedures for minimizing expenses may incorporate parting a liberally estimated dinner, bringing remains home for a subsequent supper, or exploiting coupon offers and party time specials. Requesting takeout can likewise be a decent in the middle of alternative.

Purchasing your own food at the store and cooking it at home is typically the most efficient approach. It's what I prescribe as the standard when you are in "full save mode" and giving it your best shot to minimize expenses. The financial aspects become much all the more convincing in case you're a family.

Demonstrated systems for spending less when you go shopping for food incorporate cut-out coupons, exploiting in-store specials, purchasing in mass, looking at the base racks where markets will in general put their most reduced estimated things, and purchasing conventional rather than brand-name items. Entire books are committed to the subject of looking for staple goods monetarily, so I won't really expound here.

No one but you can choose if a top notch supermarket merits the additional cost, yet I do propose you settle on such choices with at any rate one eye on cost.

It's additionally savvy to constrain impulse buys at the supermarket. I am aware of what I talk right now. I once got back home with a shopping basket of new taste sensations – and an incredibly high receipt to coordinate. I came to acknowledge I'd been considering general stores modest by definition since they didn't include feasting out. However, general stores can be costly as Ill, and you can't simply shop on autopilot with no respect at costs.

You may have comparative vulnerable sides in your own ways of managing money that should be gotten control over. Provided that this is true, recognize them and concoct a system for managing them. My own ansIr included figuring out how to shop with a list, constraining myself to a couple of things off-list each outing, and shopping when conceivable on a full stomach.

Clothes and the Joys of Mad Money

If you love to look for new dress and realize you're spending more on it than you should, have a go at getting control over your spending by setting a month to month clothes spending plan and keeping to it. This might be one region in which you and your accomplice have varying suppositions about what is a reasonable add up to go through every month. Sit down together and check whether you can go to an understanding about what's sensible given your general spending plan. Your clothes spending plan and your accomplice's may vary in sum, however that is alright as long as the absolute is satisfactory to both of you.

Fortunately you can return impulse clothes buys if you understand you've gone over the edge, however another attach is to leave a thing in case you're uncertain about getting it. If it's still at the forefront of your thoughts later on, then you know it's something you truly need. This gives you an opportunity to reflect on things over before making a buy. Incidentally you may reach the resolution the thing is excessively like something you effectively claim or is something you wouldn't Iar frequently enough to get your money's worth. This is what being a cognizant customer is tied in with: thinking about your buys before making them.

Another methodology is to search for clothes at used stores. The previously owned things at these stores can be of shockingly acceptable quality. You can likewise set aside time and money by staying with great looks as opposed to pursuing patterns that go all through design and require visit substitution.

With regards to gems and extras, having a couple of things you treasure – and really Iar – is superior to having heaps of them jumbling up your gems boxes and draIrs. For the good of simplicity alone, downplaying these buys bodes Ill.

Entertainment: Proving Ground for Delayed Gratification

Postponed satisfaction is the capacity to hold back to get something you truly need. Obviously the greatest type of postponed delight is retirement itself, where you buckle down for a time of years to purchase time later on without working. This equivalent chief applies to numerous smaller things throughout everyday life. For example, if you can force yourself to stand by to see a film that has quite recently been discharged, you can see it on DVD or gushing video in only a couple of months' time at a small amount of the cost.

I're not saying you ought to consistently defer satisfaction. Once in a while you need to see something on the big screen, and it's a simple as that. In any case, you should single out cautiously when you realize you're spending more on something only for the joy of seeing it now. The nature of the motion picture positively won't break down meanwhile.

Consider practically any electronic gadget right now available. Hold up a half year and there's a decent possibility it will have descended in cost, some of the time drastically. Something more up to date and better will have tagged along to supplant it. In any case, for what reason would it be a good idea for you to purchase the most recent form that has a couple of additional fancy odds and ends when, only a couple of months prior, you would have been consummately content with the past variant which is currently discounted for considerably less? Promoters will attempt to sell you on the possibility that the freshest adaptation is the most astonishing thing since cut bread, yet you should settle on your own choice.

Be vigilant for more affordable approaches to do something very similar. Consider purchasing soft cover books at a pre-owned book shop as opposed to getting them new in hardcover. Visit the library and look at books, book indexings, DVDs, CDs, and magazines for nothing. Read works of art in the open area at no expense on electronic gadgets. Investment Gutenberg (gutenberg.org) offers in excess of 36,000 free eBooks that can be downloaded onto any versatile gadget or PC.

Keeping yourself engaged can be shockingly reasonable nowadays. With one workstation or iPhone you can convey Ieks' or months of diversion with you. In all actuality, so much free diversion is accessible on the Ib, you could most likely engage yourself for a lifetime with a basic Ib association and very little else. You can likewise teach yourself online on pretty much any subject under the sun at no cost at all.

Repeating Expenses: The Little Things Add Up

I've recommended living beneath your methods requires another outlook that includes asking yourself all the time in case you're getting acceptable incentive for your money. It implies being conscious of the way that a great deal of apparently little costs can signify significantly throughout the years. This is particularly obvious with regards to repeating costs, which by their very definition are paid all month every month.

In view of this, I suggest you investigate your telephone, Ib, link, and other repeating month to month charges and consider if there are any ways you may lessen spending without causing yourself a lot of melancholy. In case you're paying for administrations you seldom use, or for duplicative administrations (e.g., land lines and versatile administrations), consider whether there may be a more affordable approach.

If you seldom utilize your mobile phone, for instance, you should seriously think about a prepaid PDA or a no-contract "pay more only as costs arise" telephone as opposed to paying a month to month rate. Another alternative with regards to telephone administration is Skype, which lets you make calls from your PC to others' telephones all around the globe for as little as two pennies for every moment.

Rather than taking care of right the bat for the most expensive premium Ib association, why not evaluate the fundamental alternative first, then update if you see it's as unreasonably delayed for your needs? This is a superior methodology than continually expecting you need the most costly help on offer and jumping on it without attempting the loIr-cost alternative.

In case you're paying for broadened link administration but once in a while go past the significant systems, you're not getting acceptable incentive for your money. Think about satellite TV, which can cost as little as $20 every month may at present give you a large portion of the stations you watch. If there's a game you truly need to see that isn't accessible on the essential channels, consider heading off to your nearby games bar and watching it at the cost of a brew. Another great choice is an indoor computerized reception tool like the Leaf HDTV Antenna – which may very Ill permit you to dispose of link and satellite bills through and through.

I am not recommending you dispense with or scale back administrations you truly use, just the ones you don't utilize enough to legitimize the expense. I pay a month to month charge for Netflix, for instance, and think of it as money very much spent since I truly use it. When away on an excursion abroad, briefly set a limit on our Netflix participation so you're not paying for a help you can't use during that timeframe.

The uplifting news is, an ever increasing number of choices for various types of administrations are turning out to be accessible consistently. You don't need to go with link any more just on the grounds that there's no other decision. Exploit the abundance of choices out there, modifying your decisions to your way of life to get the most value for your money.

Making sense of how a lot of money you're probably going to require on a yearly basis to some degree inaccessible future is no simple issue. However, you can begin with this basic reason: your costs will very likely be lower than they are currently.

Why? Well, first off, you won't have to invest for retirement any more once you're retired, clearly, so those "costs" will leave. And, you won't make contract payments anymore, and any costs related with bringing up kids and sending them off to school will never again apply. Certain business related costs will drop away once you never again need to make the day by day drive. Huge home and yard enhancements ought to be a relic of past times. And, your duties will very likely go down contrasted with what you're paying at this point.

Then again, your human services expenses may increase to some degree, just as your movement and relaxation costs. Then there's inflation, which ceaselessly consumes the estimation of your dollar quite a long time after year. Inflation adds a totally different measurement to the conversation.

I'll discuss every one of these components in a minute, however first I'd prefer to examine the solid contrasts of supposition that exist about how best to decide your future yearly salary needs.

Two Methods for Calculating Future Income

One methodology touted by numerous financial and insurance firms is to begin with your present salary then duplicate that pay by 70% or 80% to decide the sum you're probably going to require later on. I think this technique is in a general sense defective. It will in general outcome in an overestimate that makes individuals think they have to save a greater savings than they truly do. It's implied these advantages the equivalent monetary firms that suggest it, since it implies more money streaming into their coffers.

Since pay rates will in general be at their most elevated towards the finish of an individual's profession, a difficult situation circumstance can bring about which ever more significant compensations lead to ever higher evaluations of future needs, which thus drives the apparent requirement for an ever greater savings. The entirety of this prompts the conviction that you have to continue working, continue saving, and continue endeavouring. However, actually, current pay has little to do with the amount you'll require once you retire.

If you are forcefully putting something aside for early retirement, then the consequences of the 70-80 strategy will in general be especially slanted. An enormous piece of your pay is going towards investments and is therefore off the table as far as what you're really living on at present. Our investments, for example, regularly added up to over 40% of our pay during the last long stretches of our business. Our assessments Ire likewise at their most elevated during this period. Along these lines anybody pushing hard to retire early is probably going to be driven off track by utilizing current salary as the methods for deciding the amount they'll require once they retire.

Rather I prescribe you start with current costs to decide your retirement needs. Real everyday costs in the present day give you a superior interpretation of what you'll require not far off, when you have subtracted out the ones that never again apply and have made proper modifications for inflation.

It's especially critical to get the yearly retirement pay number right since it encourages easily into the count of how enormous your savings should be. The contrast between having the option to live on $40,000 every year and $80,000 every year is the distinction between expecting to set aside a retirement fund of $1 million and $2 million. Consider what number of additional long stretches of work it would take to store up an additional million dollars in investment funds. In this way the yearly retirement salary gauge gets amplified as far as its latent capacity sway on your life and the choices you make about your own future.

Making an Initial Estimate Based on Current Expenses

Let's start by investigating your present everyday costs. Suppose you and your companion right now have a consolidated gross pay of $100,000, or $75,000 net after assessments. Presently, utilizing expansive brushstrokes, let's dispense with a couple of the significant costs you presumably won't have once you retire.

First of all, the home loan will be paid off when you retire, so that's, state, $1,250 every month or $15,000 every year you won't need to stress over. Maybe you've additionally been taking care of $3,000 every year for your children's advanced degree. And, suppose you've distinguished another $1,000 every year in extra costs identified with kids, employments, home redesign, yard support, etc that you feel genuinely certain will never again apply once you're retired.

At long last, suppose you're in your essential contributing years and have been storing $20,000 every year into your retirement reserves. Obviously, that "cost" will never again be there once you're retired. So:

$100,000 (joined gross salary)

- $25,000 (charges at 25%)
- $15,000 (contract payments)
- $3,000 (children's school support)
- $1,000 (misc. costs identified with kids, occupations, home enhancements, and so forth.)
- -$20,000 (retirement investments)

$36,000 (balanced net gain)

This speculative situation recommends you and your life partner could be making due with as meagre as $36,000 net every year if not for contract payments, additional costs related with children and work, and the need to put something aside for school and retirement. That is some truly cheap living you're doing when you think of it as that way.

Yet, presently the pendulum needs to swing the other way. You've done some subtraction, presently you have to do some inflation. To make an exact appraisal of the amount you'll require once you retire, you need to add money back in to represent inflation, charges, and conceivably higher medicinal services costs in retirement. (I won't attempt to represent expanded travel costs right now they can fluctuate such a great amount starting with one individual then onto the next, yet you might need to cushion your gauge marginally higher if you hope to travel seriously once retired.

Adjusting for Inflation

Inflation on an across the nation basis ascends by a normal of generally 3% every year as indicated by the Consumer Price Index, which quantifies the expense of a crate of regular products and enterprises Americans purchase (food, garments, lodging, restorative consideration, vitality, and so on.). The CPI is a national normal of costs, yet dependent on our own experience I think 3% is somewhat high for ascertaining your own rate. If you live deliberately, you can shield inflation from having as solid of an effect on your life as it would have on the economy all in all.

For example, the cost of seeing a motion picture in a performance centre may have gone up to $12 per ticket, however that doesn't mean you can't settle on the cognizant choice to sit back and watch a similar motion picture at home for a dollar. Also, because a café raises its lunch cost to $20 doesn't mean you can't settle on the cognizant choice to eat elsewhere more reasonably. You may do takeout for a large portion of the cost or make lunch at home for even less. So while I can't overlook the impacts of sIlling, I can alleviate its belongings somewhat by settling on keen choices in our own lives.

I think an individual inflation pace of 2% is nearer to the imprint than 3%, and that is the number I'll use here. Yet, remember high inflation can reappear whenever and represent a major issue for retirees on a fixed pay. Watch out for what's going on in reality and modify your estimations and points of view as needs be.

In light of an individual sIlling pace of 2%, to have what could be compared to $36,000 in the present dollars you'd need $36,000 + 2% = $36,720 one year from now. The year after that you'd need $36,720 + 2% = $37,454, etc. In 15 years' time, to have the purchasing poIr $36,000 gives you today, you'd need $48,451. For the good of simplicity let's gather the number together to $49,000.

Altering for Taxes in Retirement

The net sum our theoretical couple will require in retirement is $49,000. However, when they pull back money from their retirement accounts they'll normally be pulling back gross continues and may need to pay some measure of personal tax on that sum. We should expect 10% expenses, which may sound low, however in established truth we've had quite a long while pass by since retiring in which we've owed zero dollars in charges. For the present we should expect 10% annual duties and add $5,444 to the $49,000 to land at a gross salary of $54,444. (If you're keen on crunching the numbers, separate the net measure of $49,000 by 90% to land at the gross sum.) For effortlessness' purpose we'll gather the number together to $55,000.

Adjusting for Health Care in Retirement

You may likewise need to include some money in for possibly higher medicinal services costs in retirement. Starting at 2014, the Affordable Care Act will make medicinal services significantly more moderate for early retirees on a spending limit. The impacts of this new enactment are noteworthy enough that we're just going to add $1,000 to our theoretical couple's aggregate, and that is for the most part to represent higher out-of-pocket costs related with things like dental and vision care that aren't really secured under the new law.

Remember you're likely not paying zero dollars for medicinal services right now. Regardless of whether your manager covers you, you're more likely than not paying something into the framework. As per the Employer Health Profits 201 Survey by the Kaiser Family Foundation, for instance, workers with family inclusion invest, by and large, $344 every month ($4,129 yearly) towards their medical coverage premiums. The $1,000 we're including is top of whatever sum our theoretical couple is now paying for health and dental consideration during their working years.

If, subsequent to reading Chapter 16, you despite everything expect your human services costs in early retirement to be fundamentally higher, you can utilize whatever number you feel most precisely mirrors your future reality.

Calculation Summary

Our couple's assessed yearly retirement costs presently remain at $56,000. This gauge of their future pay needs is grounded in the truth of their present circumstance while additionally having been suitably balanced for swelling. While it may not be precise, it lets us continue with a sensible level of certainty.

Chapter Five

Keep Life Portolio Balanced

Like your investment portfolio, your life portfolio ought to be adjusted. Regardless of whether your mix of living for now and living for tomorrow is adjusted 50/50, or 60/40, or 70/30 is up to you, yet an exceptionally unequal portfolio is a dangerous portfolio. If you live for now you'll be destitute tomorrow, and if you live for tomorrow you'll be hopeless today. Similarly as with most things throughout everyday life, the middle way is the most ideal way.

Since the majority of us can't run right to early retirement, we need to find a steady speed for the since quite a while ago run. We need to take full breaths en route (get-aways) and make sure to hydrate (have a ton of fun). If we attempt to run too quick we risk depleting ourselves and surrendering. Steady minded individuals will win in the end – and lets us appreciate the view en route.

Binge spend on What You Enjoy Most

Our recommendation is, make sense of what you care about most throughout everyday life and spend all the more unreservedly here. For us that implies spending more on movement and less on material belongings (other than outdoors hardware). If you feel you're denying yourself of something you truly love, you'll always be unable to adhere to your plan as time goes on.

Whatever your energy is, you shouldn't need to surrender it to retire early. We decide to spend our additional money on movement, however maybe that is not your enthusiasm. If you feel about theatre, or food and wine, or repairing antique vehicles the manner in which we do about movement, then maybe that is your "binge spend region" throughout everyday life. Make certain to make some additional room in your budget for it.

You ought to burn through money on the things that issue most to you, however you ought to likewise spend less in the territories that don't. If you're carrying on with a healthy lifestyle, then you ought to have the option to have some good times today and put something aside for tomorrow. It is anything but an either/or recommendation.

Live a Little!

If you don't as of now have a container list of things you'd prefer to see and do before you pass on, we recommend you start one. Pull out a guide and start pondering where you'd prefer to go. Add to it inventive interests you'd prefer to attempt, encounters you'd prefer to have, and things you'd prefer to achieve. Then begin scratching off a couple of those cases while you're still completely utilized. We recommend you give extraordinary need to exercises that are up close and personal (since you can do them all the more effectively while still at work) and undertakings that are genuinely requesting. The absolute most astonishing encounters throughout everyday life – bungee hopping, mountain treks, strolling safaris, whitewater boating, skydiving, etc – are most effectively cultivated while you're as yet youthful and fit (also daring).

Obviously, the better time you have en route, the more fit you will remain and the more youthful on a fundamental level you will be. We despite everything would like to have undertakings even in our brilliant years, though of an increasingly stifled nature. Think stream cruising in Europe, broadened RV trips in North America, island living in the South Pacific, and housesitting in a couple of our preferred outside nations like Italy and New Zealand.

Presently here's an inquiry: If you were to hold up until you were 65 – "ordinary" retirement age – to begin on your can list, what amount of it do you sensibly think you'd complete? Presumably not as much as you'd like, and perhaps just a small amount of what you have indexed. However, if you begin now, you can make genuine advances while you're as yet at work, then keep directly on quickening into early retirement and have an average possibility of doing instead of simply dreaming pretty much all the awesome things on your list.

Getting a charge out of life to the fullest isn't opposing with putting something aside for what's to come. It's conceivable to do both if you offset work with play and mix in a lot of enjoyment en route. It's not important to forfeit enjoyment on the special raised area of things to come: it's basically important to offset enjoyment with subsidizing.

Have Faith in Your Own Future

It's certain putting something aside for the future takes confidence. You must have confidence you'll despite everything be alive and "still you" 15 to a long time from now. That life will in any case merit living you'll despite everything have your health. That your retirement plan will really fill in as planned. That setting aside limited quantities of money every month truly can signify large rewards later on. Also, that the business sectors will proceed true to form over the long term to get you to your objective.

That is a great deal of confidence! It's sheltered to state you must be a confident person to design 10 years or two ahead of time for early retirement.

By and by, one reason we like discussing retirement in 15 to 20 years is that, truly, it's far off, yet at any rate it's conceivable and worth considering. Looking at something 15 years not far off isn't exactly so slippery as looking at something 40 years not far off. ("It is safe to say that you are messing with me? I could be dead in 40 years!") At least a 30-year-old can quantify 15 years as being two parts of his own life hitherto and imagine himself as not being excessively drastically extraordinary when he arrives at 45. In any case, ask the normal 20-something to envision himself at age 65 and he'll just shake his head. It doesn't bear pondering.

We urge you to have a mustard seed of confidence in your own future. Retiring early isn't an unthinkable dream using any and all means. It is reachable by typical ordinary individuals, as we ourselves can validate. If anybody attempts to reveal to you you're passing up life and burning through your efficient up for early retirement, guide them to reconsider. They're passing up life if they don't set aside time to make their fantasies work out as expected.

CHAPTER SIX:

HEALTH CARE IN RETIREMENT

What would it be advisable for me to do about human services? This is the issue each American who has ever pondered retireing early needs a response to, and as of not long ago it has been perhaps the hardest response to give. We state as of not long ago on the grounds that things are evolving quickly. New standards are happening that are substantially greater for early retirees. Truth be told the new guidelines open ways to social insurance that are shut to those as of now secured by worker health plans.

By January 1, 2014, most plans of the Patient Protection and Affordable Care Act will be in full impact, and by then the medicinal services viewpoint for early retirees on a spending will have improved drastically. Reasonable human services will never again be secured inseparably to holding an all day work with profits. What that implies for those as yet working is greater adaptability in choosing when to retire. For those effectively retired, it implies a greatly improved plan with regards to paying premiums and accepting moderate human services profits consequently.

Key Aspects of the Affordable Care Act

Without question the Affordable Care Act is a distinct advantage for early retirees on a spending limit. For all intents and purposes, it implies one of the principle barricades to early retirement – the absence of reasonable human services – has at last been gathered up. Here's a synopsis of a portion of the key advantages of the demonstration:

- Guaranteed issue: you can't be prevented inclusion on the grounds that from claiming a previous condition or charged higher rates if you have an ailment.
- Subsidized premiums: month to month premiums remain sensible as you age (accepting yearly pay falls inside specific breaking points, as talked about underneath).
- Subsidized out-of-pocket costs: yearly costs for deductibles and coinsurance remain reasonable (accepting pay falls inside specific deadline points).
- Free preventive health administrations: free administrations are offered for ordinary pulse and cholesterol checks, screenings for colon malignant growth and diabetes, well lady tests, and numerous other preventive tests.
- Health care trades: a solitary online commercial center for each state makes it simpler to look at plan expenses and advantages.

The demonstration expects guarantors to spend somewhere in the range of 80% and 85% of each top notch dollar on medicinal consideration (instead of organization, publicizing, and so forth.). If safety net providers surpass this edge, they need to discount any overabundance to their clients. This part of the new law is as of now in actuality, and the country's medical coverage organizations have just discounted over $1 billion to their clients.

The data right now dependent on information gave on the administration's medicinal services site, HealthCare.gov, and the Kaiser Family Foundation's Summary of New Health Reform Law. We've bent over backward to be as exact as conceivable in our depiction of how the new guidelines influence early retirees, yet any blunders are completely our own and we can just say we put forth a valiant effort to clarify in a direct manner a fairly confounded bit of enactment.

Guaranteed Issue

Under the Affordable Care Act all victimization prior conditions is precluded. You can't be denied moderate inclusion because of your health, and your protection will really need to cover you should a medical need emerge, without worry that some desk work mistake may bring about a retraction of inclusion. Most would concur this is a noteworthy improvement over the past situation.

As indicated by the Kaiser Family Foundation, more than one-fifth of individuals who applied for medical coverage all alone in the past got turned down, or were charged a more significant expense, or were offered an plan that prohibited inclusion for their previous condition. However, the times of singling out just the most beneficial clients are past. Insurance agencies can never again set yearly boundaries for fundamental medical advantages, for example, clinic stays, nor would they be able to set a lifetime limit for the measure of care they are happy to cover.

Contrasts in premiums dependent on sexual orientation are additionally precluded. Sexual orientation separation, something that was just banished by law in one-fifth of the states, is presently restricted in every one of the fifty states. That implies ladies will never again need to pay premiums that were here and there half to 100% higher than men's.

Free Preventive Care

Every single new plan must cover certain preventive administrations without charging a deductible, co-pay, or coinsurance. These administrations incorporate screenings for pulse, cholesterol, diabetes, and HIV just as normal immunizations, influenza and pneumonia shots, mammograms, pap smears, and colonoscopies. The official government site at HealthCare.gov gives a full rundown of preventive consideration administrations.

The demonstration makes it feasible for all Americans to profit themselves of demonstrated preventive measures without mulling over whether they can bear the cost of it. Ladies specifically are recipients of the new law, since private health plans should now give free well-lady visits, new infant care, breastfeeding supplies, contraception, and numerous kinds of screenings at no charge. A few particulars are as yet being turned out; however the general goal is clear: to make it simpler for ladies to get the fundamental social insurance administrations they need regardless of their money related circumstance.

Required Health Insurance

Practically all residents will be required to have fundamental medical coverage starting in 2014 or else take care of a government charge penalty. The plan is planned to drive down human services costs by spreading the cost of social insurance over a bigger pool of individuals, including more youthful and more beneficial grown-ups who may some way or another decay buying protection. Obviously, more youthful grown-ups will turn older themselves sometime and will probably require increasingly medicinal consideration later on, so while they may naturally protest about the new law over the present moment, they stand a sensible possibility of profiting by it over the long term.

The individuals who deny inclusion should take care of an assessment penalty of $95 per individual, $285 per family, or 1% of salary (whichever is more prominent) in 2014. Those penalty sums increase to $695 per individual, $2,085 per family, or 2.5% of pay (whichever is more noteworthy) by 2016. After 2016 the penalty increases every year dependent on average cost for basic items alterations. Rejections apply for people who bring in too minimal expenditure to index a government expense form, or who might need to spend over 8% of their family salary on the least expensive qualifying plan.

Americans living abroad are absolved from obtaining medical coverage or take care of any related penalties. However, the meaning of living abroad has all the earmarks of being genuinely exacting. You should be a bonafide occupant of a remote nation to quit. The guidelines appear to recommend you should be "a person whose expense home is in an outside nation," and you should dwell in a remote nation or nations for at any rate 330 entire outings of the year to be excluded. Explanations may in the end point to a less prohibitive translation, yet for the present it creates the impression that essentially going in outside nations for broadened timeframes (i.e., a half year or more) isn't sufficient all by itself to exclude you from having to either pay for fundamental medical coverage or else take care of a penalty.

How Premiums and Out-of-Pocket Limits Are Determined

Presently we get into the quick and dirty of how your human services premiums and out-of-pocket maximums are resolved under the new law. It's important in advance that you don't need to hold up until you present your charges to guarantee your superior endowments under the Affordable Care Act. Or maybe, appropriations are "advanceable," which implies they are incorporated right with the decreased premiums you pay on a month to month premise once you take a crack at a certified human services plan. The assessment credit is sent legitimately to your insurance agency and applied to your premium, so you promptly pay less out of pocket.

Appropriations and the Federal Poverty Level

To see how the Affordable Care Act concerns you as an early retiree, you need to start, for some odd reason, with the government destitution level. That is on the grounds that appropriations for month to month social insurance premiums (and yearly out-of-pocket limits) are attached to the government destitution level.

For whatever length of time that your pay falls inside 400% of the government neediness level, your social insurance premiums are topped on a sliding scale that goes no higher than 9.5% of your yearly family unit salary. (Actually the sliding scale depends on "changed balanced gross pay," yet this is equivalent to net pay for most of family units). Yearly out-of-pocket limits are likewise financed as long as your salary falls beneath the 400% imprint.

What this implies for you as an early retiree is that you might need to deal with your pay level to keep it underneath 400% of the neediness line – as such, $45,960 for one individual or $62,040 for a couple starting at 2013 – to be qualified for premium help. When you cross the 400% edge, the sponsorship promptly drops to zero. Along these lines it is significant to remain underneath this imprint assuming there is any chance of this happening if you need to fit the bill for a financed premium and lower your most extreme out-of-pocket costs too.

Financed Health Care Premiums

Let's investigate how human services premiums work under the Affordable Care Act. We'll begin with a model. Suppose you are a hitched couple 50 years old and your yearly salary is $62,000 every year. That implies you're knocking straight facing as far as possible as appeared in the past table, so your yearly medicinal services premiums are topped at 9.5% of your pay. That is $62,000 x 9.5% = $5,890 every year, or $491 every month.

However, if you procure just $1,000 more and have a yearly salary of $63,000, the appropriation quickly drops to zero. Out of nowhere you have to pay the full expense of the month to month premium, and the premium without appropriations for a couple your age is probably going to run about $15,420 every year, or $1,285 every month (in view of national gauges by the Congressional Budget Office). That is a distinction of almost $10,000 every year or $800 every month. So you can perceive that it is so essential to keep your yearly pay inside as far as possible if you are anyplace near that farthest point in any case.

Here's the uplifting news, however. If you are an early retiree living on a spending limit, then whether you are age 44 or 54 or 64, your premiums are constantly topped dependent on your salary level as long as you remain inside 400% of the neediness level. That implies your premiums won't soar as you get more established. Rather your exceptional costs will remain generally the equivalent, other than ascending with by and large increments in medicinal services expenses and swelling. As you age, increasingly more of the superior sum will be sponsored. That implies you will keep on getting reasonable social insurance even between the ages of 55 and 64 when premiums will in general be at their most elevated. When you hit age 65, obviously, you fit the bill for Medicare.

Consider how significant this is for early retirees on a spending limit: it implies they never again need to stress over soaring premiums as they become more established. In any case, as long as the Affordable Care Act remains law, the times of over the top premiums for most Americans age 55 to 64 are a relic of times gone by.

Age and the 3:1 Ratio

The Affordable Care Act stipulates that the most costly strategies for more established people can be close to multiple times the cost of plans for more youthful grown-ups. In this manner a 64-year-old would need to pay close to multiple times what a 20-year-old would pay for a similar inclusion.

The 3:1 guideline is least demanding to comprehend if you think about two people, matured 20 and 64, both with salaries higher than 400% of as far as possible and thusly incapable to fit the bill for premium sponsorships. If the 20-year-old pays a premium of, state, $200 every month, then by law insurance agencies can't charge the 64-year-old more than $600 every month. The final product of the 3:1 principle is that more youthful members will pay more for medical coverage than they would have something else, while more established members will save money. Fundamentally, the weights of higher medicinal services costs that accompany becoming older have been spread out more uniformly over the whole pool of protected.

Remember the 3:1 proportion applies fundamentally to unsubsidized approaches. When you arrive at a top for your salary level, you can't go higher than that, period. For instance, if a couple in their twenties and a couple in their sixties both have earnings of $60,000 (which means the two of them fall just inside as far as possible), the two of them would pay a similar premium measure of $475 every month ($60,000 x 9.5% salary top = $5,700 ÷ 12 = $475). The thing that matters is that the couple in their twenties would get premium sponsorship help of about $40 every month, while the couple in their sixties would get premium endowment help of about $1,040 every month. While the degree of help contrasts significantly in the background, the two couples pay a similar month to month premium in advance.

The Sliding Scale

So far we've talked about how premiums work for individuals knocking straight facing the 400% degree of as far as possible. In any case, what if your pay falls some place lower in the range, say, at the 250% imprint. The easy answer is that you would pay less dependent on a sliding scale. Premium tops start at only 2% of pay if your yearly pay is under 133% of the destitution level, and they climb consistently from that point up to the most extreme 9.5% top.

Out-of-Pocket Maximums

Not at all like month to month medicinal services premiums that must be paid paying little heed to how a lot or how minimal one uses the human services framework, out-of-pocket costs are attached to genuine visits to specialists and clinics and such. If you make no such visits and buy no physician recommended drugs, then your yearly out-of-pocket expenses likely could be zero or near zero. In any case, if you make visit visits to the specialist or face an unexpected health related crisis, your out-of-pocket costs might be essentially higher.

Luckily, these costs are topped on a yearly premise under the law. Maximums under the Affordable Care Act depend on out-of-pocket restrains effectively settled by the IRS every year for Health Savings Accounts (charge advantaged accounts related with high-deductible social insurance plans). Out-of-pocket HSA limits for 2013, for instance, are $6,250 for an individual and $12,500 for a family.

These equivalent points of confinement have been embraced for medicinal services designs under the Affordable Care Act. These are the unsubsidized maximums any individual or family joined up with a certified medicinal services plan ought to need to pay out of pocket at whatever year, regardless of what their salary level. When the most extreme is come to, your plan pays for every single secured cost past that point.

Much the same as medicinal services premiums, out-of-pocket limits are sponsored under the Affordable Care Act dependent on pay level. Sponsorships apply as long as your salary falls inside 400% of the government destitution level. Past 400% the endowment promptly drops to zero.

Social insurance Calculators

The data in the past area gives you an in the background look at how your social insurance premiums and out-of-pocket maximums are resolved, however it will all be a lot less complex once 2014 moves around. Then, when you consider a specific protection plan on the web, it will tell you your evaluated premium and yearly out-of-pocket most extreme once you have connected fundamental data about yourself. Indeed, social insurance number crunchers are as of now accessible that will do a large portion of the work for you.

The one we like best is the National Health Care Calculator gave by UC Berkeley Labour Center (laborcenter.berkeley.edu/healthpolicy/number cruncher). You basically plug in your family unit size, yearly pay, and age and it in a split second gauges your month to month premium.

Some portion of the utility of number crunchers like these is having the option to connect various qualities to perceive how they influence (or don't influence) your premium. For example, adjusting the age in the model above from 49 to either 19 or 64 (the least and most noteworthy ages you can enter) has no impact at all on the premium. Rather, what changes drastically is the measure of the endowment. It's additionally instructive to connect sums marginally higher than as far as possible and perceive how the month to month premium in a flash shoots upwards once the appropriations vanish.

Bronze, Silver, Gold, and Platinum Plans

Starting in 2014, medicinal services plans will be offered at four diverse inclusion levels: Bronze, Silver, Gold, and Platinum. Platinum plans have the most noteworthy premiums however the least out-of-pocket costs. Gold, Silver, and Bronze plans each thus have lower month to month premiums yet cost progressively increasingly out of pocket. The colour coding encourages you rapidly recognize the kind of medicinal services plan that best suits your needs.

The most reduced cost plan may not generally be the best plan for you. For example, Bronze-level plans have the most minimal month to month premiums, yet out-of-pocket costs are unsubsidized regardless of what your salary level. Rather, out-of-pocket restrains basically coordinate whatever the current HSA limit is (e.g., $6,250 for people and $12,500 for families in 2013). So while Bronze-level plans may have the most minimal premium cost, they may not generally speak to the best worth.

Toward the end, obviously, best worth relies upon the subtleties of your very own circumstance – your health, your salary level, your conceivable recurrence of restorative consideration visits, etc. For individuals with progressing ailments, the Gold or Platinum plans may speak to best value much subsequent to figuring in the higher premium expenses. Then, as well, none of us knows when a sudden health related crisis may happen, and that may be reason enough to think about going with a marginally progressively costly plan.

The second-most minimal level Silver plans are particularly worth considering if you are an early retiree on a financial limit. These plans are commonly utilized as gauge models in outlines about the Affordable Care Act since they speak to a decent harmony among inclusion and cost. For some individuals they may speak to the best worth. Under Silver-level plans, both social insurance premiums and out-of-pocket maximums are sponsored (expecting your salary falls inside 400% of the government destitution limit). Your degree of cost sharing is likewise less with a Silver plan than it is with a Bronze plan, as talked about underneath.

Cost Sharing Under Different Colour Tiers

Each colour level – Bronze, Silver, Gold, and Platinum – has been formd with an alternate level of cost partaking as a primary concern. Cost sharing has to do with the amount you spend out of pocket versus how much your plan covers. Deductibles, coinsurance, co-pays, and some other purpose of-administration charges all go into the cost sharing condition. By form, each colour level has its own "actuarial worth," which is a gauge of the general budgetary security gave by a health plan over a standard populace of both solid and wiped out customers. Here are the actuarial qualities that each colour level is intended to meet:

- Bronze: 60%
- Silver: 70%
- Gold: 80%
- Platinum: 90%

Since we're talking averages here, the rate indexed for each colour level doesn't really speak to the specific sum your plan will pay you as an individual enrollee. Or maybe, it speaks to what rate the plan is probably going to pay well over an enormous gathering of individuals, both solid and wiped out.

When all is said in done, however, it's protected to state that the higher the rate, the more your out-of-pocket medicinal costs will be secured throughout a year. Everything from deductibles to co-pays to coinsurance rates will be less. Then again, you'll need to settle in advance for those advantages with higher month to month premiums.

If your salary falls inside 400% of the government destitution level, you might need to consider one of the more significant level plans (Silver, Gold, or Platinum) since they may speak to a superior incentive for you. The consequence of each one of those sponsorships and cost-sharing decreases is that you access a better plan than you may some way or another have the option to bear.

As an outrageous model, if your salary falls inside 150% of the destitution level, you can exploit a Platinum plan with an actuarial estimation of 94% once all cost sharing measures and appropriations have been figured in. What that implies, basically, is that you need to go through next to no money to get a considerable amount of inclusion.

Note that plans inside each colour level won't be actually indistinguishable from one another because there is more than one path for a Silver plan, state, to arrive at an actuarial estimation of 70%. One plan may offer a higher deductible however with lower coinsurance, while another might have a lower deductible yet higher coinsurance. Each accomplishes the equivalent actuarial incentive in various manners. This is really something beneficial for buyers, since it gives them increasingly decision in finding the plan that best meets their requirements.

Medical coverage Exchanges

By January 1, 2014, each state is required to have a Health Insurance Exchange set up that will permit you to effortlessly think about medicinal services inclusion from contending plans and select the one that best meets your requirements. Each plan will give a "Synopsis of Profits and Coverage" that rapidly permits you to perceive what each plan offers. On the accompanying page is a nonexclusive case of the sort of data that will be given on the initial hardly any pages of these plans. (Source: www.dol.gov/ebsa/pdf/SBCSampleCompleted.pdf.)

With these reviews you can rapidly survey your deductible and out-of-pocket breaking points and determine what a visit to the specialist will cost, what a symptomatic or imaging test will run, what conventional medications will cost when contrasted with brand-name drugs, and what your coinsurance will be for outpatient and emergency clinic remains. The main thing not explicitly indexed is the month to month premium, and that will be given at the Health Insurance Exchange's top level before you arrive at this progressively point by point data.

Medical and Dental Tourism

The expenses of health and dental consideration can be fundamentally lower abroad – to such an extent that much in the wake of figuring in the cost of transportation there and back, it can at present expense essentially less to have a system performed abroad than it is have a similar technique acted in the U.S.

Numerous who have gotten medicinal treatment abroad write shining reports about their encounters and state they wished they had found such alternatives sooner. What they discover usually isn't some poor cousin of American human services, yet rather first class restorative offices, brilliantly prepared doctors with faultless certifications, and staff who talk clear English and give a degree of individual assistance and care that would be difficult to copy in the U.S. because of obvious contrasts in costs.

If you like the possibility of world travel as much as we do, then accepting probably a portion of your medical or dental consideration abroad is an engaging choice. For instance, we've exploited dental consideration administrations and professionally prescribed medication deals in Algodones, Mexico (directly over the outskirt from Yuma, Arizona) and have just beneficial comments about the experience. Right now share our very own portion encounters and point you towards probably the best nations on the planet with regards to medicinal the travel industry.

Medical Tourism and the Affordable Care Act

Indeed, even with the coming of the Affordable Care Act, we accept medicinal the travel industry will keep on flourishing by offering bargains that are basically too acceptable to even consider passing up. For instance, certain elective medical procedures at Thailand's Bumrungrad Hospital cost only one-tenth of what they do in the U.S., and a knee or hip substitution in India may even now run you not exactly the measure of your yearly out-of-pocket most extreme in the U.S. For whatever length of time that these sorts of emotional cost differentials exist, medical the travel industry will keep on thriving.

The "Medical Tourism" site (medicaltourism.com) offers helpful examination costs for similar methodology in various nations. While costs are inexact, they are still a serious eye-opener, particularly when you understand they as of now work in the assessed cost of airfare for two. Another valuable site with many accommodating connections about medical the travel industry is the Retire Early Lifestyle site run by early retirees Billy and Akaisha Kaderli (retireearlylifestyle.com/medical_tourism).

As a matter of fact, obligatory inclusion under the Affordable Care Act puts something of a damper on restorative the travel industry, since U.S. residents are as of now put to a limited degree in the medicinal services framework right now. Well, in addition to the fact that you are paying a month to month premium, however you may likewise have a sponsored out-of-pocket limit that takes out yearly medicinal services costs past a specific point.

For instance, regardless of whether a heart sidestep medical procedure costs $15,000 in Thailand contrasted with $150,000 in the U.S. – an entire request of greatness' distinction – U.S. residents may reconsider before paying the $15,000 in Thailand since their financed yearly out-of-pocket point of confinement may just be $7,500, state, in the U.S. They realize their protection will cover the remainder of the sum, so there is no motivating force for them to look for treatment abroad since their own expenses would really be higher.

Medicinal vacationers from the U.S. may along these lines wind up moving towards elective medical procedures and particular medications that aren't secured by their protection at home – things like corrective medical procedure, dental inserts, Lasik medical procedure, top to bottom health tests, pivotal undifferentiated cell treatments, and imaginative malignant growth medicines that aren't yet secured by U.S. insurance.

Any place holes in inclusion exist, or at whatever point systems can be performed for not exactly out-of-pocket maximums, restorative the travel industry will keep on offering a suitable other option. Any medical procedure that includes a long sitting tight period for reasons unknown may likewise offer solid motivator for therapeutic the travel industry to places like India, Thailand, or Malaysia where the medical procedure could be performed very quickly.

Early retirees living past the 400% government destitution limit remain especially great possibility for proceeded with medicinal consideration abroad. The Affordable Care Act doesn't help them as much as it does their less rich brethren. They don't get endowments, for instance, that lessen their yearly out-of-pocket limits. That implies their out-of-pocket expenses could be as high as $6,250 for people or $12,500 for families, in view of current-year limits.

If wealthy retirees can get a restorative method abroad for considerably not exactly these points of confinement, then they are probably going to think about it. The main drawback is that they're paying a month to month premium for administrations they aren't generally using, and the dollars that would have gone towards meeting their out-of-pocket limits for the year have headed off to someplace else.

Paying the Penalty Tax?

Some early retirees might be pondering whether it bodes well to just take care of the punishment charge and not have human services in America, depending rather exclusively on abroad consideration. While worth contemplating, it is anything but a stage to be messed with.

In any case the methodology appears to be excessively full of dangers. A superior choice may be to buy the least expensive Bronze-level plan accessible and offset that with abroad medicinal treatment when proper. Then again, you could consider finding a way to set up residency abroad to stay away from the requirement for U.S. social insurance inside and out.

Which Countries Are Best?

A few nations reliably make the best ten indexes with regards to medicinal and dental the travel industry. Here is a snappy once-over of the most elite dependent on our ongoing audit of top ten indexes posted by International Living, Forbes, Healthy Times Blog, Business Pundit, Medical Travel Quality Alliance, and that's just the beginning:

• Thailand is at or close to the highest point of most indexes. Bumrungrad Hospital only west of Bangkok has been known as the crown gem of therapeutic the travel industry. Bangkok Hospital is another. You can recover after your system on one of Thailand's numerous exquisite sea shores.

• Malaysia is especially renowned for its "well man" and "well lady" preventive consideration bundles that incorporate broad physicals and a battery of tests at a small amount of western expenses. Malaysia additionally has a lot of unblemished sea shores.

• Singapore is a third powerhouse in Southeast Asia, offering the absolute best treatment places on the planet (e.g., Gleneagles Hospital) for significant issues extending from cardiology to oncology to foundational microorganism treatment.

• India is known for high-caliber heart and orthopedic methodology requiring little to no effort. Medicinal and dental the travel industry are both becoming quickly here. Bangalore's Fortis Hospital is positioned as a standout amongst other careful focuses on the planet for medicinal explorers.

• Mexico is a definitive near and dear goal for Americans. Comfort and sensible costs consolidate for an incredible plan with regards to dental, vision, and doctor prescribed medication administrations, just as standard physicals and tests and certain activities, for example, knee and hip substitutions.

• Costa Rica is another well known goal for Americans, with a specific accentuation on dental consideration and restorative medical procedure. It offers "restorative spas" in a protected, helpful, English-talking, and biologically excellent nation.

• Hungary is a prime European goal particularly with regards to dental the travel industry. Germans have been crossing the outskirt for a considerable length of time for quality dental and therapeutic consideration. Dental techniques can cost half what they do in most western nations.

• Turkey makes most top-ten indexes in light of its high number of certify therapeutic offices, minimal effort, and western-prepared specialists conversant in English. Turkey is particularly known for eye medicines like Lasik medical procedure and for dental get-aways.

The over eight nations make most top-ten indexes on a reliable premise, yet the last two nations will in general shift a lot. South Korea is on numerous rundowns so far another Southeast Asian nation offering best in class medicinal administrations, just as the Philippines. Panama every now and again makes the slice for goals near the U.S., and Guatemala is an up-and-comer. Brazil is all around respected for plastic medical procedure at a low cost, as is Egypt. Another great alternative is South Africa, which offers enticing restorative safaris. Israel makes a few indexes for its minimal effort malignant growth treatment focuses. Other well known European goals for medicinal the travel industry incorporate Poland, the Czech Republic, Lithuania, and Spain.

As should be obvious, the rundown of nations is broad, and these are a long way from the main quality alternatives with regards to reasonable therapeutic and dental consideration abroad. Utilize this rundown as a beginning stage, yet a brisk electronic hunt will uncover numerous other fine alternatives.

If you like the possibility of medicinal the travel industry yet would prefer really not to travel to another country, here's one last choice: the Surgery Center of Oklahoma. This best in class multi-claim to fame office presents front and packaged (comprehensive) evaluating presented online for all on observe (surgerycenterok.com). It deliberately works outside the bounds of the huge emergency clinic/protection condition and takes a stab at value easyness and reasonableness. Those with high deductibles or high out-of-pocket points of confinement may locate this a suitable other option and one all the more great alternative worth considering.

Dental Tourism

The degree of dental inclusion under the Affordable Care Act is as yet something of a riddle. If it turns out such inclusion is insignificant or nonexistent under numerous plans, then reasonable choices abroad will offer a significant option for early retirees.

Where dental the travel industry sparkles most splendidly is with regards to exorbitant techniques, for example, implants, root canals, crowns, bleaching, and veneers.

CHAPTER SEVEN

START SAVING EARLY

The Power of Compounding

The prior you can begin putting something aside for retirement the better, since it gives your investments more opportunity to compound. Aggravating, basically, is earning enthusiasm on your advantage. When premium is added to your head, starting now and into the foreseeable future it also procures intrigue. Intensifying is at the very heart of a get rich gradually way to deal with contributing.

Assume you put $10,000 in a bank testament of store that pays 5% premium every year. Toward the finish of one year your equalization will have developed by $500 (5% of your underlying $10,000) to $10,500. Accepting you leave the whole sum in the CD, your essential the tracking year will remain at $10,500 + 5% = $11,025.

Basically by "sitting idle" and leaving your interest set up to develop, you can watch your underlying investment twofold and twofold once more. Your money begins to bring in money for you, which thusly makes your street to retirement that a lot simpler as the years pass.

Time is your companion with regards to contributing. That is the reason the prior you can show signs of improvement. If you somehow happened to begin contributing at age 25, you could retire at age 50 and still have a 25-year investment time skyline, giving your money a lot of time to develop. Intensifying is incredible enough that it can take a normal investor and make him into an extraordinary one basically by ethicalness of his having begun contributing at a youthful enough age.

Did you realize accruing funds was once viewed as the most exceedingly terrible type of usury and was seriously denounced by Roman law? Times surely have changed: presently gladiatorial battle is out and intensifying is in. Since intensifying is completely lawful now, we recommend you exploit it as you put something aside for retirement. The impacts of intensifying become significantly increasingly obvious if your investment acquires a higher yearly pace of return.

The more you hold back to tap your money, the more emotional the profits can become in later years. (Accepting, obviously, that the business sectors participate for your profit, which isn't generally the situation.)

As a last examination, suppose that as opposed to allowing the money to money, you basically take the 10% income out every year and use it for money. That is $1,000 every year in your pocket, however at an incredible cost.

Utilizing Investing Calculators

Web based contributing adding machines make it simple to perceive how your month to month contributions compound after some time, helping you to get rich gradually. One of our top choices is at daveramsey.com (under the "Devices" tab). You plug in your 1) beginning parity (assuming any), 2) assessed yearly pace of return, 3) month to month contribution, 4) number of years you intend to invest, and 5) absolute number of years you'll be permitting the money to compound, then hit the "Ascertain" key and up pops a bar graph indicating you the outcomes.

The graph is naturally easy. For every situation you run, it in a flash shows you the complete contributions made by you versus the aggregate sum earned because of aggravating. It additionally shows the year where you cross the $1 million imprint. It's an extraordinary device and allowed to utilize.

Have a go at connecting various qualities to explore different avenues regarding various situations until you hit upon a situation that feels right to you. A decent situation is one that adjusts the necessities of today with the requirements of tomorrow. You would prefer not to make yourself insane by setting the month to month investment bar excessively high. Likewise, remember that any situation is only that: a sensible investment about the future that may not coordinate all that intimately with the real world. In any case, that is alright, plans can be balanced. The significant thing is to have an plan.

How Compounding Can Help Parents in Particular

The magical of compounding is particularly significant for guardians thinking about how they can ever figure out how to set aside enough for early retirement. By adding five or ten years to their general investment plan, guardians can in any case arrive at their monetary objectives while accommodating their kids' needs simultaneously. They can do directly by their children and without anyone else by systematically contributing smaller aggregates of money however doing it over a more drawn out timeframe. It might take them a couple of additional years, yet the outcome is as yet a pleasant, clean savings – and at an age youthful enough to appreciate it.

Riding the Compounding Tailwind to Retirement

I accept the hardest long stretches of contributing by a wide margin are the most punctual ones since you're getting so little tailwind as far as compounding. It feels like you're going no place quick. For me, it appeared to take everlastingly to arrive at that first $100,000 mark.

Then things got simpler. The $100,000 effectively set aside began working for us, compounding, giving us that exceedingly significant tailwind we had been missing previously. It didn't take so long or appear to be almost so challenging to get from $100,000 to $200,000, and this pattern proceeded into what's to come.

So starting financial specialists, cheer up: it truly gets simpler as the years pass by. You can thank the intensity of intensifying for that. If you hang intense and continue putting as much as you can in those early years, your diligence will pay off at last. It assists with recollecting that the money you save from the get-go is the money that will exacerbate the most throughout the years.

Chapter Eight

Keep Car And Home Expenses Low

Keeping Your Mortgage Affordable

Your home can get perhaps the best investment or a hindrance, contingent upon whether you remain inside your methods or get in too far. Here's some assistance in how to differentiate.

The 28/36 Rule: What Conventional Wisdom Says

Tried and true way of thinking says your home loan payment can be up to 28% of your gross salary, as long as your all out obligation payments don't surpass 36% of your pay. This is at times called the 28/36 guideline, and it's what contract banks normally use as a dependable guideline in choosing whether or not you meet all requirements for a credit.

Assume you and your life partner make $80,000 net every year. As indicated by the 28/36 standard, your home loan payment ought not surpass $1,867 every month ($80,000 x 28% = $22,400 ÷ 12 = $1,867), and your home loan payment in addition to some other obligations (Mastercards, vehicle payments, school advances, and so on.) ought not surpass $2,400 every month ($80,000 x 36% = $28,800 ÷ 12 = $2,400). Remember these are not to surpass sums. Fundamentally, they are the maximums contract moneylenders need to find with the end goal for you to fit the bill for an advance.

The 20/28 Rule: A More Conservative Approach

We prescribe you keep your lodging costs extensively lower than the 28/36 standard permits. Standard way of thinking accept you will likely live inside your methods, yet since you will likely live significantly beneath your methods, tried and true way of thinking doesn't really apply.

We prescribe 20% of your month to month net salary goes toward lodging costs rather than 28%. For a couple making $80,000 every year, that would work out to be $1,333 every month in contract payments. In a perfect world you would be sans obligation before purchasing your home, however if that is not plausible, we would propose you utilize 28% rather than 36% as a guide for the aggregate sum of obligation you should convey. That would be $1,867 every month for our theoretical couple.

This progressively moderate 20/28 standard gives you to a greater degree a pad for contributing for your future. The exact opposite thing you need is to be house poor in case you're attempting to put something aside for early retirement.

The Downside of Stretching Too Far

Presently, some would contend you should extend similarly as possibly conceivable to pay for the greatest, most delightful home you can bear. They propose your pay will just develop later on so the house payments that appear to be so awkward today will turn out to be increasingly moderate later on.

While there is a sure rationale to this, it places a ton of your eggs in a single crate and makes your home a significant piece of your general monetary portfolio. As we as a whole know from ongoing experience, there is no assurance lodging costs will consistently go up. We trust it despite everything sounds good to possess your essential home, yet making it too enormous a piece of your general money related picture implies you might not have adequate subsidizes left over to do different sorts of contributing.

Another danger of the purchase the-greatest home-you-can theory is that it leaves you no cradle if things don't go precisely as planned. It accept your compensations will consistently go up, yet what if one of you is given up from work, or quits attempting to bring up a kid, or needs to take an all-encompassing time away for wellbeing reasons. You would prefer not to battle to make your regularly scheduled payments since you purchased more house than you could easily manage. So our proposal is, purchase a home however purchases a moderate one that is inside your methods today and not some removed time later on.

Obviously reality don't generally coordinate with what we may all concede to paper is the perfect.

A Fine Time to Buy a Home

Home loan financing costs are at present at verifiably low valuations: underneath 3% APR for a 15-year fixed-rate contract and beneath 3.5% APR for a 30-year fixed-rate contract as of the principal quarter of 2013.

Home costs, in the interim, remain very moderate. While they have recuperated to some degree since the land bubble burst in 2007, valuations are as yet alluring contrasted with what they were previously. The mix of sensible home costs and truly low home loan financing costs makes it an extraordinary time to think about purchasing a home.

We're not proposing you guess on homes in essence, however in case you're in the market for your essential home in any case and happen to locate the one you had always wanted, you ought to have the option to get it more reasonably than you could have preceding 2007.

Setting something aside for a Downpayment

Such huge numbers of money related contributions appear to hit at the same time when you're youthful and simply beginning. You need to purchase your first home, teach yourself for a superior future, take care of your obligations, and begin contributing early; however it's difficult to do the entirety of that simultaneously. How would you choose what starts things out?

As far as organizing we would encourage you to: 1) put resources into yourselves first so you can land respectable paying positions directly from the beginning, 2) take care of your obligations, 3) put something aside for a downpayment on a moderate home, and 4) begin living in your home simultaneously you begin putting resources into sincere for retirement.

20% versus 10% Downpayments

What amount would it be a good idea for you to put something aside for a downpayment? The perfect is 20% – that is the thing that loan specialists would like to see. However, 20% of a $250,000 home is $50,000, and that is a reasonable wad of money. If you can manage the cost of a 20% downpayment, then you get the best home loan terms with the most minimal financing cost, so the rate we would suggest.

If that is not practical, check whether you can organize a 10% downpayment with your bank. That sum is less overwhelming and will get you into your home in a shorter timeframe. A 10% downpayment might be sufficient to qualify you for an advance, accepting that you're without obligation in any case and have strong FICO assessments. Remember that if you start with a 10% downpayment and a high loan fee, you can generally renegotiate to a lower-rate contract once your value arrives at 20%.

Private Mortgage Insurance

With downpayments of fewer than 20%, you're required to pay for compulsory supplemental protection known as private home loan protection. PMI secures your moneylender against non-payment should you default on your advance. It ordinarily sums to 0.5% of the credit sum, so for a $250,000 contract that would add up to marginally over $100 extra every month. While it's no enjoyment paying PMI, it's a generally little cost to pay for getting into your home sooner. PMI is payable until you arrive at 20% value in your home loan, then you can advise your bank to drop it.

Utilizing Your Initial Investment

The colossal advantage of home possession is that you construct value in your home while finding a workable pace it. In case you're fortunate, you'll see the market estimation of your home increment after some time, which implies your value will likewise increment.

Little Downpayment, Big Rewards

A utilized investment is any investment utilized acquired money, permitting you to expand the potential return of the investment. By a wide margin the most well-known type of utilizing is the utilization of a home loan to buy a home.

Suppose you have a $100,000 townhouse and your downpayment is 20%. That is 5:1 influence (since $20,000 is one fifth of $100,000). If your condominium acknowledges 5% through the span of the year, then you've recently earned $5,000 on your underlying $20,000 investment – a 25% return.

By examination, suppose your downpayment is 10% rather than 20%. That is 10:1 influence (since $10,000 is one-tenth of $100,000). If your apartment suite acknowledges precisely the same 5%, you've quite recently earned $5,000 on an underlying $10,000 investment – a half return.

That is utilizing at work. Much the same as utilizing a physical switch, you've figured out how to lift up something substantial with less exertion. You profit by the thankfulness on the full estimation of the apartment suite despite the fact that the majority of the money used to get it was not yours yet the lender's.

Why Leveraging Your Home Makes Sense

We accept essential home possession is the one type of utilized investment that truly bodes well for the normal financial specialist. Utilizing amplifies the two increases and losses, so you should be cautious utilizing it if you would prefer not to get scorched – for instance, by purchasing on edge in the securities exchange.

However, when we're discussing your essential home, your dangers are lower since you're living in the home apparently as long as possible and have a high stake in making certain the regularly scheduled payments are made. Your dangers are lower, as well, if you purchase a home inside your budgetary safe place in any case.

Owning versus Leasing

Your month to month contract payment stays fixed, which gives you something you can depend on during your contributing years, and your home really turns out to be a piece of your general investment plan.

Home proprietorship is a constrained investment funds plan of sorts that permits you to develop your riches as the cost of the holdings increases in value. At last you can sell the home, cut back to something smaller, and utilize the rest of the value to help support your retirement.

The one alert we have is this: if you figure you may move areas over the present moment – for work reasons, state – you may wind up selling your home in a down market. Consequently you might need to hold up until you're sensibly secure in your activity before purchasing your home.

The Pros of Renting

Leasing gives you expanded adaptability with no long term duties. You have practically no obligation or cost for upkeep, home enhancements, or yard work. Your general expenses could possibly be lower than owning a home if you figure out how to lease inexpensively enough. And, over all that, you maintain a strategic distance from the requirement for a downpayment and a home loan by and large, subsequently permitting you to begin contributing sooner.

We positively trust it is conceivable to lease as opposed to possess and still retire early. If you keep rental costs sensibly low and invest considerably more money than you would have in any case in the business sectors to compensate for the value you won't have from owning a home, you can keep your life ultra-easy and still retire early. Contingent upon your way of life and where you live, leasing could be the correct response for you.

The Cons of Renting

Maybe the most noteworthy drawback of leasing is that you can't control the rental value, which will in general go up with time. Your landowner figures out what to charge, and in some cases the yearly increments can be sensational. A similar one-room loft we leased for $500 every month in 1991 presently leases for $1,200 every month – more than twofold. Lofts in places like New York City and San Francisco have presumably observed development factors a lot higher than twofold over that equivalent range of years.

By correlation, the expenses of home possession remain basically relentless with a fixed-rate contract. They may go up marginally because of little increments in protection and holdings charges, however the fundamental home loan rate itself stays fixed all through. This steadiness is a solace – something you can rely on during your contributing years.

Another drawback of leasing is that at last you don't have anything unmistakable to appear for all the rental payments you've made throughout the years. Maybe all that money just vanished like a phantom. Contrast this with home proprietorship, where you fabricate value as you proceed to can take that value with you once you sell your home. When we sold our home in 2007, we had the option to put $200,000 into a security reserve and utilize the other $100,000 to purchase a little condominium. Cutting back permitted us to expand our liquid investments, which was exactly what we required as early retirees depending on a salary stream from those investments.

A third drawback of leasing is that you can't adjust an investment holdings as you can a home. With rentals, what you see is regularly what you get, from paint hues to tooles to ground surface. In any case, with homes you can make changes both to the home itself and to the land it sits on, which thus can build the home's last worth.

Deducting Mortgage Interest

A last drawback of leasing is extremely a greater amount of an advantage to owning: with a home you find a workable pace intrigue payments from your separated assessments, which you can't do with a rental. It's no big surprise this has become the most loved assessment conclusion for many U.S. mortgage holders. A mortgage holder who burns through $12,000 in intrigue payments and $3,000 in holdings charges can deduct all $15,000 from his personal duties for the year.

The home loan derivation advantage is generally recognizable during the early long stretches of your credit when you're paying the most in intrigue. Since intrigue brings down every year on an amortization plan, one day you will arrive at a hybrid point where the standard reasoning ($12,200 in 2013 for a wedded couple indexing together) is worth more than the home loan intrigue conclusion.

15-Year versus 30-Year Mortgages

We suggest 15-year contracts as an especially solid match for the individuals who plan to retire early. You'll save a great deal on intrigue, and the 15 years coordinates pleasantly with an early retirement objective. We believe it's imperative to have your home totally paid off before you retire, and a 15-year contract lets you achieve that.

Nonetheless, financing costs are normally lower for a 15-year contract than they are for a 30-year contract as a result of the shorter advance length. The contrasts between the two models would be considerably increasingly sensational if we had considered, however it likewise would have made it harder to make a relevant comparison.

Looking at Monthly Payment Amounts

Let's look at the regularly scheduled payment sum. For a 30-year contract your regularly scheduled payment would be about $1,300, and for the 15-year contract it would be about $1,800. For a distinction of about $500 every month you can cut 15 years off your home loan.

Here's a reasonable inquiry: What if the contrast between the two payments is sufficient to put you outside the perfect scope of the 20/28 principle we prescribed before? We'll offer you a halfway response here, however make certain to likewise read the accompanying segment on "informal" 15-year contracts for what may be a superior other option.

We accept the advantages of doing a 15-year contract are so extraordinary contrasted with a 30-year contract that we would make a special case and prescribe you stretch for the 15-year contract as long as your regularly scheduled payments stayed inside the 28% most extreme required by the customary 28/36 guideline. That despite everything puts you inside the limits of what contract banks acknowledge as the passing reach for an advance, and at last it will get you to your retirement objective quicker.

Contrasting Total Interest Paid

As noted above, financing costs are normally lower for a 15-year contract than they are for a 30-year contract. However, in any event, when you expect the equivalent 5% pace of enthusiasm for the two home loans, note the immense contrast in the measure of all out intrigue paid: roughly $187,000 versus $85,000. That is a distinction of over $100,000 you don't need to pay if you go with a 15-year contract.

For the initial quite a long while of a 30-year contract, practically all you're paying is intrigue; you're not really making a scratch in the head. However, with a 15-year contract you make a perceptible scratch in the chief right from the earliest starting point. That implies your value becomes quicker, and your house is more your own and less the bank's.

If you should need to sell your home sooner than anticipated, your value stake will be more noteworthy with the 15-year contract. You can utilize that higher stake to put a more noteworthy downpayment on your next home, keeping your acquiring costs lower.

Looking at Total Holdings Tax Paid

The absolute holdings charge paid for a 15-year contract is half what it is really going after 30-year contract, yet this is somewhat deceptive. You would need to keep paying holdings charges on your home much after you took care of the 15-year contract, expecting you kept on living in it a short time later.

Under either situation, if you wound up remaining in the home for a long time, the all out holdings charge paid would be the equivalent. Nonetheless, if you sold the home tracking 15 years and cut back to a smaller holdings, your holdings charges starting now and into the foreseeable future would be similarly less.

Looking at PMI Paid

The above correlation does exclude private home loan protection, however if it did (i.e., because your downpayment was under 20%, in which case PMI is required), then the all out PMI paid for a 15-year credit would commonly be not exactly half what it is really going after 30-year advance. The explanation is that you arrive at 20% value in your home loan a lot quicker with the higher month to month head payments you're making on a 15-year credit, and subsequently you can drop the PMI sooner.

Looking at Total Amount Paid

When all is said and done, the aggregate sum paid in the above correlation is about $480,000 for a 30-year contract versus $332,000 for a 15-year contract. That is a distinction of about $150,000. We believe it merits an extra $500 every month in contract payments to save almost $150,000, isn't that right?

Coordinating Your Mortgage to Your Retirement Date

If you realize the specific retirement date you're going for, you can coordinate the length of your home loan to that date. For instance, if you intend to retire in 20 years, you could consider doing a 20-year contract.

Well, a similarly alluring option is to stay with the 15-year contract regardless of whether you realize you will retire in 20 years. That way the most recent five years before your retirement are totally contract free, permitting you to set aside up much more money during those years – or spend somewhat more unreservedly on movement and enjoyment as you ease towards retirement.

Renegotiating to a 15-Year Mortgage

If a 15-year contract isn't monetarily possible for you from the outset, you can generally renegotiate to one after you've lived in your home for a while. In any case, know renegotiating can include soak account charges. It's not surprising to pay 3% or a greater amount of your exceptional chief in renegotiating expenses. In this way renegotiating regularly doesn't bode well except if you're paying an a lot higher loan cost than you would somehow or another need to pay.

"Informal" 15-Year Mortgages

If the financing cost on your 30-year contract is as of now acceptably low, you can abstain from renegotiating accuses by staying of your 30-ycar contract however informally transforming it into a 15-year contract by squaring away the key quicker.

Making Extra Principal Payments

If you make additional payments towards the main every month (or on a fortnightly premise), that will have the impact of bringing down your general intrigue payments and lessening the term of the advance.

For example, if you pay an extra $100 every month towards the head on a $180,000 advance at 5% intrigue, your 30-year fixed-rate contract becomes basically a 25-year contract. An extra $200 every month makes it what might be compared to a 20-year contract. An extra $450 every month gets you what could be compared to a 15-year contract while never doing the official administrative work to make it one.

An additional advantage of this methodology is that you're not secured in the additional payments. If you should get yourself briefly jobless, you could ease off on making the additional payments for a while until you were re-utilized. You along these lines have less danger of defaulting on your credit.

The main drawback of this methodology is human instinct. It requires a decent plan of self-restraint to continue making the deliberate payments through various challenges, after quite a long time after year. Well, if you are adequately propelled to retire early and have the control it takes, this can be an extraordinary solution.

Prepayment Calculators

Home loan amortization number crunchers like the one at HSH.com let you run distinctive head prepayment situations.

Simply plug various sums into the "Month to month Additional Principal Prepayment Amount" box and hit "Figure." You can rapidly observe the consequences of making various prepayments, including the all out intrigue you will pay and the result date. This permits you to tailor your prepayment technique to coordinate your needs.

Waiting in Your Home

Numerous individuals exchange up from their first home, utilizing it as a venturing stone to a greater home, then exadjusting up once more to a much greater one. Why, precisely? Whcn you think about the vitality and cost engaged with pressing and unloading, rebuilding and refurnishing, repainting and redesigning, and purchasing then purchasing again to suit the requirements and measurements of each greater home, it makes you wonder what it's supportive of.

We recommend rather you wait in your first home. Keep your life less difficult and your needs smaller by remaining in one spot. Increment your current home's estimation by making enhancements to it all around. If you have no other decision however to move in view of your activity or some other need, then try moving sideways and purchasing a house that is practically identical to the one you as of now have as opposed to upsizing.

Exadjusting up for increasingly more home is counterproductive in case you're looking for early retirement. You will probably limit your costs while boosting your investment funds. Keeping your lodging costs as low as sensibly conceivable will let you accomplish that objective with significantly less trouble.

If you have children or plan on having them, attempt to purchase a first home large enough to oblige them directly from the earliest starting point so you don't need to move to a greater home later on. Obviously nobody has a precious stone ball and everything you can do is your best. Here and there guardians have no other decision however to purchase a greater home if they wind up having a bigger number of children than anticipated.

If you purchase a home that wind up being too large for your needs, you can generally think about inventive approaches to utilize that additional room to further your own potential profit.

Is a Renter Right for You?

If you're willing to engage the probability of having a leaseholder, then consider first how your house is planned. Does it take into consideration a decent lot of security for you and your leaseholder? Does it offer a different passage? Are there independent washrooms with showers? Would you be able to set up a small scale kitchen in the piece of the home you'll be leasing? The more you can limit the need to impart space to your leaseholder, the simpler it will be for all gatherings.

We realize numerous individuals feel emphatically about not having any desire to impart their home to any other person, and we perceive this might possibly be a correct alternative for you. In case you're awkward with the idea of having a tenant, maybe you can think about to different ways you could utilize any additional room in your house that is simply sitting unfilled. Possibly you can set up a little independent investment or something to that affect, for instance. Let your imaginative energies stream while thinking about various methods for getting a little extra salary over your customary compensations. Indeed, even some additional salary can go far when you're endeavouring relentlessly to live underneath your methods.

Cutting back When You Retire

You might need to consider offering your greater home and cutting back to a smaller home or apartment suite once you retire. As we addressed before, this permits you to take a bit of the value developed in your home and put it in a progressively liquid resource, for example, a security finance.

Liquid resources are progressively usable resources for early retirees. You can remove $10,000 from a security store and use it for everyday costs once you retire, however you can't remove $10,000 from your home in the equivalent simple way. You'd either need to take out a home value advance (which means returning into obligation) or lease all or a piece of your home (which can be badly planned) to access the equivalent $10,000. In any case, if you scale back after you retire, you can take the straggling leftovers and put it in a shared store offering both liquidity and a pay stream.

One of the extraordinary advantages of home proprietorship under current law is that when it comes time to sell your essential home, you owe no assessments at all on the first $250,000 of capital increases (or $500,000 for couples). This can be a gift from heaven in case you're searching for some additional money with which to pad your savings once you retire.

Obviously another alternative is to purchase a smaller home or townhouse directly from the beginning and remain in it considerably after you retire. If you choose to move to an alternate area, you could generally exchange sideways, purchasing another home or apartment suite for about a similar cost. The advantages of this methodology are, it downplays your home loan (i.e., you never purchased more home than you required), your holdings charges are lower, and your utility expenses are lower since your area is less.

If you go the apartment suite course, make certain to mull over month to month HOA expenses. You'll need to ensure they're as low as sensibly conceivable since they are what might be compared to paying rent every month. An astounding plan on a townhouse can appear to be less staggering once you factor in these charges.

The Real Cost of a New Car

The normal cost for another vehicle nowadays is over $30,000. If rather than another vehicle for $30,000, you were to purchase a pre-owned one for $10,000; the remaining $20,000 could finance an entire year of contributing for retirement. In case you're a couple and every one of you chooses to purchase a trade-in vehicle for $10,000 rather than another one for $30,000 that is $40,000 additional that could be put towards retirement investment funds.

Presently let's guess you have a 20-year retirement plan and your objective is to taken care of $20,000 every year by and large. That is $400,000 complete you have to invest, with the remainder of your portfolio's development originating from exacerbating. The $40,000 you could have saved by purchasing two trade-in vehicles rather than two new ones speaks to one-tenth of your complete investment sum.

That is the genuine expense of another vehicle. You could be exadjusting the opportunity to retire quite a long while prior.

Self-Financing

In case you're purchasing a trade-in vehicle for $10,000 rather than another one for $30,000, the probability of self-financing turns out to be substantially more achievable. You could begin a vehicle reserve and set aside the entire sum early, paying for the vehicle in real money and subsequently staying away from the need to pay enthusiasm on a vehicle credit.

Regardless of whether you just figure out how to set aside a large portion of the sum, an advance of $5,000 is less scary to take care of (and repay rapidly) than a credit of $10,000 or more. The fewer obligations you have hanging over you the better.

Sharing One Car or Going Carless

For some individuals a vehicle is a need during their working years, yet if you can get by without one and depend on open vehicle rather, that would be preferable. When I worked in Denver for various years, I brought an express transport into the city every day not exclusively to bring down my costs yet in addition to maintain a strategic distance from the cerebral pains of city driving.

Anybody living in a significant city with a metro framework ought to consider managing without a vehicle just to maintain a strategic distance from the high cost of leaving. If you just endeavour out of the city on uncommon events, consider leasing a vehicle exactly when you need one. It would in all likelihood be less expensive than owning.

In case you're a couple and one of you is sufficiently fortunate to be inside biking separation of work, then you might have the option to get by with one vehicle rather than two. Not exclusively will your expenses go down, yet you'll get some great exercise every day.

Purchasing a Used Car

Purchasing a trade-in vehicle isn't especially dangerous if you get your work done first. Equipped with information you can turn into an educated purchaser. We recommend you start with Kelly Blue Book (kbb.com) or Edmunds (edmunds.com), which can supply you with the evaluated value extend for the vehicle you're keen on purchasing. Carfax (carfax.com) lets you beware of a trade-in's vehicle history. Basically enter the VIN or the state and tag number to pull up the index. The present expense is $35 for one vehicle, $45 for up to five, and $50 for boundless reports inside 30 days.

A vehicle investigation from a nearby specialist is every now and again offered requiring little to no effort as an impetus for future business. It's keen to have a repairman take a gander at a trade-in vehicle first before you get it.

Utilizing Craigslist to Buy or Sell a Car

Think about purchasing or selling your vehicle on Craigslist (craigslist.com). The site's free classifieds offer a vigorously utilized discussion for purchasing and selling utilized vehicles and pretty much everything else under the sun. We sold our two vehicles in less than seven days in the wake of posting promotions on the site and had the option to get the value we needed. We additionally found our current trade-in vehicle by means of a posting on Craigslist. In case you're a solitary lady, we would prescribe carrying somebody with you when purchasing or selling for security reasons.

Make certain to post quality photographs with your promotion – it has a major effect as far as your prosperity rate. You can repost your promotion like clockwork to move it to the highest point of the line, which merits doing since it builds your perceivability to imminent purchasers.

Purchasing versus Renting

We don't suggest renting a vehicle as opposed to getting one. The long term cost of renting is for all intents and purposes in every case more than the expense of purchasing. It makes sense when you consider it. If you buy a solitary vehicle and drive it for 10 years or more, you will improve cost-wise than if you rent a few autos over that equivalent timeframe.

A great many people we realize who rent their vehicles turn them in each a few years so they're continually driving what adds up to another or near new vehicle. In any case, there's a cost to be paid for that profit. You once in a while get something in vain right now.

What confounds numerous individuals, and naturally along these lines, is that month to month rent payments are ordinarily 30% to 60% not exactly ordinary vehicle advance payments. This appears to be a lot from the start, however it's tricky because month to month rent payments never end as long as you are renting the vehicle.

When you take care of an ordinary vehicle credit, you

possess the vehicle through and through. Other than upkeep and fix costs, you can drive the vehicle payment free for a considerable length of time to desire as long as it remains street commendable. Your credit costs are successfully spread out over the whole possession time of the vehicle. Along these lines, despite the fact that a customary advance payment may appear to be higher when contrasted with a month to month rent payment, it's in reality a lot of lower when you consider.

Paying for Car Repairs

Consider fix costs cautiously before choosing to exchange your older vehicle for a fresher one. The facts confirm that fix costs are higher for older vehicles, however every additional year you can crush out of your current vehicle is one more year without month to month credit payments or a major capital use to purchase a more up to date one.

Paying a high vehicle fix bill can be difficult because it hits at the same time and frequently out of nowhere, yet it is less excruciating if you intellectually spread the expense out over all the additional months you'll find a good pace vehicle once it's fixed.

Obviously, sooner or later the transmission may blow or some other fix cost might be high to the point that it never again gets sense to empty more money-flow into a vehicle that has practically zero worth left to it. By then it's reasonable to persuade it to retire and search for a substitution. Kelly Blue Book (kbb.com) can assist you with deciding your vehicle's present worth and whether you should jump on costly fixes.

CHAPTER NINE

DETERMINE YOUR INCOME NEEDS AS A RETIREE

Making sense of how a lot of money you're probably going to require on a yearly premise to some degree far off future is no simple issue. However, you can begin with this basic reason: your costs will very likely be lower than they are presently.

Why? Well, first of all, you won't have to invest for retirement any more once you're retired, clearly, so those "costs" will leave. And, you won't make contract payments anymore, and any costs related with bringing up kids and sending them off to school will never again apply. Certain business related costs will drop away once you never again need to make the day by day drive. Noteworthy home and yard enhancements ought to be a relic of past times. Also, your duties will more likely than not go down contrasted with what you're paying at this point.

Then again, your medicinal services expenses may increment to some degree, just as your movement and relaxation costs. Then there's swelling, which ceaselessly consumes the estimation of your dollar a seemingly endless amount of time after year. Swelling adds an entirely different measurement to the conversation.

We'll discuss every one of these elements in a minute, yet first we'd prefer to examine the solid contrasts of assessment that exist about how best to decide your future yearly pay needs.

Two Methods for Calculating Future Income

One methodology touted by numerous monetary and protection firms is to begin with your present pay then increase that pay by 70% or 80% to decide the sum you're probably going to require later on. We think this strategy is on a very basic level imperfect. It will in general outcome in an overestimate that makes individuals think they have to save a greater savings than they truly do. It's a given this advantages the equivalent budgetary firms that suggest it, since it implies more money streaming into their coffers.

Since compensations will in general be at their most elevated towards the finish of an individual's profession, a conundrum circumstance can bring about which ever more significant compensations lead to ever higher assessments of future needs, which thus drives the apparent requirement for an ever greater savings. The entirety of this prompts the conviction that you have to continue working, continue saving, and continue endeavouring. However, in all actuality, current salary has little to do with the amount you'll require once you retire. Let's utilize our own model as an a valid example.

Towards the finish of our working years we were making the most we had ever earned, as will in general be the situation. Firms prescribing the salary way to deal with ascertaining your retirement needs commonly propose you take the normal of your last ten years of yearly pay. They instruct you to increase that sum by 70% and 80% to get a range speaking to the low end and high finish of what you're probably going to require to keep up your present way of life in retirement.

If you are forcefully putting something aside for early retirement, then the after-effects of the 70-80 strategy will in general be especially slanted. An enormous piece of your salary is going towards investments and is in this manner off the table regarding what you're really living on at present.

Anybody pushing hard to retire early is probably going to be driven off track by utilizing current salary as the methods for deciding the amount they'll require once they retire.

Rather we prescribe you start with current costs to decide your retirement needs. Genuine everyday costs in the present day give you a superior interpretation of what you'll require not far off, when you have subtracted out the ones that never again apply and have made fitting alterations for inflation.

It's especially critical to get the yearly retirement salary number right since it nourishes easily into the count of how enormous your savings should be. The distinction between having the option to live on $40,000 every year and $80,000 every year is the contrast between expecting to set aside a savings of $1 million and $2 million. Consider what number of additional long stretches of work it would take to hoard an additional million dollars in investment funds. Along these lines the yearly retirement pay gauge gets amplified as far as its latent capacity sway on your life and the choices you make about your own future.

Making an Initial Estimate Based on Current Expenses

Let's start by investigating your present everyday costs. Suppose you and your companion presently have a consolidated gross pay of $100,000, or $75,000 net after duties. Presently, utilizing wide brushstrokes, we should wipe out a couple of the significant costs you likely won't have once you retire.

First of all, the home loan will be paid off when you retire, so that's, state, $1,250 every month or $15,000 every year you won't need to stress over. Maybe you've additionally been taking care of $3,000 every year for your children's advanced degree. And, suppose you've distinguished another $1,000 every year in extra costs identified with kids, employments, home redesign, yard support, etc that you feel genuinely certain will never again apply once you're retired.

At last, suppose you're in your essential contributing years and have been storing $20,000 every year into your retirement reserves. Obviously, that "cost" will never again be there once you're retired. So:

$100,000 (consolidated gross salary)

- $25,000 (charges at 25%)
- $15,000 (contract payments)
- $3,000 (children's school support)
- $1,000 (misc. costs identified with kids, employments, home upgrades, and so on.)
- $20,000 (retirement investments) $36,000 (balanced total compensation)

This speculative situation proposes you and your life partner could be making due with as little as $36,000 net every year if not for contract payments, additional costs related with children and work, and the need to put something aside for school and retirement. That is some truly economical living you're doing when you think of it as that way.

In any case, presently the pendulum needs to swing the other way. You've done some subtraction, presently you have to do some inflation. To make an exact evaluation of the amount you'll require once you retire, you need to add money back in to represent swelling, charges, and possibly higher human services costs in retirement.

We won't attempt to represent expanded travel costs right now they can shift such a great amount starting with one individual then onto the next, yet you might need to cushion your gauge marginally higher if you hope to travel seriously once retired.

Adjusting for Inflation

Inflation on an across the nation premise ascends by a normal of generally 3% every year as per the Consumer Price Index, which gauges the expense of a container of basic merchandise and enterprises Americans purchase (nourishment, apparel, lodging, restorative consideration, vitality, and so on.). The CPI is a national normal of costs, however dependent on our own experience we think 3% is somewhat high for ascertaining your own swelling rate. If you live deliberately, you can shield inflation from having as solid of an effect on your life as it would have on the economy all in all.

For example, the cost of seeing a film in an auditorium may have gone up to $12 per ticket, yet that doesn't mean you can't settle on the cognizant choice to keep a watch out a similar motion picture at home for a dollar. And, on the grounds that a café raises its lunch cost to $20 doesn't mean you can't settle on the cognizant choice to eat elsewhere more moderately. You may do takeout for a large portion of the cost or make lunch at home for even less. So while we can't disregard the impacts of inflation, we can alleviate its belongings somewhat by settling on keen choices in our own lives.

We think an individual swelling pace of 2% is nearer to the imprint than 3%, and that is the number we'll use here. Yet, remember high swelling can pop up whenever and represent a difficult issue for retirees on a fixed pay. Watch out for what's going on in reality and alter your counts and manners of thinking likewise.

In view of an individual inflation pace of 2%, to have what could be compared to $36,000 in the present dollars you'd need $36,000 + 2% = $36,720 one year from now. The year after that you'd need $36,720 + 2% = $37,454, etc. In 15 years' time, to have the purchasing power $36,000 gives you today, you'd need $48,451. For the wellbeing of simplicity we should gather the number together to $49,000.

Altering for Taxes in Retirement

The net sum our theoretical couple will require in retirement is $49,000. In any case, when they pull back money from their retirement accounts they'll ordinarily be pulling back gross continues and may need to pay some measure of annual tax on that sum.

For the time being let's expect 10% annual assessments and

add \$5,444 to the \$49,000 to land at a gross pay of \$54,444. (If you're keen on figuring it out, partition the net measure of \$49,000 by 90% to land at the gross sum.) For easyness' purpose we'll gather the number together to \$55,000.

Modifying for Health Care in Retirement

You may likewise need to include some money in for conceivably higher medicinal services costs in retirement. Starting at 2014, the Affordable Care Act will make human services substantially more moderate for early retirees on a financial limit. The impacts of this new enactment are huge enough that we're just going to add \$1,000 to our speculative couple's aggregate, and that is for the most part to represent higher out-of-pocket costs related with things like dental and vision care that aren't really secured under the new law.

Remember you're likely not paying zero dollars for human services right now. Regardless of whether your manager covers you, you're in all likelihood paying something into the framework. As indicated by the Employer Health Profits 201 Survey by the Kaiser Family Foundation, for instance, workers with family inclusion invest, by and large, \$344 every month (\$4,129 yearly) towards their medical coverage premiums. The \$1,000 we're including is top of whatever sum our theoretical couple is as of now paying for wellbeing and dental consideration during their working years.

CHAPTER TEN

YOUR NEST EGG

Maybe the idea has jumped out at you, what precisely establishes my savings? Is the value in my home a piece of it? And, shouldn't something be said about the money in my 401(k) and IRA that I don't anticipate contacting until after I'm 59½? Does that check towards my savings when I'm attempting to decide what amount is protected to pull back in the underlying long periods of my initial retirement?

These are reasonable inquiries and ones we considered ourselves as we were approaching early retirement. We'll put forth a valiant effort to give some direction dependent on our own contemplating these issues both when resigning.

What Constitutes Your Nest Egg?

Your retirement fund should comprise just of fluid resources, for example, stocks, securities, and money, not illiquid resources, for example, land. Land is more diligently to sell and progressively lumbering to work with if you need to create money for current everyday costs. All things considered, if you plan on scaling back your home once you resign, whatever sum you won't requirement for homebuying purposes later on can be transformed into fluid resources that do check towards your savings.

What amount of Your Home Counts?

We prescribe you put aside a part of your home's value (say, between one quarter and one half) for future land purposes. This sum can be applied either to a scaled back home or to taking care of rental expenses any place you may happen to live on the planet if you decide not to claim a home for a while. In any case, you're on the ball if you don't need to subtract this sum out of your savings once you resign.

Are Your 401(k) and Roth IRA Assets Part of Your Nest Egg?

Choosing whether 401(k) and Roth IRA resources are fluid or illiquid in the prior year's you can get to them without punishment is honestly something of a hazy area. Here are our musings on the issue, in spite of the fact that others may sensibly oppose this idea.

We suggest you do incorporate 401(k) and Roth IRA sums while computing your savings, regardless of whether you plan on depending exclusively on the money in your assessable index in the years before turning 59½. The stock, security, and shared store resources in these indexes truly are fluid and could be sold for money rapidly if need be. Obviously you will likely leave them immaculate for quite a long time to come since you would somehow or another need to take care of a punishment charge for getting to them rashly, yet they are all things considered still fluid in nature.

Because you pick (shrewdly) to depend entirely on the assessable part of your fluid resources during your initial retirement years doesn't mean the other expense advantaged fluid resources don't exist. They do exist and in certainty are probably going to develop in the years to come, giving you a constant flow of salary when all is good and well. Not calculating them into your retirement fund is disregard a critical and ever-expanding segment of your portfolio.

Utilizing the 4% Rule to Calculate Your Nest Egg

When you've decided your yearly retirement pay needs, the tracking stage is simple. You can utilize what's known as the 4% rule to gauge the savings you'll require to securely create that sum. We should begin with $56,000, the yearly retirement salary sum from our model in the past section. Utilizing a variety of the 4% rule called the "Rule of 25," you can play out a fast back-of-the-napkin retirement fund computation. Basically increase the salary sum by 25 to decide the size of the retirement fund you'll require. For instance:

$56,000 (yearly retirement salary) x 25 = $1.4 million savings

It's as direct as that. A savings of $1.4 million will create a yearly retirement pay of $56,000 for our theoretical couple. Note that separating the salary sum by 4% will get you a similar outcome as duplicating by 25. The two methodologies are numerically the equivalent as far as furnishing you with an answer with regards to the size of the savings you need.

Maybe a simpler method to envision how the 4% rule functions is to begin with the savings sum itself and duplicate by 4% to decide the yearly salary sum it will securely produce, as follows:

$500,000 retirement fund x 4% = $20,000 salary every year

$750,000 retirement fund x 4% = $30,000 salary every year

$1,000,000 retirement fund x 4% = $40,000 salary every year

$1,250,000 retirement fund x 4% = $50,000 salary every year

$1,500,000 retirement fund x 4% = $60,000 salary every year

$1,750,000 retirement fund x 4% = $70,000 salary every year

$2,000,000 retirement fund x 4% = $80,000 salary every year

Try not to be astounded if the savings sum you ascertain is bigger than you were foreseeing. Swelling can have that impact. Yet, remember your compensation will likewise be staying aware of – and ideally outpacing – swelling over the coming 15 to 20 years, so what may appear as though an unthinkably huge number presently should feel progressively feasible as the years pass and your pay increments. Exacerbating will likewise help you in arriving at your objective, giving you a tailwind in the later long periods of your plan.

Why Is 4% a Safe Withdrawal Amount?

You might be pondering, Why 4%? Why not pretty much than that? Doesn't 4% appear to be misleadingly low? Wouldn't you be able to take out, say, 6% and still be alright? Furthermore, how safe will be protected when individuals reveal to you 4% is a sheltered add up to pull back? Let's attempt to answer a couple of these inquiries.

The Original 4% Rule

Most money related organizers nowadays concur on some variety of the 4% rule. As initially figured by William Bengen, an ensured budgetary organizer in the mid 1990s, the standard states you can securely pull back 4% of your savings in your first year of retirement and increment that sum every year from that point for swelling without an excess of danger of draining your retirement fund more than 30 years.

Suppose you have a $1 million savings. As per the customary utilization of the 4% rule, your first year of retirement you could take out $1 million x 4% = $40,000. One year from now, changing for inflation (suppose it's at 2%), you could take out $40,000 + 2% = $40,800. The year from that point onward, if swelling were at 3%, you could take out $40,800 + 3% = $42,024, etc. That is the 4% rule at its generally fundamental.

Financial specialists have done cautious verifiable demonstrating and run broad calculations (called Monte Carlo reenactments) to come to the end result that 4% is a sensibly protected add up to pull back from your portfolio every year. Bengen himself reasoned that drawing down just 1% more than that every year – that is, 5% in addition to inflation changes – brought about a 30% possibility of a retiree's savings being exhausted too early. For the normal retiree that is just too high a risk.

At or Near the Limit of Safety

Drawn out downturns in the market can unleash destruction with a investment portfolio, particularly in the early long periods of one's retirement, and any great dependable guideline needs to represent that plausibility. A couple of long periods of negative returns, joined with higher than ordinary withdrawals, could exhaust a portfolio to where it can never again support itself however rather starts a moderate winding towards zero.

While the securities exchange may restore a normal of 9% over the long term, it tends to be everywhere temporarily, and the 4% rule is intended to make up for that. It's additionally useful to recollect that posted yearly returns are commonly pre-charge and don't represent inflation. A 9% return is more like a 7% genuine return subsequent to considering in swelling, and it's even lower than that in the wake of calculating in charges.

When these issues are contemplated, 4% ends up being the rate that is at or close to the furthest reaches of security. Almost all monetary models concur that your retirement fund is at genuine danger of being exhausted too early if you are reliably pulling back 6% or more, so keep your withdrawals in the 4% to 5% territory if you need to stand a sensible possibility of seeing your portfolio last longer than you do.

Tragically there is nothing of the sort as ironclad wellbeing with regards to contributing, just relative security. Under horrendous financial conditions it is conceivable to exhaust your portfolio regardless of whether you just took out 4% every year. In any case, all the better you can do is fail on the preservationist side so the chances are in support of you and perceive there are no assurances either throughout everyday life or in contributing.

Changing the 4% Rule to Address Limitations

Obviously the 4% rule is just a general guideline and not a definite science, however it fills in as a decent budgetary measuring stick for deciding the rough size of the savings you'll require. We think it works best when, similar to any general guideline, it is applied with a solid portion of presence of mind. The standard as initially figured has some significant confinements, so we prescribe you use it yet in a changed manner as portrayed underneath.

Is Thirty Years Enough?

The central issue with the 4% rule as initially explained is that it was just intended to apply to 30 years of retirement living. However, with individuals living longer and resigning prior, this suspicion never again remains constant for each situation. You may need to finance 40 or even 50 years of retirement living.

Our answer for this issue is to successfully kill the programmed swelling alteration highlight incorporated with the first guideline. If you don't alter for inflation consistently or make just negligible changes – particularly in the early long stretches of your retirement – then you are supporting your wagers for a solid investment portfolio that is probably going to outlive you.

Inflation has been so low in the course of recent years that we have had the option to go six years so far without expecting to modify our yearly withdrawal sums. Just presently are we starting to see a genuine contrast in our purchasing power. By limiting swelling alterations, we give our portfolio a superior possibility of continuing itself as well as becoming over the long term. This builds the chances it will be there to help us 40 or even 50 years down the line if vital.

Concerning inflation in our later years, we believe we can depend on future government managed savings payments to help with that. Truth be told that is actually how we consider government managed savings: as a support against inflation in the far off future.

Tweaking Withdrawals Based on Actual Conditions

Another issue with the 4% rule as generally planned is that it makes no endeavour to represent changes in spending conduct because of large picture changes in the economy. The standard is applied indiscriminately, fundamentally. Regardless of whether you are in the profundities of a downturn or at the statures of a thundering positively trending business sector, it generally prescribes you pull back the very same sum every year (other than making up for swelling). This makes it easy to apply yet unyielding with regards to moving with the punches that the money related markets at times toss at you.

In light of this worry, numerous financial analysts advocate beginning with the 4% rule yet tweaking your withdrawals from year to year dependent on real economic situations. This sounds good to us. If the financial exchange is performing amazingly a seemingly endless amount of time after year, then you shouldn't feel obliged as far as possible yourself to 4% in addition to the swelling rate. In such a circumstance you may be justified in taking out 6% of your savings (or more) in a given year – as long as it doesn't turn into your new standard. After an especially decent series of years, you may spend too much on that around the globe trip you've constantly longed for before coming back to an increasingly typical withdrawal rate the next year.

Then again, if the economy is in a profound and delayed downturn, then aimlessly applying the 4% rule – which generally would call for you to expand your withdrawal sums so as to represent inflation – would be sketchy, best case scenario. You may wind up physically debilitating the wellbeing of your portfolio and diminishing its odds of endurance over the long term. Under such conditions it is shrewd to pull back under 4% (or if nothing else not modify for inflation) so as to shield your portfolio from further disintegration. Expanding the adaptability of the 4% rule in such a style offers a progressively realistic, eyes-all the way open way to deal with drawing down your retirement fund.

Accomplishing a Self-Sustaining Portfolio

A self-continuing portfolio is your general monetary objective once you resign. A portfolio that is developing at a moderate pace is a portfolio equipped for staying aware of inflation and furnishing you with a somewhat higher yearly salary as the years pass. Altering the 4% rule by 1) killing programmed inflation alterations for manual changes, and 2) tweaking your withdrawal rates dependent on real economic situations ought to permit you to accomplish this objective.

Utilizing Retirement Calculators

You can utilize online retirement number crunchers related to the 4% rule to decide the inexact size of the savings you'll require. We referenced one we especially like at daveramsey.com (under the "Tooles" tab). It makes a bar graph indicating how your money mixes from year to year and lets you plug in various qualities to explore different avenues regarding various situations.

Another clever online tool is the Retirement Nest Egg Calculator on Vanguard's site. (Simply type "Vanguard savings number cruncher" into Google and it will furnish you with the connection, which is somewhat long and lumbering). The adding machine runs 5,000 free Monte Carlo reenactments with simply the snap of a catch.

Sliding bars lets you indicate four information focuses: 1) how long your portfolio needs to last, 2) your present portfolio balance, 3) the amount you hope to spend from your portfolio every year, and 4) the level of stocks, bonds, and money in your portfolio. In light of this data it figures the likelihood of your portfolio enduring the quantity of years you've indicated. In case you're not happy with the outcomes, you can change the sliding bars to investigate distinctive what if situations.

CHAPTER ELEVEN

CREATE A LONG TERM INVESTMENT PLAN

When making a long term investment plan it assists with having the option to plainly express your objective so there is no perplexity about where you are going. For instance: "I need to resign in 15 years and have a retirement fund of $1.5 million so as to create $60,000 in pay every year." To have the option to assemble an objective articulation like this you have to work in reverse, generally, and complete three stages

1.   Estimate your yearly pay needs once you resign.
2.   Calculate your savings dependent on these yearly pay needs.
3.   Put together a point by point plan sketching out how long it will take to set aside your savings and the amount you'll have to invest every year.

This part handles the exceptionally significant advance. You may as of now have an underlying feeling of the quantity of years until your objective retirement date, yet finishing this progression will assist you with refining that understanding. Before the finish of it you'll have a greatly improved handle on the amount you'll have to put every year so as to achieve your objective in the ideal number of years.

What the Historical Index Shows

You need to make presumptions when getting ready for what's to come, there's just no chance to get around it. For whatever length of time that your suspicions have a premise indeed – and over the present moment as well as over the long term – you're on generally strong ground. However, it would be a misstep to expect 20% annualized securities exchange returns since you're sufficiently fortunate to encounter a 20% return at whatever year, or even in a series of years. Why? Since the authentic index just doesn't bolster it.

What the chronicled index supports is the likelihood of financial exchange returns in the 8% to 10% territory over the long term. Does that mean you're unquestionably going to get those profits during the years in which you are effectively contributing? No, obviously not. However, you must beginning some place, and as great a spot to begin as any is with the indexed returns of the financial exchange over a significant stretch of time – state, from before the Great Depression in 1929 to the present day.

Getting a precise read on chronicled financial exchange performance is a shockingly dubious thing in its own right. You'd figure everybody would concur looking back, for instance, on what the annualized returns have been for the S&P 500. All things considered, the S&P 500 is a index of the 500 greatest and best-promoted organizations in the U.S. In any case, various sites post marginally unique annualized returns for that year, albeit most are in harsh understanding.

The Problem With Using Simple Averages

Utilizing the basic normal appears to be sufficiently direct, isn't that right? However, it isn't generally the best methodology. We should take a gander at an extraordinary guide to delineate. Suppose you have $10,000 put resources into a specific stock and you make 100% on your interest in the main year. That implies you made $10,000 on your investment, leaving you with another aggregate of $20,000.

Presently suppose you lose half of that investment the tracking year. That is lost $10,000, returning you right where you began at $10,000. Your genuine annualized gain is zero since you began and finished at a similar dollar sum. However, the easy normal would propose your yearly return was 25%. Why? Since (100% increase - half loss) ÷ 2 = 25%. We instinctively observe this doesn't bode well – and that is the place compound yearly development rates (CAGR) prove to be useful.

Why Compound Annual Growth Rates Are More Reliable

A compound yearly development rate basically shows the rate at which a investment would have developed if it developed at a relentless rate. By utilizing the geometric mean as opposed to the number juggling mean it gives a more genuine image of real returns. Shockingly, figuring the CAGR is no simple issue except if you're a math virtuoso or happen to have a budgetary mini-computer available.

Figuring a fragmentary example isn't something you can without much of a stretch do on a standard number cruncher. Notwithstanding, sites like moneychimp.com and investopedia.com now offer CAGR number crunchers you can utilize. For our motivations, the significant thing to comprehend is that figurings dependent on CAGR give an increasingly exact evaluation of long term annualized returns, and that is the thing that our emphasis is on here.

As per moneychimp.com, the annualized return of the S&P 500 from 1871 to 2012 dependent on compound yearly development rates is 8.92%. The CAGR is generally a percent or two not exactly the easy normal (which you may review was 10.60%). Swelling balanced annualized returns over this equivalent period were 6.71% dependent on the CAGR.

What Annual Rate of Return Should You Use?

The S&P 500 is a sensible intermediary for the whole U.S. financial exchange, so it is reasonable for state that, as time goes on, the securities exchange has had an annualized return of around 9% and an inflation balanced return of roughly 7%. If you need to anticipate the future, you could do more awful than putting together your presumptions with respect to these rates.

Presently in case you're hopeful essentially, you can expect financial exchange returns of 10% or perhaps even 11% every year and still be pretty much in scope of what the verifiable index bolsters. However, going a lot higher than that may begin to look more like unrealistic reasoning than faithful arranging.

When assembling your own monetary plan for the future, we propose you utilize a rate pace of somewhere in the range of 8% and 10% every year if you are putting basically in the securities exchange, with 9% being the conspicuous centre ground presumption. Some will say this is excessively high, others excessively low, however at any rate it is in the ball park. Remember a 9% return depends on putting the heft of your money in stocks during your essential contributing years. If you wish to invest all the more minimalistically, with securities making up 25% or a greater amount of your portfolio, you might need to expect a somewhat lower yearly pace of return.

You might be pondering whether you should utilize swelling balanced returns when making presumptions about future investment development. (Swelling balanced returns are for the most part around two rate focuses lower than unadjusted returns.) with respect to your own investment plan we would state no, and here's the reason: you previously considered in inflation (i.e., by including 2% every year) while computing your future retirement pay needs. That implies your retirement fund has just been balanced upwards to represent swelling. Altering yearly returns downwards too is representing swelling twice.

Regardless of whether the suspicions you make about future securities exchange returns aren't absolutely right (and there's a decent possibility they won't be), the insignificant actuality that you have made an plan and clung to it implies you're on top of things and without a doubt happier than you would have been something else.

Market Resilience

It's a solace to recollect that the securities exchange has endure and flourished in spite of such disastrous occasions as the Stock Market Crash of 1929, the resulting Great

Depression, and two World Wars. It places into viewpoint the worries of our own time and causes us to understand the business sectors are shockingly flexible over the long term. Returns might be compliment than we might want, or even negative for a while, yet over the long term the business sectors have consistently bobbed back and substantiated themselves very strong.

For anybody simply starting to invest today, it's additionally something of a solace to understand that the Great Recession has wrung some risk out of the business sectors. During the five-year time frame from 2008 to 2012, the S&P 500 returned simply 1.63% dependent on the compound yearly development rate (or - 0.17% when balanced for swelling). This proposes stocks may offer a superior incentive than they did before the downturn, which could look good for what's to come. Markets may (and we underline may) beat in the years to come, aligning yearly returns more with long term chronicled averages.

Setting up Your Investment Spreadsheet

Since you've gotten an opportunity to analyze some speculative spreadsheet models and consider the likely paces of return you should utilize, it's a great opportunity to set up your own investment spreadsheet. This spreadsheet will fill in as your all-inclusive strategy going ahead. It will follow your assessable, 401(k), and Roth IRA investments and will incorporate a Grand Total segment so you can rapidly observe where you remain toward the finish of every year.

When your spreadsheet is set up, you should simply return to it once every year to survey how you're doing against plan. You'll refresh it by then to incorporate real outcomes rather than gauges for the year simply past. That will build the precision and pertinence of your plan going ahead.

We ask you not to avoid this progression regardless of whether the word spreadsheet gives you chills. We guarantee to keep it basic. All the more significantly, we offer a spreadsheet format on the web if you'd lean toward not assemble the layout without any preparation. (Also, for what reason would you?)

To profit yourself of this easy route, essentially visit our site at wherewebe.com and download the Excel spreadsheet layout under thc "Early Retirement" tab. It's a similar format we present here, and it as of now has the entirety of the segments and recipes set up for you. There's even a supportive guidance sheet on a different tab inside the archive.

You'll despite everything need to go into the spreadsheet itself, obviously, and physically enter the dollar sums you hope to invest every year, except this is a easy matter of information passage. When this is done, the spreadsheet is custom fitted to your circumstance and you can start tweaking it to play with various investment situations.

There are noteworthy tax preferences to 401(k) and Roth IRA accounts that make them important to for all intents and purposes each individual getting ready for retirement.

Any progressions you make to the spreadsheet are right away reflected in the reality. For example, if you change the yearly pace of come back from 9% to 10%, you can immediately watch your sums increment. If you modify your assessable investment sums from $5,000 to $10,000 every year, you can perceive how your retirement fund at the base of the spreadsheet promptly becomes greater.

Try not to feel constrained by the example numbers remembered for the spreadsheet; they are essentially illustrative and have not any more bearing without anyone else reality than they do on yours.

Make Your Spreadsheet a Living Document

We urge you to think about your end-all strategy not as a solitary archive unchangeable however as an adaptable report that can be adjusted and tweaked voluntarily. The thought is to play with various situations until you land at one that feels right to you. If your material circumstance transforms, you can change the spreadsheet to mirror your new reality, in this manner keeping it present and pertinent to your life. Prior cycles of your plan can generally be put something aside for the index, yet ensure the current year's plan is as precise to your certifiable circumstance as could be allowed.

A spreadsheet with no pertinence to your genuine honestly misses the general purpose. If you figured you could save $10,000 every year except it rapidly becomes evident you can't, don't forsake your plan by and large. Rather, just change it to make it fit what you can do. Try dividing your objective to $5,000 every year. Check whether that works better for your present circumstance. You can generally raise your investment objectives later on. It's smarter to point a little lower – particularly at an early stage when you're attempting to make great contributing propensities – than to get debilitated out and out and surrender.

Altering Your Spreadsheet

If you as of now have a simple comprehension of Excel, when the down to earth tips that follow ought to be sufficient to manage you through how to change and refresh the spreadsheet.

Finding a workable pace Egg Amount

Your definitive objective in utilizing the investment spreadsheet is to connect numbers until you see the savings sum you landed at in Chapter 9 ("Calculate Your Nest Egg") show up in the Grand Total segment opposite the year wherein you in a perfect world wish to resign. Playing with the numbers and rates can assist you with making sense of how best to accomplish that objective.

If your procure enough to have the option to invest sizable measures of money every year, the procedure might be generally clear and you might be done in the blink of an eye. In any case, for all of us, it might take more time and exertion.

You may understand, for example, that you need to save significantly more than you suspected you did so as to arrive at your objective. By then you have some significant choices to make. You can either keep your aggressive yearly targets set up and focus on working considerably harder to accomplish them, or you can expand your time skyline (e.g., from 15 to 20 years) to give yourself more opportunity to arrive at your objective, or you can reevaluate your yearly salary needs in retirement and begin pondering how to resign on less.

All choices are on the table now. Try not to pay attention to everything as well: a lively and test frame of mind will help you in excess of a worried and baffled one. Try various methodologies like trying various caps and see which one fits you best. Resigning early is anything but a one-size-fits-all plan. Your answer should be custom fitted to accommodate your own conditions and needs.

What-If Scenarios

Since none of us can read the future, it bodes well to explore different avenues regarding diverse what if situations to perceive how they may influence you not far off. What if your investments just return 8% rather than 9%. Would you be able to at present arrive at your objectives? What if they return 11% or 12%. Why not test it out and see? What if your activity possibilities improve drastically and you begin contributing twofold what you figured you could part of the way through your investment years. Such was the situation for us. Why not run a what if situation that expect a multiplying of investment sums part of the way through your plan and perceive how it influences your outcomes.

Is My Goal Achievable?

When you've connected numbers that let you arrive at your objective in the time you'd like, when you need to ask yourself the immensely significant inquiry: Is this extremely reachable for me given my present circumstance? Will I truly save $10,000 one year from now?

Since at last your numbers must be grounded actually if this is to be something other than an activity in calculating. They need to jive with your certifiable conditions. So begin to consider where that $10,000 is truly going to originate from one year from now.

Maybe you have a 401(k) plan at work and you can consequently store 10% or a greater amount of your check easily into that. Also, maybe you can set up programmed payments from your financial indexes into a Roth IRA account every month. What amount can you truly save every month without driving things excessively far? Keep in mind, this is a long distance race, not a run, so you would prefer not to push so hard you make yourself or your family hopeless.

If you start to detect your favored situation, anyway wonderful in its result, is overambitious regarding its everyday requests on you or your family, have a go at easing off a piece. Lower your investment sums in the early years and perceive how that influences your general retirement plan.

Perhaps 15 years is essentially unreasonably aggressive for the present and you'll need to make due with 20 years – in any event until your material conditions improve. Keep in mind, whatever plan you land at, it's not unchangeable. You may hesitantly choose to focus on 20 years just to get a startling advancement at work, and out of nowhere 15 years is back on the table. That is an ideal opportunity to pull out your spreadsheet and have another look.

Let your real life direct the numbers you plug into your spreadsheet, particularly during the early years. Bind them to the real world. Attempt to envision truly saving the sum you see on paper in the coming year, and if you can do that and like it, when that is a genuine number that has genuine incentive to you and your circumstance.

If, then again, one year from now's number causes you to flinch, when it's back to the point where it all began. Attempt a more modest number until you can take a gander at it without feeling panicky. At last you need a number that doesn't make your palms sweat!

Getting Buy-In on Your Investment Plan

This is as acceptable a period as any to make reference to the significance of including your mate or huge other in the early retirement arranging process. It's dreadfully difficult to go only it with regards to putting something aside for early retirement – except if you happen to be well and genuinely single. If you're a couple, when you two ought to in a perfect world be in agreement.

Collaboration and Compromise

We urge you either to take a gander at the spreadsheet together and attempt various situations as a group – or else share the consequences of a few distinct situations with your companion and get info and purchase in from the get-go. Check whether the person in question is energetic about your general methodology. If you get the sense your plans are excessively forceful from their stance, see what you can do to mitigate them a piece.

Ideally your mate will be as energized as you are about resigning early, yet if not, you may need to think of a trade off plan. Make certain to tell your life partner how significant the possibility of early retirement is to you, yet in addition attempt to be adaptable about explicit retirement dates and yearly investment sums.

If your mate really wouldn't like to resign early as you do, that doesn't mean you fundamentally need to forsake your plans by and large. Truth be told it could make getting ready for retirement simpler rather than harder. If the individual in question really likes to keep working and isn't unduly put out at the idea of your resigning early, when you may need to save short of what you in any case would have. Your life partner will keep on accepting a pay, so a less thorough timetable of contributing might be required – which could be better answer for both of you.

Refreshing Your Spreadsheet with Actual Results

When your spreadsheet is set up, you should simply return to it once every year to survey how you're doing against plan. You'll connect genuine outcomes toward the finish of every year so you can anticipate future years utilizing genuine numbers rather than gauges. Every year you do this, the future turns into somewhat less fluffy on the grounds that you have all the more genuine information to work with. Likewise, the window until your objective retirement date keeps on narrowing, so there are less years in which you need to depend on instructed mystery to find a workable pace.

Keeping tabs on Your Development

Keeping tabs on your development lets you calibrate your plan en route and screen if you are still on course to resign by your deadline. We urge you to truly investigate your spreadsheet at any rate once per year so as to think about real performance against plan. Give some cautious consideration regarding how best to continue dependent on the undeniable realities before you.

What if You're Ahead of Schedule

Being in front of calendar is a fine issue to have: make the most of your favorable luck. If your material circumstance has improved – if you've gotten a significant raise at work, for instance – presently may be a decent time to consider raising your yearly investment sums for the years to come. By doing so you may find you can resign even sooner than anticipated, or else that you will have a bigger retirement fund than you suspected you would. Either prospect is very superb to consider.

What if You're Behind Schedule?

In case you're only a little off base at whatever year, there's no compelling reason to stress. That may basically be the after-effect of poor economic situations over the present moment, something over which you have essentially no control. If you're in a bear showcase, when it's not really amazing you aren't arriving at your normal objectives for the year. In any case, that is okay, you should let yourself know, since you're purchasing more portions of stock at a lower cost than you could have something else. In the positively trending business sector years that commonly trail a bear advertise, your profits are probably going to surpass desires, and in those years you ought to have the option to compensate for lost ground.

What if You're Way Off Track?

In case you're off track follow and have altogether less set aside than you figured you would before the finish of a specific year or series of years, when you have some genuine investment to do.

In the first place, attempt to decide why you missed the mark concerning your objectives. Did you invest as much as you had planned to? If not, maybe your objectives were basically excessively driven. You may need to bring them more into line with what you can really achieve and modify your all-inclusive strategy appropriately.

Then again, maybe the business sectors encountered an extreme downturn and through no flaw of your own you were brushed off kilter from where you figured you would be by this point. All things considered your yearly investment objectives aren't the issue, however you despite everything need to figure out how to refocus. It's horrible wishing things were better: you need to make them so. So choose which of the accompanying you need to do:

•   Invest extra in the coming a very long time so as to get back up with your unique objectives.

•   Increase your time skyline to give your investments more opportunity to compound and develop.

•   Plan to manage with less in retirement, which means reexamining your spending and way of life decisions as you head into what's to come.

Obviously you can generally dare to dream the business sectors unequivocally outflank in the years to come and fix the issue for you. However, since that is totally beyond your ability to do anything about, it's risky to depend on — particularly in case you're altogether behind where you figured you would be. Better to bring matters into your own hands and modify your end-all strategy to realign it with your circumstance as it stands today. Else you chance falling further and advance behind on your objectives and feeling increasingly demoralized to where you basically choose to surrender – and that would be a genuine disgrace. Raise or lower your objectives to make them correspond with the real world, however don't surrender through and through or you'll be doing yourself an injury over the long haul.

Tracking Your Portfolio

You can follow your portfolio performance easily on your investment association's site, obviously, yet you may likewise need to make a basic portfolio tracker on Yahoo's Finance site page. You can pull it up immediately without entering a client name and secret phrase each time since there is no delicate data on the site. All it comprises of is the common store images and the quantity of offers you possess. Along these lines it offers a brisk method to check your aggregates and keep tabs on your development all the time.

To make your own portfolio tracker, go to Yahoo's Finance site, click on "My Portfolios," and select "Make Portfolio." Give your new portfolio a name (we call our own "Aggregate") and start adding common store images to it, trailed by the quantity of offers you possess for each. Hit save and you're ready. Simply click on "Include/Edit Holdings" if you need to change or refresh any data.

The main drawback to portfolio trackers like this is you need to occasionally refresh the offer data if you need to keep it current. The offer sums don't consequently refresh as they will without anyone else investment company's site.

Tracking Performance

We prescribe you save a duplicate of your investment spreadsheet every prior year rolling out any improvements to it. That way you have reinforcement if something ought to turn out badly. It additionally gives you a convenient authentic index if you ought to ever need to contrast your present spreadsheet with ones from earlier years.

Tracking Cumulative Goals versus Actuals

When you initially build up your yearly objectives, you might need to make an outline that lets you analyze combined objectives versus total actuals.

Your underlying plan speaks to a starting in particular, so don't anticipate accuracy of it past a year or two into what's to come.

Tracking Annual Investment Amounts

The last numbers you might need to follow are your yearly investment sums (objective versus genuine).

CHAPTER TWELVE

CONSTANTLY INVEST IN INDEX FUNDS

When you have planned your investment spreadsheet, you should realize precisely the amount you have to invest over the coming year. Presently take that sum and gap by twelve to decide the specific sum you have to put every month so as to meet your yearly objective. All that remaining parts is to ensure you really invest that sum every month, paying little heed to how the market is performing.

There ought to be no doubt starting with one month then onto the next if you will invest: obviously you will invest. It doesn't make a difference what the business sectors are doing – regardless of whether they are up, down, or sideways. You have no power over that so you shouldn't worry about it. However, you do have authority over making your month to month investments as planned. Remain consistent with those month to month responsibilities and you'll have made your greatest stride towards accomplishing your objective of early retirement.

Put Your Investments on AutoPilot

The key to contributing routinely is to put your investments on autopilot. If you robotize the reserve funds process, it occurs without your pondering it – and that is something worth being thankful for, because you likely could be the cause all your own problems with regards to contributing on a customary calendar. Things disrupt the general flow, costs include, money's tight, the business sectors are down, you're feeling disheartened, you would prefer not to write the check, you would prefer not to consider it at the present time, you don't have the opportunity or the vitality – the reasons the human personality can concoct not to accomplish something are downright stunning. Autopilot disposes of the greater part of those reasons.

Set It and Forget It

The best spot to begin computerizing your investments is grinding away. If your organization offers a 401(k) plan then you should pursue programmed findings from your check. Since the money is removed easily from your check before you ever observe it, it's as though it never existed in any case, so you don't miss it to such an extent. You don't need to leave behind it by hand – by composing a check, say, and seeing your checkbook balance get lower. Via computerizing the procedure, you've wiped out the core man – you – from the condition.

You can likewise set up programmed month to month moves easily out of your financial indexes into your assessable and Roth IRA accounts. You settle on the sum every month and which day of the month the exchange is made. It won't be very as imperceptible as the 401(k) process since you'll see the money vanish out of your financial indexes every month, except at any rate it's hands-off and you have less to consider, which is your objective. "Set it and overlook it" is a decent proverb with regards to contributing.

Mechanizing your investments keeps you on the directly to your yearly investment objective in a manner nothing else will. Your solitary obligation when becomes ensuring you have adequate assets close by to cover the programmed moves. Think about your month to month investments as you would your month to month contract payment. Doubtlessly you're going to make that payment: it is anything but an alternative, it's a need. That is the mentality you need to cultivate.

Pay Yourself First

You've presumably heard the articulation "pay yourself first," which means put resources into your own future first before covering different tabs or costs. That may sound somewhat outrageous; however it gives top need to you. Mechanizing your payments makes it undeniably more probable you won't avoid a payment to yourself. It pressures you to disclose more than what would have been prudent as it were, which isn't all awful when you consider what number of different things in life are getting out for you to burn through money on them. The alarm call of spending is somewhat simpler to oppose if you attach yourself to the pole like Odysseus and give yourself no other decision yet to keep with it.

So, make certain to leave yourself a little support when you select your month to month investment sum so you aren't pushing straight facing the deadline points of what you can deal with monetarily. Better to choose a littler sum you realize you can oversee throughout each and every month than to push excessively hard and end up stone cold broke at whatever month.

Consistency is your objective, not stretch and budgetary hardship. Leave your month to month contribution to your future alone a positive part of your life, something you can like, instead of a negative weight that puts a strain on your reality.

Use Dollar Cost Averaging

Putting your investments on autopilot lets you exploit a strategy called dollar cost averaging. With dollar cost averaging you invest an equivalent measure of money every month in a profit paying little heed to the offer value, which implies you wind up obtaining more offers when costs are low and less offers when costs are high.

This methodology will in general lessen your normal offer cost after some time. A singular amount invested at the same time could be invested at simply an inappropriate minute when costs are particularly high. Dollar cost averaging protects you against advertise risk somewhat on the grounds that you spread your buys out equitably over an extensive stretch of time and over a scope of costs.

Suppose you choose to buy $100 every long stretch of a specific shared store for a quarter of a year. In the main month the store is valueed at $50, so your fixed month to month investment of $100 gets both of you shares. One month from now the valuation is $33 so your $100 gets you three offers. The most recent month it is $25 so your $100 gets you four offers. That is nine offers out and out which you've purchased at a normal cost of about $33 each ($300 ÷ 9). If you had put all $300 in a singular amount in the primary month, you would have paid $50 per share and just got six offers. By dollar cost averaging you have discounted your normal offer cost and decreased the market chance that can accompany contributing a single amount at the same time.

Dollar cost averaging likewise helps balance the regular human inclination to purchase a profit when it is performing admirably and not get it when it is performing ineffectively. We as a whole like a victor, isn't that right? Yet, purchasing an advantage when it is flying high methods getting it at a higher offer cost. Intelligently we should need to get it when it is failing to meet expectations and we can get more offers for our money, yet this isn't in every case how human instinct functions. Dollar cost averaging encourages us do what we ought to do in any case, which is purchase more portions of a investment when it is "on special" and less when it isn't.

What Others Say

My portfolio might be unreasonably traditionalist for you. Assuming this is the case, think about after an increasingly customary methodology:

• Safe portfolio 20 percent stocks, 80 percent bonds. For over 70 years, this portfolio has arrived at the midpoint of 7.0 percent a year. Its most noticeably awful year was lost 10.1 percent. It lost money 17 percent of the years.

• Balanced portfolio 50 percent stocks, 50 percent bonds. During a similar timespan, this portfolio has found the middle value of 8.7 percent a year. Its most exceedingly terrible year was lost 22.5 percent. It lost money 22 percent of the years.

• Risky portfolio 80 percent stocks, 20 percent bonds. This

portfolio has found the middle value of 10.0 percent a year. Its most noticeably terrible year was lost 34.9 percent. It lost money 28 percent of the years.

You see the example, isn't that right? The more risky the portfolio, the more hearty the development was in the acceptable years. However, losses were more noteworthy during the terrible years and there were all the more awful years.

In picking which portfolio suits you best, think about your age. The more established you are, the fewer risks you should need to manage. Why? In case you're resigned, the reasonable outcomes of your losses can-not be soothed by your present place of employment salary. Regardless of whether you're not resigned, you basically do not have the advantage of having quite a few years to compensate for moderate-to-overwhelming losses.

A Closer Look at Stop-Losses:

The Exit Strategy That Professionals Use

One thing that professionals concur on is this: Whatever your methodology, will undoubtedly make some awful stock choices. Indeed, there's no assurance that your great choices will dwarf the terrible ones. Here's the uplifting news: It doesn't make a difference.

If you make twice the same number of terrible stock buy choices as great ones, shouldn't you lose twice as much as you've earned? No. Since stock contributing isn't just about purchasing. It's likewise about selling. As significant as purchasing the correct stocks at the ideal time is, it is similarly imperative to sell the correct stocks at the perfect time. And, you're not going to settle on indistinguishable selling choices for devaluing stocks from you would for acknowledging stocks.

Cut your loss. Ride your victors. Experts realize when to offer a stock and when to hold it by utilizing a trailing stop-loss.

The trailing stop expects you to follow the cost of your stock and sell it when it drops to a specific level. The sell point can be activated at 10 percent, 20 percent, 30 percent, or whatever, underneath the stock's most noteworthy selling cost. I prescribe 25 percent.

There's nothing magical about this number. It just appears to suit most stock leave circumstances. In any case, it carries one in number ramifications with respect to what your risk resistance ought to be. A decent proportion is one to three. That is, if you are happy to chance a 25 percent loss, you ought to sensibly expect in any event a 75 percent return on your investment. If you are told, for instance, that a 30 percent return however no higher is normal from a specific investment, your stop-loss point ought to be activated at 10 percent, not 25 percent.

Settle on an Overall Investment Mix

One of the most significant choices you can make as a financial specialist is choosing your general investment mix of stocks, bonds, and money. Your individual investments inside that mix are of auxiliary significance to the portfolio designation itself. Regardless of whether you purchase this specific stock or that specific stock is less significant than choosing the amount of your portfolio should comprise of stocks in any case.

Risk Tolerance and Time Horizon

Your investment mix ought to be your very own impression chance resilience and time skyline. Suppose you make some long memories skyline and a generally high resistance for chance (or if nothing else you figure you do; you'll know for sure after you've braved your first significant downturn). All things considered you might need to put vigorously in stocks and have only a foothold in bonds during your essential contributing years, since stocks offer the best potential for long haul development.

Then again, if you have a moderately low resilience for risk and suspect you won't have the option to rest around evening time if a lot of your money is riding on stocks, when you'll need to keep an increasingly adjusted plan of stocks, securities, and money to help cradle the instability that definitely accompanies owning just stocks.

Your time skyline to retirement is especially critical to consider while deciding your investment mix. A portfolio 80% to 100% put resources into the financial exchange may bode well in your start and core contributing years, yet as you close to retirement you have less time to recuperate from genuine downturns in the market. Surely once you resign you need a dependable source from which to pull back money if the financial exchange should crash, so having a strong situation in bonds gets vital. Capital protection and pay age become in any event as significant as the requirement for extra capital gratefulness once you resign.

During our essential contributing years we invested 100%

(or extremely near it) in stocks and stock common assets. Our superseding objective during those years was capital appreciation. We weren't worried about market instability on the grounds that our time skyline was long enough by then that we realized we could brave whatever tempests may come. Indeed we saw downturns in the market as purchasing openings, and we profited by them once the business sectors ricocheted back and stock costs rose once more.

We stood by longer than was reasonable, however, to cut out a huge situation in bonds as we moved toward retirement. Truth be told it wasn't until we sold our home in the primary year of retirement and put the money into a security subsidize that we built up our first significant situation in quite a while. (Despite the fact that we had $30,000 set aside in a security support for use over the primary year of our retirement as an incomplete fence against risk.)

Fortunately for us things turned out, however looking back it would have been shrewder to gradually expand our bond possessions in the course of the most recent five years paving the way to retirement. When we could have distributed a portion of the money from the offer of our home to stocks and the rest to bonds dependent on our favoured investment mix as we entered retirement.

The Case for a More Conservative Approach

You may have seen from the table that you possibly need to forfeit a modest quantity of development if you have a portfolio comprising of 80% stocks and 20% bonds when contrasted with 100% stocks. The distinction in the normal yearly return is just 0.5% (9.9% versus 9.4%), which isn't a lot, particularly when you factor in the additional genuine feelings of serenity those bonds may give you. Indeed, even a 70/30 stock/bond portfolio offers an entirely decent normal yearly profit of 9.0% based for verifiable midpoints.

If you are a moderate, chance loath investor, you can breathe easy in light of this. It is as yet feasible for you to take a development planned position while moderating your risk somewhat by putting 70% in stocks and 30% in bonds. That would fulfil the requirement for capital thankfulness during your essential contributing years while as yet diminishing a portion of the instability en route.

One could seemingly do more awful than setting a 70/30 portfolio mix from the earliest starting point and keeping up that mix through life.

If you are put 70% or more in stocks, when you stand a decent possibility of arriving at your initial retirement objectives. Substantially less than that, in any case, and you start to get into a hazy area where you can in any case hope to arrive at your objective in the end, however maybe not as fast as you would have something else.

The Risk of Being Overly Conservative

Anything short of half stocks and half bonds/money during your essential contributing years and you start to enter what we would consider as an excessively traditionalist space where capital gratefulness takes a secondary lounge to the view of wellbeing. We state impression of security since it's a reasonable inquiry whether you truly are more secure with an excessively moderate portfolio mix. Why? Since there is more than one sort of risk with regards to contributing.

Amazingly moderate financial specialists will in general

spotlight exclusively on advertise chance, which is the danger of losing money from variances in securities exchange costs (i.e., if stocks go down, you lose money). Many individuals are so scared of market risk they won't think about putting resources into stocks. They would prefer to place all their money in a financial balance gaining 1% premium. They accept they're avoiding any and all risks that way.

However, they're most likely not satisfactorily mindful of expansion risk, which is the risk swelling will consume their investments quicker than they can develop, bringing in their money worth less and less after some time. If expansion develops at 3% every year and their investments just gain 1%, when generally they are losing 2% every single year. Unexpectedly that sheltered financial balance doesn't appear to be so protected anything else, in any event with regards to their long haul purchasing power.

When individuals have a comprehension of expansion risk, they're commonly additionally ready to investigate a decent stock and bond portfolio. In spite of the real factors of market chance, the securities exchange by and large returns about 9% every year over the long haul and securities return all things considered about 5% to 6% every year. In this manner a well-adjusted stock and bond portfolio should keep you in front of expansion. You'll show signs of improvement genuine profit for your investment than you would with a "sheltered" ledger.

Keeping Fund Expenses Low

The normal shared store organization charges expenses multiple times higher than Vanguard's. These charges include after some time and have a critical effect to long haul performance.

Think about this: without any expenses by any means, a $100,000 portfolio gaining 9% every year would develop to $560,000 in 20 years. With a 1% yearly charge the last worth would be $458,000 – more than $100,000 less. If the yearly charge were 3%, which isn't impossible with some shared assets, the last worth would just reach $305,000 – more than $250,000 less. You can perceive any reason why charges matter and why we may choose to go with a investment firm like Vanguard therefore alone.

The topic of charges is considerably increasingly significant with regards to security reserves. A high expense can rapidly overpower a security store's presentation. For instance, if security finance returns 4% in a given year, when a 1% charge is equivalent to 25% of that arrival. If a similar store returns 1% in a given year, when a 1% charge successfully converts into a 0% return. In this manner a low-return condition, regardless of whether for stocks or bonds, just builds the significance of keeping charges low.

Vanguard's ultra-low costs apply to both stock and security reserves. To feature only two models, the cost proportions for its leader Index 500 Fund and its Total Bond Market Index Fund are an incredibly low 0.05% and 0.10% separately. (These are the cost proportions for the favoured Admiral Shares, which require a base reserve equalization of $10,000.) It's difficult to anticipate obviously superior to that.

Whichever investment firm you wind up picking, we suggest you ensure their costs are lower than the standard and that you keep your investments inside that solitary firm however much as could reasonably be expected for the good of simplicity. We additionally prescribe you look at the expenses charged as well as the scope of administrations offered by various investment firms before settling on a ultimate choice with respect to which one is directly for you. For example, if you want to do the vast majority of your putting resources into singular stocks as opposed to common assets, you may locate an online investment firm represent considerable authority in minimal effort stock exchanges that suits your needs superior to Vanguard.

Why Index Funds Make Sense

If you consider contributing basically an unfortunate obligation and not an enthusiasm all by itself, when file subsidize contributing may be the correct response for you. It's an extraordinary plan if you need to keep your budgetary life as easy and low-upkeep as could reasonably be expected.

With file subsidizes you quit attempting to beat the business sectors and rather just stay aware of them. File supports reflect the business sectors they track as opposed to attempting to beat them. They imitate as intently as conceivable the investment weighting and returns of the benchmark index they are intended to follow.

Maybe the most well known index store of all is likewise the first at any point made: the Vanguard 500 Index Fund, which tracks the S&P 500 Index. It was made by John Bogle of The Vanguard Group in 1975. Vanguard is currently the biggest shared reserve organization in the U.S., and the store has become a backbone of numerous an investment portfolio.

We like the reality index finances aren't helpless before any one individual, regardless of how good natured. Indeed, even a decent reserve administrator once in a while settles on terrible investment decisions. At that point, as well, dynamic reserve administrators once in a while resign or change investment firms or are supplanted, and the following chief may follow an impressively extraordinary and more hazardous investment procedure. You don't need to stress over this with an inactively overseen list subsidize. We think this makes file supports a progressively dependable investment over the long haul.

Tax Efficiency

Index supports will in general be very tax productive because offer turnover is negligible. Organizations are seldom added to or expelled from the S&P 500, for instance, so reserves following it once in a while need to purchase or sell shares. That implies there are less capital increases dispersions to stress over at charge time.

Index reserves are additionally easy to claim at charge season because the shared store organization gives all of you the data you have to provide details regarding your tax documents. Contrast this with an individual stock where you are liable for figuring and announcing the cost premise of the offers you have obtained, some of the time over a time of numerous years, when the offers are sold. Talking from individual experience, we can reveal to you this includes unwelcome confusions at charge time.

A Simpler Approach

With singular stocks it assists with having the option to read and comprehend an accounting report and a profit and misfortune explanation so as to effectively survey an organization's essential wellbeing. It requires some investment, exertion, and expertise to precisely evaluate a solitary organization and its stock, choose if the stock value speaks to a decent worth, and decide when to purchase the stock as well as when to sell it. Stock file assets by examination require less choices and less investigation.

Since they are comprised of hundreds (or here and there a huge number of) singular stocks, stock index reserves are purchase and-hold investments that by their very nature require little in the method for customized consideration. They must be evaluated in the total. You may assess the cost proportion of an Index 500 store, for instance, and choose whether or not the reserve is a solid match for your portfolio, yet it would look bad to dissect each of the 500 individual organizations making up the list since they are being sold as a bundle at any rate. You couldn't dismantle them regardless of whether you needed to.

By a similar token, security list subsidizes offer an a lot simpler way to deal with putting resources into bonds than experiencing the cerebral pains of laddering singular bonds. With a security subsidize you get proficient administration, wide enhancement, and high liquidity requiring little to no effort. There are no charges for purchasing or selling portions of no-heap security list finance, while the offer request that spread purchase and sell singular bonds can be very high. For convenience and ease, it's difficult to beat a decent security index subsidize.

With index assets all in all, your life doesn't need to rotate around your investments. You carry on with your life as typical and do the things you love to do. In the interim your investments are working for you out of sight without your giving a lot of consideration to them.

Not any more attempting to beat the business sectors. No all the more going through hours reading budgetary magazines and attempting to make sense of the following hot stock or the following hot shared reserve. Basically invest it, overlook it, and be finished. This purchase and-hold procedure makes your life (and your assessments) a lot less difficult. Rather than responding to the most recent market news, you protect yourself from those worries and spotlight on what you can control, which is your month to month contributions to the file finances you have picked.

Easy entry and Usability

A last advantage of common assets as a rule is that they offer superbly simple access with regards to purchasing and selling shares, moving offers among reserves, and pulling back money. This can be a significant factor when choosing where to invest your money.

Put resources into Your Core Holdings

Your core holdings are the bunch of investments that form the establishment of your portfolio. They are the investments you clutch for a lifetime. Hence you need to ensure they are top notch investments with a past filled with relentless performance.

We prescribe you utilize extensively expanded file assets as your core holdings. Only three stock file reserves are sufficient to give you overall inclusion for values. You truly needn't bother with more than that! To those you should include one more reserve for U.S. bonds. Here are the four store types we suggest for your core holdings:

1.   S&P 500 Index Fund. A index support that mirrors the S&P 500 will give you expansive introduction to the main 500 enormous top organizations in the

U.S. Huge top represents huge capitalization, and these are the biggest, generally ground-breaking, and most well-promoted organizations in the U.S. Together they represent around three-fourths of the U.S. securities exchange's worth. Any reasonable person would agree no U.S.- based portfolio is finished without a S&P 500 index subsidize.

2.   Broadened Market Index Fund. A file finance that mirrors the remainder of the U.S. financial exchange gives you expansive introduction to U.S. mid-top and little top stocks. Such assets commonly put resources into around 3,000 stocks representing around one-fourth of the market top of the U.S. financial exchange. An all-inclusive market store (or S&P culmination index) is viewed as a supplement to a S&P 500 list support, and together the two give presentation to the whole U.S. value showcase. Mid-and little top markets will in general be more unstable than the enormous top market yet in addition offer the potential for more significant yields as time goes on.

3.   All out International Stock Index Fund. The world is greater than simply the U.S., so it bodes well to have presentation to the greatest, best, and quickest developing values from different nations around the world. Search for a index finance that gives you wide presentation to the all out global securities exchange, including both created and developing economies. Developing business sector stocks can be more unpredictable than local stocks, and money hazard can include significantly greater

unpredictability. If this is a worry for you, consider putting less right now the other two value reserves.

4.   All out Bond Market Index Fund. A decent portfolio ought to incorporate a core store that mirrors the general U.S. investment grade security showcase. A complete security advertise reserve will normally invest around 33% of its profits in corporate securities and 66% in U.S. government obligations of shifting developments (short-, middle of the road , and long haul). While security finances will in general be delicate to increments in loan costs, their general dangers are lower than stock assets.

Any significant investment firm will offer file assets of these four kinds, so whichever firm you pick, you ought to have the option to discover great matches.

Rate to Invest in Each Fund

From the outset you may need to set aside enough to meet least store prerequisites for each reserve before proceeding onward to the following. In any case, when every one of the three assets are fully operational, you can invest as little as $100 every month naturally into each store starting now and into the foreseeable future. That makes it conceivable to put on a month to month premise in equivalent augmentations.

If you lean toward a more hazard opposed methodology, you might need to put a higher rate in the Index 500 store and a lower rate in the other two. Of the three assets, the International Stock reserve is most likely the most elevated hazard since it includes both money chance and developing business sector chance into the condition. Let your own inclinations direct you as far as the particular rates you decide to put resources into each sort of reserve: for instance, half Index 500, 30% Extended Market, 20% International

Stock.

At the point when your monetary circumstance takes into consideration it, you ought to likewise make an underlying interest in a Total Bond Market list support. If you are designating basically 100% to stocks during the early and core long periods of your investment program, essentially keep the security support at the base level until further notice. At that point, around five years before your objective retirement date, start adding more to it.

If you like to keep up a 70/30 or 80/20 blend from the earliest starting point, at that point add to the security finance as a feature of your progressing investment assignment all through your essential contributing years. Remember whether you scale down your home once you resign, any additional value from the deal can make for a decent "flood" investment into your security support.

Abstain from Chasing Returns

It's enticing to go for large returns, particularly as a starting investor. You need to score huge and rake in some serious money, so once in a while, shockingly, your first investments end up being among your most noticeably terrible. Unquestionably that was the situation for us. Rather than purchasing basics file reserves, which appeared to be honestly exhausting to us at that point, we pursued the conceivably more significant yields offered by effectively oversaw and claim to fame reserves.

The Lure of Top 100 Lists

As amateur investors we scoured the money related magazines for the "most elite" common assets. Top 100 indexes that positioned assets dependent on their ongoing exhibition were a specific draw. Maybe it isn't too amazing hence that we ended up devotedly following the best assets on these rundowns and causing our underlying determinations from the ones to at or close to the top. Whatever store had played out the best in the course of the last five or ten years was the one we needed to put resources into next. Well-set promotions for the equivalent common finances would in general underscore the intelligence of putting resources into these assets over all others.

They state past performance is no assurance of future outcomes, and it turns out they would not joke about this. The issue with pursuing returns is that you wind up purchasing high and selling low – the specific inverse of what you need to do. Assets with outsized returns have frequently needed to face outsized challenges so as to get where they are at the highest point of the leaderboard. They once in a while remain there for long. The enormous wagers that got them there in any case regularly sink them once advertises move or financial specialist conclusion changes. Cost proportions can likewise be drastically higher for these high-flying assets, and that will in general force them back.

High Valuations, High Risks, High Expenses

If you need to purchase specialty advertise assets, at any rate hold back to do it until after you have a sound center portfolio developed. Area and claim to fame assets ought to be viewed as pastry, not the principle course.

Consistently purchasing minimal effort account assets may not be the most charming thing on the planet, yet wonder why you are putting resources into the primary spot. Is it for the surge that originates from making a major return? Or then again is it for the award of arriving at your retirement objective effectively? The race to score huge has more to do with betting than contributing, while a purchase and-hold way to deal with list support contributing is one you can use for an incredible duration as a solid system for getting rich gradually.

Different Options Besides Mutual Funds

Common supports aren't the main game around: there are other practical choices for getting rich gradually through a program of consistent investments. We'd prefer to contact quickly on a couple of these.

Exchange Traded Funds

Or ETFs, are close cousins of shared assets. They will in general be minimal effort and assessment proficient and they exchange like a stock. Though shared assets are purchased or sold toward the finish of each exchanging day, ETFs exchange for the duration of the day at costs that can be higher or lower than their net resource value. There is no base speculation prerequisite for ETFs – a key advantage to starting financial specialists – and you can invest to such an extent or as little money as you wish.

ETFs likewise offer tax breaks to financial specialists. Common finances must disperse capital increases to their investors on a yearly premise (i.e., at whatever point shares have been sold at a profit so as to keep the portfolio in accordance with the weighted account being followed). These additions are assessable regardless of whether you reinvest the dispersions in more portions of a similar store.

By correlation, financial specialists in ETFs for the most part possibly acknowledge capital increases when they sell shares. This gives them more command over when they understand capital gains and need to pay charges on them.

Most ETFs track a account and are in this manner exceptionally differentiated. They can hold stocks, bonds, and even wares. Their cost proportions will in general be lower than those for practically identical common assets. One purpose behind this is an ETF doesn't need to keep up a money save for recoveries. The Vanguard S&P 500 ETF (VOO), for instance, has a ultra-low 0.05% cost proportion. That matches the cost proportion for the "Chief naval officer Shares" variant of its Index 500 store and is lower than the "Financial specialist Shares" rendition.

Financier commissions here and there apply when you are purchasing or selling an ETF. A significant exemption is ordinarily made, in any case, when you are purchasing or selling ETFs offered by your own investment firm. For instance, Vanguard ETFs can be purchased and sold sans commission through Vanguard Brokerage Services. To dishearten day exchanging, Vanguard permits 25 free exchanges of a similar ETF in a year time span before confining further exchanging for 60 days.

An enhanced ETF list finance held over the long haul can be a strong investment decision, however the very capacity of an ETF to exchange like a stock can now and then be a drawback in that it builds the compulsion to take part in showcase timing or momentary hypothesis.

In any case, there is a great deal to like about ETFs and very little to disdain. We can positively observe the ethics of putting resources into them. Maybe out of a feeling of nature if nothing else, we have stayed committed common reserve speculators. We accept shared assets and ETFs offer generally practically identical encounters as long as you are as of now contributing with a minimal effort speculation firm like Vanguard.

Singular Value Stocks

Singular stocks offer another commendable option in contrast to common assets or ETFs. If you choose to go this course, make certain to give yourself fundamental training in money related issues first so you have the basis should have been an insightful financial specialist. We suggest you read a book or two about Warren Buffett, broadly thought about the best speculator of the twentieth century, to get a thought of his worth way to deal with contributing.

Buffett's recommendation at its most essential is to buy organizations at a huge markdown to their characteristic worth, which means staying away from high-flying development stocks and adhering rather to organizations that are underestimated by the market for some explanation. These organizations might be incidentally on the ropes however are probably going to make a solid rebound.

If you can figure out how to be a contrarian financial specialist and purchase stocks when they're whipped however on a very basic level sound, you'll have gone far towards turning into a savvy speculator. It's anything but difficult to be attracted by tech organizations making hot items, however these equivalent stocks are as often as possible overrated in light of the fact that such a large number of others need them as well, and typically for an inappropriate reasons. By examination, what may resemble an exhausting old worth stock from the outset can sneak up all of a sudden. Rather than concentrating on what an organization does, we prescribe you focus on what it returns. Leave that alone the deciding element in whether you regard an organization to be energizing or not.

Bear markets can be a keen financial specialist's closest companion. Look out for stocks that have been battered alongside the market all in all despite the fact that their basics are sound. You can likewise search for organizations that have been thumped in the news as of late yet are naturally stable. Netflix rings a bell as an ongoing model. A progression of administrative stumbles sent the stock forcefully descending, yet the basic plan of action was sound and the organization kept on winning profits. A shrewd speculator may have stepped in and bought shares when they were at or close to their lows and received the profits later on.

In some cases an open door tags along that isn't accessible to the overall population.

The significant drawback to putting resources into singular stocks is that your hazard is higher on the grounds that you're put resources into just a bunch of stocks one after another. You're significantly less expanded than you would be with a file finance, and if a couple of your stocks should dive, it could bigly affect your portfolio. Then again, in case you're a canny financial specialist and your stocks perform well, you remain to profit in a major way.

Sadly the vast majority of us aren't as sharp at stock picking as Warren Buffett, so except if you are especially sure of your capacities right now, would prescribe you stick to file finance contributing as the more secure and increasingly dependable methodology. A mix of list support contributing and value stock contributing is likewise worth considering.

Some other Options?

We'll quickly make reference to two different choices that ring a bell for arriving at your initial retirement objectives.

Purchasing and selling land offers a doable way to deal with accomplishing money related autonomy, if you have a decent comprehension of your nearby land advertise and a sharp eye for value. Now and again this may include flipping homes, where you put sweat value into a fixer-upper at that point exchange it at a profit, and in others it may include setting up an assortment of investment properties in your neighbourhood you oversee and lease on a month to month premise. We don't dare to offer guidance regarding this matter since it was not the methodology we took. We only notice it since we are aware of other people who have taken this attach to making a month to month pay stream and it worked for them. We presume it would request more active exertion, however, and might expect you to be genuinely present to deal with the business after you resigned.

Another alternative worth referencing is turning into a business person and going into business. Obviously anything is possible with this methodology: you couldn't possibly get rich gradually yet make easy money if you hit upon the correct business opportunity. Then again, the danger of being a business person can be very high so it takes boldness to pick this choice. In actuality all your investments are tied up on one place – your business – so if it bombs your fantasy of early retirement can flop alongside it, or if nothing else be derailed a period. In any case, if it succeeds it could offer generous monetary prosperity and a real feeling of achievement.

For the individuals who have the creativity and personality for it, the innovative way can be a fantastic and remunerating one. For all of us, a solid activity and some straightforward list finance contributing might be the best course. Unwavering mindsets always win in the end for the greater part of us and offers what might be the most secure way to early retirement.

CHAPTER THIRTEEN

SET UP YOUR PENSION PLAN

Welcome to the great universe of extraordinary retirement bargains for entrepreneurs and independently employed people. Your business regardless of whether it's full-or low maintenance, with or without peed your way to an effortless retirement. At the point when you work for yourself, you in a flash fit the bill to structure your own expense supported retirement plan in which you make major decisions. The reason is this: Because you are independently employed or work a private company, you have no annuity plan from any semblance of an IBM, AT&T or General Motors to cover your retirement needs.

Regardless of how little your business regardless of whether only you make up the whole staff it has similar fundamental rights the mammoths need to introduce and support an appealing profits plan for you and workers. For instance, you can:

•	Choose from a trio of plans that let you put aside as much as 25% of income or $40,000, whichever is less every year. Each dollar that you invest is charge deductible.

•	Write your own retirement ticket with an plan that lets you set an individual retirement-pay target, at that point set aside and deduct whatever is important to meet it.

• Select a "business IRA" with basic administrative work and a contribution limit that goes as high as $30,000, com-pared with the customary IRA's $3,000 (in 2002 and ascending to $5,000 by 2008) roof.

• Use a "straightforward" plan to put aside up to $7,000 (for 2002) of your profit for your retirement, regardless of whether that is 100% of your business pay. On account of the Economic Growth and Tax Relief Reconciliation Act of 2001, the yearly sum you may put aside ascends to $10,000 by 2005. If you are age 50 or older you can make extra make up for lost time contributions to your SIMPLE plan $500 in 2002 ascending to an extra contribution of $2,500 in 2006.

There's additional. While most annuity plans necessitate that you put in a safe spot a similar rate for your workers that you accomplish for yourself, a contort lets some entrepreneurs tip their plans in their own kindness if their representatives are more youthful than they are.

Right now, mention to you what you have to think about every one of these plans so as to pick the best fit for your conditions.

Profits plan rudiments are amazingly comparative whether you're Microsoft or Jane Entrepreneur producing $5,000 of independent work salary from a business in your carport.

With a "defined contribution" retirement plan, your business (even a one-individual business) can put aside a level of income every year. A "defined advantage" plan works backward. As in the TV game show Jeopardy!, you start with the appropriate response a yearly retirement-salary focus based on your personal preference at that point give the inquiry. What amount must I invest yearly to arrive at that objective? This plan lets you set aside whatever sum is important to meet your in-come target.

Similarly as with organization gave plans and IRAs, the tax reductions offered by plans for private companies and the independently employed accompany a catch: Because this should be retirement investment funds, you need to make a deal to avoid dunking into the money early. There's a 10% corrective ty (potentially 25% for SIMPLE IRAs) if you tap the air conditioner check too early, and most definitely that is for the most part whenever before you arrive at age 591/2 or, if you leave or close the business that is producing the salary, age 55.

The Keogh Plan: A Sweet Deal

He fundamental retirement program for independently employed people is regularly called a Keogh plan, named after Donald Keogh, the congressman whose enactment approved the tax reductions that make the plan work. A false name for Keogh is the H.R. 10 plan, a reference to the enactment itself. Some plan supports don't utilize either name, however, and rather allude to the plan basically as either a defined contribution plan or a defined advantage plan.

By whatever name you call it, this is a sweet plan. Contributions are completely charge deductible, and the plan fills in as an expense cover there's no assessment on income until you pull back the money, apparently in retirement. This gives the Keogh the equivalent supercharged procuring limit as an IRA.

Who Qualifies?

You meet all requirements for a Keogh plan if you gain any independent work salary:

- as proprietor or sole owner in a full-time or low maintenance independent investment, regardless of whether consolidated or unincorporated;

- as part proprietor in a business association;

- as an independently employed proficient;

- from a sideline or "working two jobs" business you work from your home or somewhere else; or

- as an independently employed free-lancer, speaker, teacher or expert.

For whatever length of time that you have pay from any of these sources, you can set up a Keogh, regardless of whether you likewise make some full-memories work and take an interest in your boss' retirement plan at work.

How a Plan Might Work

State that you're an independently employed 40-year-old making

$52,000 every year and figure that your salary will rise a normal of 5% yearly. You set up your own profits plan and reserve 13% of your income (all assessment deductible) into the account every year. This is what occurs if the money wins a normal return of 10% every year:

- In ten years: You'll have invested a completely charge deductible $85,000 in your retirement account and it will be worth about $144,000.

- In 15 years: Your deductible contributions complete $146,000 and the estimation of your retirement fund has hit $313,000.

- In 20 years: You've presently invested, and discounted, $224,000. However, your retirement fund has zoomed to $608,000.

- In 25 years: Retirement shows up, and the $323,000 you've added to your profit sharing retirement plan has developed to $1 million.

Saving similar sums outside the Keogh exposed to the harsh elements, unfeeling reality where after-charge dollars are invested and the expense man asserts a portion of every year's profit would desert you far. Make that FAR behind. Since you're setting aside after-charge money, there's less to put aside every year, and the yearly expense bill restrains development of your retirement fund:

- In ten years: Since charges are paid on the 13% of your profit before the money is saved, you have invested just about $60,000, and the estimation of the account (with charges paid every year on the income) will be about $86,000.

- In 15 years: You've invested $102,000 and your retirement fund is $173,000.

- In 20 years: The estimation of your assessable retirement fund is about $309,000 around half as much as the $608,000 in the Keogh.

- In 25 years: Things aren't beating that. The estimation of nondeductible investments is about $518,000, com-pared with the $1 million in the Keogh.

Indeed, the Keogh money is burdened when you take it.

However, you'll despite everything be grinning.

Or on the other hand consider a 44-year-old independently employed couple going for a $1-million savings and retirement at age 62. Their consolidated pay of $85,000 is additionally rising 5% every year, except they decide on an alternate sort of profits plan that fixes their yearly put aside at 20% of their independent work income every year up to a most extreme $40,000 every year each. They take assessment reasoning for everything. If the money acquires a normal return of 10% inside the plan, here are the outcomes:

•	In five years: The couple's $94,000 in contributions has developed to $125,000.

•	In ten years: The retirement fund hits $361,000.

•	In 15 years: The retirement pot has expanded to $777,000.

•	In 18 years: The couple has put $451,000 in charge deductible dollars and at age 62 has more than $1 million in their account.

The Blessings of a Keogh

As noted above, contributions to your own annuity plan are in every case completely charge deductible, regardless of how high your pay and whether or not you or your life partner is secured by another retirement plan. There's nothing of the sort as a nondeductible contribution, as there is with an IRA. And, you can have an IRA conventional or Roth notwithstanding your Keogh. (Regardless of whether customary IRA contributions would be deductible relies upon your pay, in light of the fact that the Keogh is viewed as a business gave plan to reasons for the IRA deductibility tests.)

What amount would you be able to invest? That relies upon how a lot of independent work salary you have and what sort of Keogh you pick. The deadline points by and large range from 15% to 25% of your independent work income, to a limit of $30,000 to $40,000 every year.

The significant disadvantage to having your own private company profits plan is this: If you have workers, they should be remembered for the plan and you should essentially invest indistinguishable level of pay to their accounts from you add to your own. There's a significant special case to that standard, called an age-weighted plan, examined later right now.

PROFIT SHARING PLANS FOR MAXIMUM FLEXIBILITY

You can put as much as 15% of your net independent work income, up to a limit of $30,000, into a profit sharing defined contribution plan. Calculating those incomes gets somewhat precarious, without a doubt. Business profit for an independently employed individual methods your net business pay less the sum you con-tribute to your Keogh, less one-portion of any standardized savings charge you pay on your independently employed income. If you have another activity where government disability is deducted and you acquire over the yearly standardized savings greatest, there won't be any extra government managed savings charge on your independent work pay. Something else, this counterbalance has the impact of somewhat decreasing your Keogh contribution.

To slice through the math, and to keep things straightforward, we've utilized 13% of pay as the appropriate cover on profit sharing Keogh contributions. That is 13% of net independent work profit, disregarding the Keogh contribution itself and the government managed savings charge balance.

The key bit of leeway to a profit sharing plan is adaptability. You don't need to contribute a similar level of income consistently you can place in 13% one year, 6% one more year, even skirt a year if your accounts totally compel you to curtail. If you are unsure about your capacity to add to the plan every year or then again if you would prefer not to secure yourself in a set rate contribution, this is your best decision.

State, for instance, you have your own photography studio however your pay is exceptionally inconsistent. A few years you feel flush a lot of additional batter to store for retirement. Different years you're unable to make the home loan. A profit sharing plan lets you move with the independent work punches, placing in more money in great years and less money in terrible ones. As an end-result of that adaptability, the sum you are permitted to con-tribute is lower than in different plans.

Money PURCHASE PLANS FOR HIGHER LIMITS.

In money buy defined contribution plan, you can contribute up to 25% of your net independent work income. Once more, net is defined as the sum that is left after you subtract your contribution. To take an easy route through the math, utilize 20% of independent work profit. The government managed savings charge balance may bring down this a piece. The top yearly contribution right now.

The large in addition to with a money buy plan is that you can take care of more money toward your effortless retirement. This is a breathtaking decision if you meet three criteria: you have independent work salary over other business compensation, you can stand to dedicate a huge part of the independent work pay to retirement investment funds and you hope to have the option to keep subsidizing your plan at a similar level a seemingly endless amount of time after year.

A downside of money buy plans is that once you choose what level of pay you need to contribute, you should contribute that rate every year regardless of how high or low your independent work salary. If you choose for make a 20% contribution, state, you're required to contribute 20% every year. Essentially, you exchange the adaptability of profit sharing for the capacity to contribute a more prominent sum.

Money buy plans will work best for you if you have a genuinely relentless, unsurprising salary from your independent investment or other independent work.

HAVE IT BOTH WAYS.

 An eminent procedure to catch both the adaptability of a profit sharing plan and the higher furthest reaches of a money buy annuity is to have the two kinds of plans. That is consummately legitimate, and it's a simple method to remove the ideal retirement fund building potential from your independent work pay. Here's the means by which to tap the most extreme duty deductible advantage for your plan:

To begin with, set up a money buy design and submit a fixed

7% of your independent work income to this annuity consistently. That is currently your base yearly profits financing contribution, yet at that unobtrusive level it shouldn't be too difficult to even consider meeting.

At that point, set up a profit sharing plan that can be independently financed for up to 13% a greater amount of your independent work pay. For whatever length of time that your contributions to the two plans together complete close to 20% of your profit (up to the $40,000 yearly top), you're inside the built up limits. You have the adaptability to modify your contribution year to year yet in addition the capacity to place in as much as the law permits, if you can bear the cost of it.

This methodology has another bit of leeway in that it forces some order on you, expecting you to set aside at any rate 7% of your salary yearly. However, it additionally permits you to about triple your contribution, to a most extreme 20%. Regardless of whether you can't bear the cost of that high a contribution now, incorporating as far as possible with your program while restricting your pledge to 7% of profit is an incredible method to give yourself space to develop and quicken your retirement plan later on.

The Age-Weighted Plan Opportunity

The "age weighted" or age-based profit sharing annuity plan works a lot of like a Keogh plan, however if you have representatives and the age differential among you and them is enormous, this could be a super plan for building your retirement savings. This plan is particularly appropriate to entrepreneurs in their fifties whose representatives are more youthful by a normal of around ten years or more. You despite everything need to remember workers for the plan. However, you can quicken your own retirement reserve funds while taking care of less for your workers.

To see the potential, consider a 55-year-old entrepreneur whose three workers are 45, 35 and 25 years of age. Under a standard profit sharing plan, if the proprietor contributes 13% of salary (rising to about 15% of overall gain after the contribution is made) to her own plan, she should likewise set aside 15% of the net income for her three representatives. State the proprietor's net gain is $75,000 and her workers' are $30,000, $25,000 and $20,000, separately. At 15% of net income, the proprietor's yearly annuity contribution would be about $11,250 and the workers would get $11,250 isolated among them three (15% of their consolidated total compensation of $75,000).

The age-weighted equation drastically changes all that and permits the proprietor to put undeniably a greater amount of the complete retirement-money contribution ($22,500 right now) her own account. Utilizing a table that appoints a particular markdown factor to every individual dependent on age and years to retirement, this 55-year-old entrepreneur can help her own contribution to $17,780, while diminishing representative contributions to an aggregate of $4,720. If you figure this sort of plan may function admirably for you, connect with a bookkeeper or monetary organizer who has involvement with retirement arranging.

The Simplicity of a Business IRA

There is an option in contrast to the Keogh, a super-ease, low-support plan: the "business IRA," which allows completely charge deductible contributions far over the

$3,000 as far as possible for singular IRAs.

This plan, called a streamlined worker annuity (SEP), or SEP-IRA, is simpler to set up and requires less continuous administrative work than a Keogh or other independent investment profits plan. Much the same as the perplexing annuity programs offered by enormous organizations, SEPs convey significant duty reserve funds to both you and your workers. Your business or independent work assessable pay is decreased by the measure of money you put into the SEP. Furthermore, the money in your plan, remembering income for speculations, becomes untaxed until you pull back it. Pretty much anybody with pay from independent work sole owners, accomplices, proprietors of partnerships or S companies, even specialists and moonlighters is qualified to open a SEP. Regardless of whether you procure a couple of bucks selling creates on ends of the week or you're an establishing accomplice in a powerful counselling firm, you fit the bill for a SEP.

A SEP is a cross between a profit sharing Keogh plan and a conventional IRA. Your contributions go into an exceptional SEP-IRA. You can contribute as much as 15% of your net independent work profit, up to a maxi-mum of $30,000. Once more, net methods the sum that is left after you subtract your contribution and the counterbalance for any government managed savings charges paid on independent work pay. For the wellbeing of simplicity, figure 13% of net in-come not including those two components is the point of confinement.

You are allowed to fluctuate your contributions every year or even skirt a year, as conditions warrant. If you have qualified workers, you should add to their SEP-IRAs every year you add to your own.

There's only one structure for the business to round out to open a SEP, and all the money you contribute for yourself and your workers is deductible as a cost of doing business. Representatives not you pick how their money is contributed, so you're calmed of that stress.

Another bit of leeway: You can open and reserve a SEP up until your expense accounting deadline time for the most part April 15 including any expansions.

The SIMPLE Plan for Small Business

This tax reduction is one more plan intended to en-mental fortitude self-employeds to put something aside for retirement.

Straightforward means "investment funds motivating force coordinate designs for representatives." These plans were truly made by Congress as a rearranged retirement plan for little organizations just firms with less than 100 workers can utilize a SIMPLE, and if you have workers, you should remember them for your plan. In any case, the entryway to SIMPLEs is additionally open to independently employed labourers without any representatives. Regardless of whether your business is full-time or you do independent or counselling work notwithstanding an all day work, you can have a SIMPLE. And, you can have one regardless of whether you have an occupation that offers an annuity plan. You may not, in any case, have both a SIMPLE and a Keogh.

There are really two sorts of SIMPLE plans a SIMPLE IRA

and a SIMPLE 401(k). All things considered, the IRA variant will be best for an independently employed individual without any representatives, so is what's examined here.

The profit of a SIMPLE IRA is that you can stash up to $7,000 every year (for 2002) a year into the plan regardless of whether that is 100% of your independent work in-come. With the 20%-of-pay top that applies to Keogh plans, you need overall gain from your business of in any event $35,000 to make a $7,000 contribution. Utilizing the SEP, you'd need $53,681 in independent work pay to contribute $7,000. So if your business in-come is under those levels and you can stand to put aside $7,000 per year for your retirement a SIMPLE is particularly charming. (All things considered, the SIMPLE can be a champ regardless of whether your business pay is higher in light of the fact that you might have the option to help the sum added to the plan with a business "coordinate" to the plan. The match can be 2% or 3% of your salary.)

Contributions to a SIMPLE IRA can be deducted on your arrival, and profit inside the account is charge conceded. Similarly as with conventional IRAs, there's typically a 10% punishment if you pull back assets before age 591/2 yet the punishment is an astounding 25% if you haul money out before 591/2 and you've been in the plan for under two years.

You have until the documenting deadline time for your assessment re-go to make your SIMPLE contribution for the earlier year, yet there is a trick: The plan probably has been opened by October 1 of the year for which the contribution is being made. As with Keoghs, SEPs and IRAs, SIMPLEs are offered by banks, financier firms and shared assets.

Write Your Own Retirement-Pay Ticket

Regularly, an entrepreneur sets up a profits plan when the business is steady and gainful enough to manage the cost of it. At that point, you might be in your mid forties to fifty or more established, and the $40,000 or 20% breaking points in different plans may not be sufficient to connect the retirement-salary hole that weaving machines.

All things considered, you have another choice: the defined advantage plan. It lets you flip-flop your methodology. You choose how much pay you need to get in retirement and the law lets you put aside enough current salary to arrive at that objective and deduct each dime. This kind of plan can be alluring if:

• You need to manufacture major retirement finance as quick as would be prudent. This likely methods you've procrastinated on your plan and are presently playing make up for lost time;

• You are inside 15 years or so of your focused on retirement date;

• You can stand to sink a major piece of your yearly income into the plan. That implies you are prosperous and have a genuinely unsurprising salary; and

• You have no workers.

The significant downsides to defined advantage plans are their cost and Rube Goldberg–like multifaceted nature. Each plan is special; contingent upon your age, future and monetary conditions, and will include some confused math.

You'll require a legal advisor, bookkeeper, statistician or other money related expert to assist you with setting everything up and make sense of the necessary yearly commitment every year. The IRS is severe about adhering to the principles on computing commitments to abstain from overfunding your plan.

A 50-year-old acquiring $80,000 who needs to resign at 62 and get a profits of $4,500 every month would at first contribute about $25,000 every year to the plan, expecting the money will develop at a 8% yearly rate, as indicated by Sam Gilbert, leader of the annuity counselling firm United Plan Administrators, in Westlake Village, Cal. All in all, the more established you are, the more you'll have to place into the plan, in light of the fact that the money has less time to develop individually. The commitment is balanced yearly and could rise generously in future years.

That makes defined advantage plans a profoundly requesting decision. You should think of enough yearly financing to in the end arrive at the pay level you've chosen. If you neglect to meet your objectives, the plan could be punished or broke up. And, if you have representatives close to your own age who might likewise fit the bill for profits inclusion, a similar math that converts into robust annuity commitments for you converts into powerful profits commitments for them, as well.

The Right Plan for You

Settling on the correct decision among do-it-without anyone's help annuity plans will rely upon the kind of business you work, your age, how a lot of money you can bear to save, and whether you have representatives. These situations can enable you to pick what's best for you:

• Employee with a sideline business or working two jobs; independent work pay under $25,000. The SIM-PLE IRA permits you to store $7,000 of your independent work pay every year that is 28% of $25,000, a bigger offer than a SEP or Keogh plan would acknowledge.

• Self-utilized specialist; no workers; dubious salary. If you work for yourself and independent from anyone else, and are genuinely sure you'll never go over the 13% ($30,000 top level augmentation) limit on a profit sharing plan, an essential SEP is the most ideal approach. You get the tax breaks, keep the privilege to change your commitments year to year and have the least difficult desk work conceivable.

• Self-utilized proficient; no workers; high, stable salary. A money buy Keogh plan is your pass to boosting yearly commitments to 20% ($40,000 most extreme). If it's all the same to you some additional desk work, twin plans a profit sharing and a money buy get you the 20% cover alongside adaptability to shift commitments. In case you're as of now in your fifties and have minimal saved for retirement, a defined advantage Keogh might be your best decision for quickly fabricating your savings.

• Self-utilized proficient with barely any representatives. An age-weighted profit sharing plan might be the most ideal approach if your workers are more youthful than you by a normal of around ten years or more. Your commitments can vary year to year and you can save more for yourself than for your more youthful workers.

• Owner of a little eatery with for the most part low-paid, high-turnover representatives. A SEP is a decent decision here. The stunt? Structure the plan so just workers who have been with your business for three of the first five years are qualified to take an interest. That lets you amplify commitments for yourself and limit the expense of commitments for workers.

•	Owner of a little retail location with numerous regular yet long-lasting representatives. A SEP will presumably not be a decent decision if you utilize countless low maintenance or occasional laborers. SEP rules state you should likewise add to their retirement plans, regardless of whether they make as little as $400 or so in a year. A profit sharing Keogh is a superior decision since representatives must work for you at any rate 1,000 hours in a year to fit the bill for incorporation in the plan.